UNDEMOCRATIC

Rogue, Reckless and Renegade: How the Government
Is Stealing Democracy One Agency at a Time

JAY SEKULOW

HOWARD BOOKS
AN IMPRINT OF SIMON & SCHUSTER, INC.

New York Nashville London Toronto Sydney New Delhi

Howard Books
An Imprint of Simon & Schuster, Inc.
1230 Avenue of the Americas
New York, NY 10020

Copyright © 2015 by Jay Sekulow

First Howard Books trade paperback edition February 2016

HOWARD and colophon are trademarks of Simon & Schuster, Inc.

For information about special discounts for bulk purchases,
please contact Simon & Schuster Special Sales at
1-866-506-1949 or business@simonandschuster.com.

The Simon & Schuster Speakers Bureau can bring authors to your
live event. For more information or to book an event, contact the
Simon & Schuster Speakers Bureau at 1-866-248-3049 or visit our
website at www.simonspeakers.com.

Interior design by Jaime Putorti

Manufactured in the United States of America

10 9 8 7 6 5 4 3

Library of Congress Cataloging-in-Publication Data

Sekulow, Jay.
   Undemocratic / Jay Sekulow.
      pages   cm
      1. United States—Politics and government—2009–   2. Abuse
of administrative power—United States.   3. Bureaucracy—United
States.   4. Civil rights—United States.   I. Title.
   E907.S398   2015
   353.4'60973—dc23   2015001876

ISBN 978-1-4767-9567-6
ISBN 978-1-5011-2308-5 (pbk)
ISBN 978-1-4767-9568-3 (ebook)

*The first edition of this book was dedicated to my
mother, Natalie Wortman Sekulow, because it was
a hardback. That was a family reference.*

*I dedicate this edition not only to my mother, but
also to her grandchildren and great-grandchildren.
So they can live and thrive in a free America.*

CONTENTS

INTRODUCTION
The Bureaucratic Blockbuster   1

CHAPTER ONE
One Day in May   21

CHAPTER TWO
America, Still Exceptional?   41

CHAPTER THREE
The IRS: At War with Conservatives   59

CHAPTER FOUR
The IRS: Auditing Adoption, Breaking the Law   90

CHAPTER FIVE
The VA: When Incompetence Kills   113

CHAPTER SIX
The Department of Justice--Making It Up as They Go Along   130

CHAPTER SEVEN
The Department of Justice—Permanently Rigging the Game   148

CHAPTER EIGHT
The EPA: The World's Least Democratic Agency   166

CHAPTER NINE
The NLRB: Does Overreach Have Its Limits?   191

CHAPTER TEN
The Blueprint: Resist, Reform, and Restore   207

CHAPTER ELEVEN
Resist: The Government Can Be Beaten   214

CHAPTER TWELVE
Accountability and Democracy:
The Mandatory Elements of Reform   231

CHAPTER THIRTEEN
Restore or Perish   243

AFTERWORD   256

Notes   269

Acknowledgments   295

Index   297

THE BUREAUCRATIC BLOCKBUSTER

Hollywood could not have written a better script.

In fact, for more than twenty years, Hollywood has been stealing ideas from the soap opera surrounding the Clintons, with movies like *Primary Colors* and shows like *Madam Secretary* and *The Good Wife*. And who can blame them? It makes for great drama. If it weren't happening in real life, before our very eyes, the recent saga of Hillary Clinton would seem too fanciful, too outrageous for the silver screen or our flat screens.

And yet, our inept, incompetent, corrupt, partisan, and bloated bureaucracy has enabled and empowered Hillary Clinton to carry on—protecting her from the level of transparency and accountability required of public servants on the other side of the political aisle.

Don't believe me? Let's examine the script.

It's the story of how our bureaucracy blocks justice and the rule of law.

It features leading lady Hillary Clinton, who has had perpetual political power for more than three decades, as First Lady of Arkansas from 1983 to 1992; First Lady of the United States from 1992 to 2000; U.S. senator from New York from 2000 to 2009; U.S. secretary of state from 2009 to 2013; and 2016 candidate for the Democratic nomination for president of the United States.

It involves the Clinton Foundation, a global network of charities and other international work that received nearly $2 billion in donations from the world's wealthiest people, foundations, and even foreign entities since its inception in 2001 at the end of Bill Clinton's presidency.[1] Many of the donors were the same ones that bundled money for both Clintons' political campaigns. Other donors were foreign individuals, companies, or nations that cannot legally give to U.S. presidential campaigns, but definitely had a stake in U.S. economic and foreign policy decisions that affected their political and economic power.[2]

It's a story that meets at the intersection of big government, big business, and the bureaucracy that entrenches them all. Billion-dollar decisions. Life-or-death conditions. Top-secret, classified information about U.S. national security interests, and the actions of our allies and enemies around the world.

And it all centers on a private email server widely reported to have been stored and operated out of a bathroom closet in a loft apartment in Denver, Colorado.[3]

The conflict at hand is not the location of the server itself, but the recklessness with which Secretary of State Clinton operated her email. And the story only gets worse. It's not even a political issue—it's a legal one. Hillary Clinton could have violated numerous civil and criminal laws that are intended to do one vitally important thing: ensure our government operates effectively in its most important obligation—keeping our nation secure and safe—which Hillary Clinton failed to do.

It's a story too farfetched to believe. But it's better than Hollywood. It's real life.

Dereliction of Duty in an Era of Cyberwarfare

In the twenty-first century, technology allows us to communicate with anyone, from anywhere, on nearly any electronic device. But enemies of freedom frequently target technological infrastructures to wreak havoc and collect any personal and classified information they can. For example, in 2014, millions of Americans faced the hassle of compromised credit when online hackers accessed the records of everyone who used a credit card at Target or Home Depot over the course of several weeks.

And now, due to the recklessness of the Obama administration and former secretary of state Hillary Clinton—*the chief diplomat in charge of national security* for President Obama's first term—our national security is at risk.

While retail hackers steal personal information and cost consumers the inconvenience of several hours, it's minor compared to what hackers accessed when they breached the U.S. government's Office of Personnel Management (OPM) database in late 2014.[4]

The OPM hack—allegedly led by the Chinese government[5]—stole personal information from more than 20 million Americans and U.S. officials, information that could, at best, lead to identity fraud and, at worst, endanger the lives of U.S. intelligence officers and assets around the globe by providing our enemies with a spy-recruiting database.[6] The hackers were in our system for so long that it will take our government months to figure out exactly what was stolen.[7]

One of the victims was me. I worked for the U.S. Treasury Department in the IRS Chief Counsel's office right out of law school back in the 1980s. One of my former colleagues recently told me that our personnel records from more than thirty-five years ago were among the files hacked.

Sadly, this hack is yet another example of how our federal bureaucracy is incompetent at best and downright corrupt and deceptive at worst.

Information released by the government about the OPM hack has been contradictory and full of lies—all in a desperate attempt to downplay what really took place. In the coming months we will discover more about who and what is responsible for this incredible incompetence but right now, the answers are not easy to come by.

This is why Senator Ben Sasse of Nebraska asked OPM, the Department of Homeland Security (DHS), and the Office of Management and Budget (OMB) if information was stolen from the military or intelligence community. What does it mean for our national security? How does the government plan to respond now? How is it going to deter future attacks? Again and again, his questions went unanswered.[8] But these are the questions we must continue to ask and our federal government must answer. Unfortunately, they have an incentive to remain silent. The bureaucracy's playbook prioritizes waiting out the ever-faster-spinning news cycle, assuming another scandal will pop up and new questions will be asked. They assume this scandal will simply drift out of the public's consciousness.

Just as other agencies in our bloated bureaucracy evade direct questions about their operations, these departments continue to deflect and downplay this hack, which some are calling the 9/11 of cyberattacks.[9] By not paying attention and not enforcing proper protocols, the administration left our most valuable assets—defense secrets and personal information—vulnerable.

It is against this backdrop that then–secretary of state Hillary Clinton used an unsecured, private e-mail server for classified and "top secret" State Department emails.

How is that even possible? How could our nation's top diplomat, someone who has held power and security clearance for decades, make such a rookie and likely illegal mistake—one that could put our national security and millions of lives at risk?

The answer is simple: she is using our federal bureaucracy as partisan protection to ensure that a faux-inquiry is conducted instead of a full, thorough, and independent investigation.

How could the Department of Justice and the FBI possibly allow this when the stakes are so high?

Here's how.

The Facts of the Case

The facts started to come to light when congressional investigations and various governmental transparency organizations and media entities made Freedom of Information Act (FOIA) requests.

Requests made under the FOIA, "often described as the law that keeps citizens in the know about their government,"[10] along with congressional investigations, ensure that our government's operations are efficient and effective in serving the will of the people. This is crucial to what our Founding Fathers envisioned for our nation. The process provides a transparency that is necessary for holding the government accountable to its citizens and safeguarding popular sovereignty in the United States.

We must not forget: information is vital so the people can rule. It positions the voting public to make informed decisions about which government officials should remain in power, which should be given the opportunity to rise to higher office, and which should be removed from authority once and for all.

So, congressional committees, media organizations, and public advocacy organizations asked the State Department for a wide range of documents related to Mrs. Clinton's actions in office. The requests included:

- How decisions were made;
- How talking points were decided;

- How certain top aides to Hillary Clinton were allowed
  to serve in the State Department while also holding
  private sector jobs that could have raised conflicts of
  interest.[11]

Some of these materials were eventually given to congressional committees or gradually released through court order. But the documents were missing something vital: emails from Hillary Clinton's private server. Not a single one was delivered.

It turns out that when the State Department was looking for the requested documents, it could not search the email account of former secretary of state Hillary Clinton.[12]

As the *New York Times* reported in early March 2014, because Secretary Clinton maintained a private server, it was shielded from State Department searches done in compliance with records requests—meaning the State Department couldn't obtain emails housed there. This arrangement provided other benefits to Hillary Clinton as well. Whether the requests came from congressional committees or civil, criminal, or administrative proceedings, it meant Clinton and her lawyers could object on numerous grounds to any disclosure of the emails.[13] And the State Department's hands were tied because they had no way to access potentially classified and top-secret government data on her private server.

What did the State Department do? Did they enforce the rule of law? Did they demand that all state secrets be turned over immediately? Did they work with the Department of Justice (DOJ) to subpoena the email server to ensure national security and state secrets were protected and no laws were broken? *No.*

Instead, they issued a request to Secretary Clinton to turn over only the emails she was legally obligated to surrender, essentially allowing her aides, her lawyers, and who knows who else to sift through classified and top-secret material to determine what needed to be relinquished to the State Department and what could be deleted.[14]

Secretary Clinton and her spokespeople have repeatedly insisted none of the emails sent using her private server were classified when they were transmitted. Read that again. The former secretary of state—our nation's top diplomat—asserted that no emails sent or received during her time traveling the world and conducting U.S. foreign policy were classified.[15]

Hard to believe, isn't it? Do they really think the American people buy her assertions? Because they don't.

And this raises another very important question: How does Hillary Clinton think she can get away with this?

I'll tell you how. She believes the Obama administration's State Department and the Justice Department would never dare fully investigate and, if applicable, indict her for breaking numerous civil and criminal laws.

In other words, Hillary Clinton is betting the bureaucracy will be on her side and that she will never have to be held accountable.

The scary and simple truth is, she may be right.

Here's why. The bureaucratic and political machine to defend Hillary Clinton kicked into high gear. Her spokespeople and the State Department insisted that Secretary Clinton's practice was not out of the ordinary, pointing to former secretary of state Colin Powell's use of a personal email account as well. But new regulations passed in 2009 applied to Secretary Clinton and not Secretary Powell.[16] Those regulations stated that any agency allowing employees to conduct official business on nonofficial email accounts had to ensure any records sent using private email systems are preserved "in the appropriate agency recordkeeping system."[17] Moreover, it is a fundamental principle of our legal system, and the rule of law, that potentially illegal activity unnoticed in the past does not justify illegal activity in the present.

Originally, in March 2015, Secretary Clinton said she had no intention of turning over the email server because she had already voluntarily handed in around fifty thousand pages of emails to the State Department, having deleted the rest and wiping them from the server because they were about personal matters such as wedding planning, yoga, and more.[18]

But then, at the end of July 2015, an internal government review found something important, and not that unexpected, among a small sample of emails Hillary Clinton had turned over to the State Department. The inspector general of the intelligence community concluded that at least four emails from her personal account contained *classified* information.[19] Because of these findings, the inspector general referred the matter to the FBI's counterintelligence division.

There are three levels of classified information regarding national security. The most recent order[20] specifies that information whose release would cause "exceptionally grave damage to the national security" is classified TOP SECRET; information whose release would cause "serious damage" is classified SECRET; the lowest category of classified information currently in use is CONFIDENTIAL.[21]

For less than twenty-four hours, news reports alleged that there was an FBI criminal investigation into Hillary Clinton and the email server.[22] But by the next morning, the Clinton machine alerted the *New York Times* and other publications that Hillary Clinton herself was not under inquiry and it was not actually a criminal investigation.[23]

The *Wall Street Journal* reported in July 2015:

> As a result of the findings, the inspector general referred the matter to the Federal Bureau of Investigation's counterintelligence division. An official with the Department of Justice said Friday that it had received a referral to open an investigation into the potential mishandling of classified information. Initially, a Justice Department official said

Friday morning the investigation was criminal in nature, but the department reversed course hours later without explanation.

"The department has received a referral related to the potential compromise of classified information. It is not a criminal referral," an official said.[24]

It seems the bureaucracy had come to Secretary Clinton's rescue.

The investigation was ongoing. Information was still being collected. Emails were still being examined. How, then, could the Justice Department declare that the referral was not criminal in nature and instead only an investigation into "potentially compromised classified material"?

The FBI's Role

In order to understand what happened, one must better understand the FBI's authority.

A series of statutes and executive orders have established broad authority for the FBI to carry out investigations into not only criminal matters, but also threats to national security.

> The FBI has a range of legal authorities that enable it to investigate federal crimes and threats to national security, as well as to gather intelligence and assist other law enforcement agencies;
>
> The FBI has authority to investigate threats to the national security pursuant to presidential executive orders, attorney general authorities, and various statutory sources. Title II of the Intelligence Reform and Terrorism Prevention Act of 2004, Public Law 108-458, 118

Stat. 3638, outlines FBI intelligence authorities, as does
Executive Order 12333; 50 U.S.C. 401 et seq.; 50 U.S.C.
1801 et seq.

This combination of authorities gives the FBI the
unique ability to address national security and criminal
threats that are increasingly intertwined and to shift between the use of intelligence tools such as surveillance or
recruiting sources and law enforcement tools of arrest and
prosecution.[25]

But this is where the bureaucracy comes into play.

It is the FBI's job to conduct investigations into federal crimes
and our national security. Because of the potential threat to national
security, the Clinton investigation was referred to the FBI. Yet the
DOJ—the executive agency that houses the FBI—continued to
minimize the investigation while clearing Mrs. Clinton of any possible criminal wrongdoing.

Even as of October 2015, the Obama Justice Department continued to assert that the ongoing investigation does not involve
Hillary Clinton herself, is not criminal in nature, and furthermore
is merely looking into potential violations of handling classified information.

The Justice Department is lying.

Either that, or it's conducting a faux-investigation with no intention of following the leads to their logical conclusions and prosecuting lawbreakers for violating civil and/or criminal laws.

It's actions like this that prove the corrupt and unaccountable
bureaucracy that is supposed to be responsible for enforcing our
laws and maintaining fairness in our country. Instead this bureaucracy allows preferential treatment that undermines our Constitution and the very fabric of our nation.

But with each new development, the Obama administration has
an increasingly difficult time justifying its ineptitude on this case.

—

In August 2015, Hillary Clinton finally turned over her email server to federal authorities.[26] She had refused for months to do so, claiming it had been wiped clean of all personal emails. But the inspector general had subsequently contacted Congress and informed them that some emails contained "top secret" information.[27] Certain reports indicated that some of this information potentially included satellite photos of North Korea's nuclear program.[28]

Other sources have speculated that it could be data about U.S. drone strikes, undercover CIA agents, and any other number of highly sensitive topics.[29] All classified—and potentially top secret—information. If Hillary knew she received and or sent these emails, then how could she have possibly said she never sent or received classified information through her private server?

There is only one reason Hillary eventually reversed course and handed over the supposedly wiped-clean server: she was given the option to turn it over voluntarily or else it would be subpoenaed. And yet the Justice Department still insisted there was no criminal investigation and Hillary herself was not being investigated. Meanwhile, as the State Department continued to examine and release more of Clinton's emails, more of her lies were exposed.

She claimed that she started using the private server on March 19, 2009, but there are emails showing she used her private email address (hdr22@clintonemail.com) as early as January 28, 2009.[30]

Cheryl Mills, Clinton's chief of staff at the State Department, emailed classified information to a staffer at the Clinton Foundation in 2012.[31] Team Clinton maintained its unconvincing talking point that the information was not classified at the time it was sent but was marked classified by the State Department years later.

This reveals yet another way Hillary Clinton is continuing to hide behind our bumbling bureaucracy. Individual agencies have the authority to deem materials classified at various points in time, with each agency having different levels of classification, unique processes for declaring items classified, and full independence to do so. Hillary Clinton and others are using this bureaucratic loophole, stating it's simply too confusing to determine what is classified and when.

Unfortunately for her, being secretary of state means more than just flying around the world on foreign affairs business. Being secretary of state brings along with it responsibilities and legal obligations.

But Hillary Clinton has nothing to fear because the Obama administration's Department of Justice is responsible for investigating and potentially prosecuting any legal violations. Which means that Mrs. Clinton has very little reason to fear she will ever face any indictments.

The Surrendered Server

By the end of September 2015, the number of the former secretary of state's surrendered emails containing classified information totaled more than four hundred, with three of them marked secret because their subject matter involved discussions about the Iranian nuclear program.[32] Other classified topics discovered in the emails ranged from the NATO intervention in Libya and WikiLeaks disclosures, to the Arab Spring movement.[33]

Then, in October 2015, the FBI expanded its probe to a second technology company responsible for maintaining Clinton's private server.[34]

For the sake of our national security, we must know if these technology company employees had access to this classified and top-secret information without security clearance.

The FBI also seized four computer servers from the State Department headquarters to reportedly analyze how top-secret information was sent to Clinton's email servers by State Department aides.[35] Again, this was to determine if classified information passed through unsecured personnel and servers.

And not surprisingly, news reports in October 2015 revealed that Clinton's private server itself was targeted by the cyberattacks originating in China, South Korea, and Germany.[36]

With each new development, it's ever clearer that our national security was put at risk by Secretary Clinton's private email server setup. While the FBI is reportedly inspecting, we can't be confident that it's anything but a faux investigation to keep voters at bay while the 2016 presidential election cycle gets under way. Just as the bureaucracy has stalled and delayed any efforts to get to the bottom of Lois Lerner's emails and the IRS scandal discussed later in this book, the FBI, DOJ, and other bureaucratic branches seem to be doing whatever it takes to ensure limited fallout for Mrs. Clinton's presidential campaign.

Fortunately, we have both civil and criminal laws designed to punish individuals who put our national security at risk.

The Legal Case Against Hillary Clinton

As I've said all along, the question about former secretary Clinton's emails is not a political issue. In fact, the only people with political bias are those preemptively declaring Hillary Clinton innocent without a thorough investigation. Yes, she is innocent until proven guilty, but far too many in the federal bureaucracy and the media have declared her innocent with no possibility of culpability whatsoever.

That is not how lawyers and lawmakers should act. They should stick to the facts, and then apply them to the law—where everyone is concerned.

Based on the facts, we must ask: Have any crimes been committed? Have any laws been violated? Should the Department of Justice and the FBI even be conducting a criminal investigation?

While there are at least a dozen regulations and laws that could be relevant as more facts come to light, we will focus on those statutes most connected to the facts presented above. As you'll see, former secretary of state Clinton's actions could be deemed felonious.

As secretary of state, Hillary Clinton's private email server likely put our national security at grave risk. There are laws designed to defend such risks.

Leaders Must Follow the Law

There is a civil statute, more than half a century old, that all federal agency heads must obey. It's intended to ensure proper recordkeeping of all government business for the purpose of transparency and accountability.

The Federal Records Act, 44 U.S.C. § 3101, was originally passed in 1950. It requires:

> The head of each Federal agency shall make and preserve records containing adequate and proper documentation of the organization, functions, policies, decisions, procedures, and essential transactions of the agency and designed to furnish the information necessary to protect the legal and financial rights of the Government and of persons directly affected by the agency's activities.[37]

The State Department itself made clear in 1995 that emails are considered records that must be preserved:

> Another important modern improvement is the ease of communication now afforded to the Department world-wide through the use of E-mail. . . . All employees must be aware

that some of the variety of the messages being exchanged on E-mail are important to the Department and must be preserved; such messages are considered Federal records under the law. (5 FAM [Foreign Affairs Manual] 443.1)[38]

In 2009, the National Archives codified a regulation that required any employees sending and receiving official emails using systems not operated by the agency to ensure those records were still preserved in the appropriate agency record-keeping system.[39]

If Hillary Clinton violated this law, civil suits in federal court could force public disclosure of her emails.

But the most significant concern is her potential criminal violation of numerous statutes designed to protect our national defense.

The top-secret information found in some of Hillary Clinton's emails suggests that she violated 18 U.S.C. § 793. If Hillary Clinton knew, or should have known, that her private email server was not a proper place of custody for this information, then she committed a crime that could potentially indict her.

Statute 18 U.S.C. § 793 is intended to protect all information relating to our national defense. Violating this statute is a felony and carries with it fines and/or imprisonment for up to ten years.

(f) Whoever, being entrusted with or having lawful possession or control of any document, writing, code book, signal book, sketch, photograph, photographic negative, blueprint, plan, map, model, instrument, appliance, note, or information, relating to the national defense,

(1) through gross negligence permits the same to be removed from its proper place of custody or delivered to anyone in violation of his trust, or to be lost, stolen, abstracted, or destroyed, or

(2) having knowledge that the same has been illegally removed from its proper place of custody or delivered to

anyone in violation of its trust, or lost, or stolen, abstracted, or destroyed, and fails to make prompt report of such loss, theft, abstraction, or destruction to his superior officer—

Shall be fined under this title or imprisoned not more than ten years, or both.[40]

Federal regulations (18 CFR 3a.11) define "Top Secret" as:

Top Secret refers to national security information or material which requires the highest degree of protection. The test for assigning Top Secret classification is whether its unauthorized disclosure could reasonably be expected to cause exceptionally grave damage to the national security. Examples of *exceptionally grave damage* include armed hostilities against the United States or its allies; disruption of foreign relations vitally affecting the national security; the compromise of vital national defense plans or complex cryptologic and communications intelligence systems; the revelation of sensitive intelligence operations; and the disclosure of scientific or technological developments vital to national security. This classification is to be used with the utmost restraint.[41]

It is perfectly reasonable for information of this kind to be sent to or from the secretary of state of the United States. It's part and parcel to the responsibilities of the job. However, some reports have confirmed that spy secrets that should have been classified as top secret were sitting on the private email server.[42] The fact that information that could cause "exceptionally grave damage to national security" was sitting on an unsecured server at Secretary Clinton's house should be of concern to every American.

Statute 18 U.S.C. § 1924 is the most likely criminal statute of relevance because it punishes officers of the United States who knowingly remove classified information to unauthorized locations:

Whoever, being an officer, employee, contractor, or consultant of the United States, and, by virtue of his office, employment, position, or contract, becomes possessed of documents or materials containing classified information of the United States, knowingly removes such documents or materials without authority and with the intent to retain such documents or materials at an unauthorized location shall be fined under this title or imprisoned for not more than one year, or both.[43]

This is the same statute to which General David Petraeus pled guilty in April 2015 for improperly handling classified material in his journals by keeping them at an unsecure location at his home and providing them to his biographer instead of turning them over to the CIA or Defense Department.[44]

The first point of 18 U.S.C. § 1924 is clear: Secretary Clinton was an officer of the United States.

All the evidence also indicates the second element—whether or not the information was classified—has also been met. While Clinton continues to insist that none of the information was classified when it passed through her email server, unbiased observers looking at the facts should have a hard time finding this credible now—simply because classified information has already been uncovered in the few emails that were previously released.

The third element in the statute—"knowingly removes material"—begs the question: Did Hillary Clinton knowingly remove this material to an unauthorized location? Yes. Because emails containing *classified* information passed through this *unsecured* and unauthorized location. No amount of playing dumb, shrugging one's shoulders, and blaming the vast right-wing conspiracy can get her out of this one.

And finally, the fourth element: Did she remove said classified material without authority? It certainly appears so.

Statute 18 U.S.C. § 2071 declares it a felony when a custodian of any official government "record, proceeding, map, book, document, paper, or other thing, willfully and unlawfully conceals, removes, mutilates, obliterates, falsifies, or destroys the same."[45] Violating this statute can result in fines and/or imprisonment for up to three years.

Most interesting is the final provision of the statute, which states that anyone found in violation of it "shall forfeit his office and be disqualified from holding any office under the United States."[46]

My friend Shannen Coffin, a former senior Justice Department official, discusses this unique provision more in depth:

> The crime is punishable by up to three years in prison. And interestingly, Congress felt strongly enough about the crime that it included the unusual provision that the perpetrator shall "forfeit his office and be disqualified from holding any office under the United States." The requirement for specific intent in this criminal law—"willfully and unlaw-fully"—and the fact that Loretta Lynch [U.S. attorney general] would ultimately decide whether to bring prosecution, makes it doubtful that charges would be filed. But the better question is how could Hillary Clinton, in light of this pro-hibition, decide that this was a good (or legal) idea? Setting up a shadow e-mail server to conduct all official business as secretary of state is an action plainly undertaken for the purpose of evading federal-records laws. And Clinton was successful at that, avoiding congressional and citizen de-mands for review of her record during her term in office.[47]

Once again, why would the partisan establishment step in and enforce the rule of law if doing so could derail the historic elec-tion of the Democratic front-runner to be the forty-fifth president of the United States? The answer is clear: they want to maintain the status quo, a bureaucracy designed to give them unprecedented power and limited accountability.

The stakes have never been higher for our nation's legal framework. Yet bureaucracy continues to undermine it at every turn.

James Madison famously wrote in *Federalist* No. 51, "If men were angels, no government would be necessary. In framing a government which is to be administered by men over men, the great difficulty lies in this: you must first enable the government to control the governed; and in the next place oblige it to control itself."

We know men are no angels and the law cannot be manipulated to shield the truth. Hackers try to undermine our national security every day. The mishandling of classified documents by a secretary of state is criminal. We have a right to know what happened and to hold those responsible to the fullest extent of the law.

As our nation's unaccountable and unelected bureaucrats' power continues to grow exponentially, the ability of the government to control itself and those in power continues to deteriorate. If we don't do something about it before it's too late, we risk a dangerous transformation—from a nation of laws into a nation of men and women corrupted by power and incapable of justice.

And that may just be a script that not even Hollywood wants written.

1

___

ONE DAY IN MAY

I have a unique vantage point from my office in Washington, D.C. My building, in the heart of Capitol Hill, is directly across the street from the Supreme Court of the United States. The Justices literally drive by my office each day that the court is in session. From my window I can see the chambers where the Justices and law clerks spend their days crafting legal opinions that impact all of us. There have been many nights when I have seen the glow of the lights emanating from those chambers as the final touches are put in place. It is an awe-inspiring location. From the white marble columns on the exterior to the expansive courtroom where the oral arguments take place, the building represents power and stability. One of the most impressive aspects of the building is the depiction of great lawgivers carved into the marble. Each time I enter the courtroom, I glance up at those lawgivers, including Moses holding the Ten Commandments written in Hebrew.

For three decades I have had the privilege of arguing cases before the Supreme Court representing a wide range of legal issues including: religious liberty, prayer and Bible clubs in public schools, free speech, and defending the unborn's fundamental right to life, and campaign finance reform. I even argued a case before the Supreme Court involving the Ten Commandments Monument in Utah. My team and I won 9–0. Admittedly, it is one of my favorite cases, as I was able to reference the Supreme Court building's own depiction of Moses holding the Ten Commandments.

The judiciary, our third branch of government, is powerful. After all, the Supreme Court interprets the Constitution and that impacts each of us. It is not, however, the most powerful branch. From my office, I also have a great view of the Capitol dome. I have often taken guests up to the top floor of our building to view the Capitol. The lit dome in the evening sends the clear message that legislators are handling serious business. The Senate office buildings are just across the street from the front door to my building. In fact, after the terrorist attacks on September 11, 2001, the security perimeter was moved directly in front of our offices. When the anthrax attack took place days after 9/11, the surveillance devices and air monitoring equipment were placed just a few feet from our main entrance. The security in the area is still very tight, as it should be—these are the buildings that house our legislature, our second branch of government. This branch represents the people, and it's where our laws are constructed. And yet, as powerful as the legislative branch of government is, it is not the most powerful branch.

I can hop into a cab and after a short five-minute drive I am at the White House. I have had the incredible privilege of being in the Oval Office, discussing major issues with President Bush, ranging from judicial nominations to terrorism. It is an experience that is hard to put into words. When you are seated next to the president of the United States, the commander in chief of our armed forces, you realize quickly that what takes place in that office not only impacts each of us, the impact is felt around the globe. The executive branch of government and the president are powerful. There is no doubt about it. But I submit to you that the executive branch is not the most powerful.

The most powerful branch of our government is located around the corner from the Supreme Court building, a few streets over from the Capitol, and a couple of blocks from the White House. These buildings are scattered around D.C. house agencies—the Internal Revenue Service, the Department of Justice, the Environmental Protection Agency, the Department of Health and Human Services, Veterans Affairs, the Labor Department, and many others. These agencies are run by bureaucrats. And these unelected, unaccountable bureaucrats destroy our liberty and threaten our democracy. We are in serious peril because of this— the most powerful branch of government we did not even learn about in high school civics class.

The problem is, the Constitution does not provide for a fourth branch of government. Yet we have one. We have created an unconstitutional, self-sustaining monster that is swallowing our democracy. Our constitutional republic hangs in the balance. I keep a diary with me where I note significant events in my legal practice. My entry on May 10, 2013, was a game changer.

The first email—marked "URGENT"—hit my inbox at 10:17 a.m., just minutes before my radio program goes live on air. The message was simple: Lois Lerner, then the head of exempt organizations at the Internal Revenue Service, had "apologized" to conservative and Tea Party groups for intentionally subjecting them to heightened IRS scrutiny.

My first feeling was vindication. More than a year earlier, dozens of Tea Party and other conservative groups had contacted me, all telling me the same story. The IRS was delaying their tax exemption applications and requiring them to answer—under penalty of perjury—appallingly broad questions, questions that violated the constitutional rights of American citizens.

The IRS delayed at least one pro-life group because the

agency subjectively determined[1] that the group's "presentations make substantial use of inflammatory and disparaging terms and express conclusions more on the basis of strong emotional feelings than of objective evaluations"—as if the liberal nonprofit organizations like Planned Parenthood or the American Civil Liberties Union don't make arguments "on the basis of strong emotional feelings."

We took the cases, notified the IRS of our representation, and publicly called on Congress to take action, by holding hearings to investigate IRS abuse. In response, the IRS denied all wrongdoing, and the mainstream media of course backed the Obama administration's taxing agency, with the *New York Times* even claiming that in scrutinizing the Tea Party, the IRS was merely doing its job.[2]

But with Lois Lerner's apology, everything changed—for a few days, anyway. Every major network carried the apology, every major newspaper wrote articles and analyses, and even President Barack Obama went to the White House podium and expressed his deep outrage.

And the IRS's actions were outrageous. In fact, they were criminal. And, for a time, the Obama administration seemed to agree. Within days of the IRS's apology, Attorney General Eric Holder declared that the IRS's conduct was "outrageous and unacceptable" and ordered a criminal investigation.[3]

The conduct of the IRS was, in fact, "outrageous." Over a period of years, the IRS singled out conservative and pro-life individuals and organizations for extraordinary audits, unconstitutional questioning, years-long delays in processing applications, and selective leaks of private information.

Ultimately, we discovered the IRS went so far as to try to collude with the Department of Justice to prosecute conservatives, to attempt to "piece together" (to borrow a term from an actual IRS email[4]) prosecutions of American citizens without a single shred of evidence or a single specific complaint of illegal activity.

On May 10, we knew only part of the story, but we knew enough to know the IRS was out of control.

Our work on several IRS cases revealed that before approving conservative groups for the same nonprofit status long granted to large liberal organizations like Planned Parenthood, MoveOn.org, and the ACLU, the IRS was not only delaying applications for years, it was asking questions that were themselves unconstitutional.

- It wanted to know the names of children tutored by a constitutional education nonprofit.
- The IRS wanted log-in information and passwords for conservative websites.
- It wanted to know the identity of donors, even when the law allowed donors to remain anonymous.
- It demanded to know the details of all communications between conservative nonprofits and any elected official, demanding even details of "indirect" communications (whatever those were).
- It demanded an accounting of all the nonprofit work of even family members of Tea Party leaders, including their membership on church boards.[5]

It attacked pro-life speech as "propaganda," and it demanded to know the content even of pro-life prayers.

And that was just the tip of the iceberg.

My first job out of law school was in the Office of Chief Counsel, Internal Revenue Service. My experience taught me that the IRS's attacks on the conservative movement went straight to the top of the agency. In her apology,[6] Lois Lerner claimed that the misdeeds were the fault of "line" workers in Cincinnati—low-level employees. But we had in our possession letters from IRS offices in California and in Washington, D.C. Some of these letters were signed by Lois Lerner herself.

Lerner also implied that the IRS's wrongdoing had stopped, that when the agency learned what the low-level workers were doing, it called a halt to all improper activity.

Nothing could be further from the truth. In fact, even as Lois Lerner spoke, multiple conservative groups were still waiting for IRS approvals and continued to receive intrusive questions. Some are still waiting for approval years after the "apology." For others, it took filing litigation in federal court to get the IRS to do the right thing.

Even worse, the very day before she spoke, emails revealed that Lois Lerner was plotting with the Department of Justice and chief of staff of the IRS commissioner to criminally prosecute conservatives for violating tax laws—*even without any evidence that the laws had been violated.*

This misconduct was not some minor annoyance for conservatives. It was so widespread—affecting every single conservative group that applied for nonprofit status—and so egregious that scholars from the American Enterprise Institute argued it may have had a material impact on the 2012 election.[7]

Writing for the AEI's online journal, Stan Veuger explained:

> The bottom line is that the Tea Party movement, when properly activated, can generate a huge number of votes— more votes in 2010, in fact, than the vote advantage Obama held over Romney in 2012. The data show that had the Tea Party groups continued to grow at the pace seen in 2009 and 2010, and had their effect on the 2012 vote been similar to that seen in 2010, they would have brought the Republican Party as many as 5–8.5 million votes compared to Obama's victory margin of 5 million.
>
> President Obama's margin of victory in some of the key swing states was fairly small: a mere 75,000 votes separated the two contenders in Florida, for example. That is less than

25% of our estimate of what the Tea Party's impact in Florida was in 2010. Looking forward to 2012 in 2010 undermining the Tea Party's efforts there must have seemed quite appealing indeed.[8]

In other words, had the Tea Party continued its proportionate impact on Republican voting, it could have well made up the difference in key states. Instead it found itself under sustained assault from the IRS, an assault that had a real impact.

Veuger goes on to explain how the IRS targeting choked off funds that would have gone to Republican candidates:

As a consequence [of IRS targeting], the founders, members, and donors of new Tea Party groups found themselves incapable of exercising their constitutional rights, and the Tea Party's impact was muted in the 2012 election cycle. As Toby Marie Walker, who runs the Waco Tea Party, which filed for tax-exempt status in 2010 but didn't receive approval until two months ago, recounted recently: "Our donors dried up. It was intimidating and time-consuming." The Richmond Tea Party went through a similar ordeal, and was only granted tax-exempt status in December, right after the election—three years after its initial request. Its chairman explained the consequences: the episode cost the Richmond Tea Party $17,000 in legal fees and swallowed time the all-volunteer network would have devoted to voter turnout, outreach in black and Latino neighborhoods and other events to highlight the constitution and "the concept of liberty."[9]

The bottom line? A rogue IRS may well have helped keep Barack Obama in the White House. In fact, Lois Lerner in an infamous email said she had hoped to get a job with President Obama's reelection campaign.

There is much more to say about this scandal later, but I raise it now to explain a deeply troubling reality, a reality that is shaking our American democracy to its foundations, a reality that could mean the end of American exceptionalism, an end to the concept of American self-government intended by our Founders and lived through our citizens for almost 240 years.

When the IRS scandal broke, my phone seemed to ring for days straight. I don't think I've ever gotten as much email before or since. And there was one question that was on everyone's lips: "What did the president know and when did he know it?"

In other words, the scandal was viewed through the prism of Watergate, the legendary scandal that ended the Nixon presidency, with the assumption that it was only truly "real," only truly important, if it could bring down the president of the United States.

But I was more disturbed by a different thought, a concern that transcends the current occupant of the White House:

What if the IRS—arguably the nation's most powerful domestic agency—didn't actually *need* a presidential directive to engage in its nationwide persecution of conservatives? What if the IRS acted largely on its own initiative to target Americans, harass them, audit them, humiliate them, and try to prosecute them merely because the IRS disagreed with their political beliefs?

That is a much larger problem than the corruption of a single agency. That is the corruption of an entire system of government.

And that is the theme of this book.

While Americans have been robustly engaged in political debates—and participating in vast numbers in elections—a new branch of government has been growing in the shadows. A branch that is elected by no one, ignored by the media, protected by the courts and by a complex web of laws and regulations: with job security so great that some federal employees are more likely to die on the job than they are to be fired.

This new branch of government—personified not just by the IRS but by the entire array of federal agencies, like the Department of Justice, the Environmental Protection Agency, the National Labor Relations Board, the Federal Communications Commission, and many others—is *the federal bureaucracy*; it possesses a staggering amount of power, and it is not only increasingly partisan, it is increasingly corrupt and incompetent.

Imagine if Congress wrote and enacted far more laws than it does now, but you could never vote the lawmakers out of office.

You don't have to imagine it. It's happening.

Imagine if congressmen were systematically corrupt, abused their power, and demonstrated rank incompetence, but by law they never had to face the voters.

That's our bureaucracy.

Imagine if a congressman, once in office, was allowed to hold power until death or retirement, whichever came first.

Imagine if elections mattered less and less because there existed a permanent, partisan political class that continually pushed the nation to the Left regardless of who occupied the White House or who held the House and Senate.

That's our bureaucracy.

Imagine if elections mattered less and less because there existed a permanent, partisan political class that continually pushed the nation to the Left regardless of who occupied the White House or who held the House and Senate.

That's our bureaucracy.

We are at a constitutional tipping point. If we wait much longer to introduce democratic accountability to the encroaching, vast federal bureaucracy we'll lose the America we know, and our electoral politics will become a sideshow, a meaningless spectacle that enter-tains the masses while the anonymous but powerful bureaucrats do the *real* work—governing the United States of America.

In short, unless the American people take action, even the pres-ident of the United States will matter less and less. He'll become a figurehead, someone not unlike the queen of England, a ceremonial leader presiding over a government that has no concern for the be-liefs and opinions of the titular head of state.

In short, unless the American people take action, even the president of the United States will matter less and less. He'll become a figurehead, someone not unlike the queen of England, a ceremonial leader presiding over a government that has no concern for the beliefs and opinions of the titular head of state.

Think that's too dramatic? Too alarmist? Hardly.

A primary goal of this book is quite simply to educate, to teach you how the United States is actually governed and how that gov-ernment can impact every aspect of your life. You need to learn how America is actually governed, how your freedom is threatened, and how your tax dollars are wasted or misused by a bureaucracy that is increasingly corrupt and partisan. You are paying for the permanent political class that is disrupting and endangering our constitutional republic.

But to understand why a growing bureaucracy represents such a clear and present danger to our Constitution, we must first recognize three critical truths about our government: there is no real gridlock, there is no real accountability, and there is nowhere to hide.

Truth 1: There Is No Real Gridlock

We've all heard the complaint. Our government does nothing. It's gridlocked. When one party holds all or part of Congress, and the other party holds the White House, the cries of gridlock are especially loud. In fact, in May 2014, President Obama's frustration with this apparent "gridlock" boiled over into critiques of the Founders' "structural" design of our government.[10]

The claim has a certain surface appeal. After all, in a divided government, it's much more difficult to pass new bills, and public fights—like the government shutdown battles of the past five years—occupy the headlines.

But that's deceptive.

Let me be clear: if someone tells you our government is "gridlocked," they typically mean that they can't get *everything* they want.

If someone tells you our government is "gridlocked," they typically mean that they can't get *everything* they want.

Because our government is anything but gridlocked.

Consider this fact: from 2009 to the end of 2012, the federal government's bureaucracy created more than 13,000 new regulations—each with the binding force of law.[11]

Even in 2012, one of the lowest rulemaking years of the last twenty (and the peak of the alleged "gridlock" in Washington, as President Obama battled a Republican House during a hotly contested election), the federal bureaucracy finalized 2,482 rules.[12]

That's a staggering number of new laws.

And not one American voted for any of the regulators who drafted, evaluated, and approved those new laws.

Not one American voted for any of the regulators who drafted, evaluated, and approved those new laws.

Unelected regulators are now so powerful that Congress will often write laws that contain intentional gaps, allowing for regulators to come in and fill in the relevant details.

Case in point: the Department of Health and Human Services' (HHS) abortion-pill mandate.

The two most egregious aspects of ObamaCare, the most contentious bill in modern American history, were the individual mandate—which required individuals to purchase health insurance—and the abortion-pill mandate, which required even religious employers to violate their religious conscience and purchase certain abortifacients (pills that can cause abortions) for their employees.

The abortion-pill mandate constituted the most grave threat to religious liberty in modern American history and represented the government's effort to draft its Christian citizens into its radical pro-abortion agenda. Under the mandate, Christian business owners were forced to buy so-called contraceptives that were actually abortifacients, drugs or devices that kill children.[13]

Yet the HHS mandate wasn't actually in ObamaCare. Our elected representatives didn't vote for it or against it. Instead, it was the creation of unelected bureaucrats in the Department of Health and Human Services—handed down with the full force of law.

In 2010, Nancy Pelosi, then Speaker of the House, famously declared[14]—about ObamaCare—that "we have to pass the bill so that you can find out what is in it." She was relentlessly mocked for the comment and deservedly so. Every legislator should carefully read a bill—especially one that purports to overhaul approximately one-sixth of our national economy[15] and 100 percent of our health care. At the same time, however, she was right.

Yet the HHS mandate wasn't actually in ObamaCare. Our elected representatives didn't vote for it or against it. Instead, it was the creation of unelected bureaucrats in the Department of Health and Human Services—handed down with the full force of law.

There was no way to tell what the bill truly meant until after it was passed and after the regulators had issued hundreds and hundreds of new rules—rules like the abortion-pill mandate.

In fact, given the length and complexity of this process, it's entirely possible that Americans will still be confused about what ObamaCare truly means for several more years, as HHS writes and rewrites its rules and as doctors struggle to keep up.

ObamaCare as passed was more like a skeleton, providing the framework for the flesh and bones constructed by the regulators—far away from public debate and public accountability.

But our bureaucrats don't need to pass rules to impact our lives. Sometimes they do so through a combination of incompetence and corruption.

In the spring and summer of 2013, Washington was rocked by a series of revelations that employees of the Department of Veterans Affairs were manipulating patient wait lists to conceal their own failure and inefficiency from the public. Even as the VA was touting allegedly decreased wait times, in reality even gravely ill veterans were put on much longer wait lists that were "off the books," and several of these veterans died without receiving the care they needed.

Bureaucrats were taking action, but the actions they were taking were designed to hide their incompetence. Rather than thinking creatively to shorten wait times and improve patient care, a number of VA employees dedicated their time to "gaming" the reporting system so that they could receive bonuses even as veterans suffered.

Incompetence (unnecessarily long wait times) led to corruption (manipulating wait lists), and veterans paid the price.

Another example: the Department of Justice.

Did you know that we can blame rogue federal prosecutors for ObamaCare? Less than two weeks before election day in 2008, federal prosecutors secured a conviction on public corruption charges against Senator Ted Stevens, an Alaska Republican.[16]

Stevens—who had been popular in Alaska prior to the prosecution—lost a close race to Democrat Mark Begich.

Begich went on to vote for ObamaCare, casting one of the sixty Senate votes that gave President Obama the filibuster-proof majority he needed to pass his "signature" health-care law.

There is, however, one problem with this story.

Ted Stevens was innocent.

Prosecutors, intent on bringing down Stevens, failed to disclose evidence that vindicated Stevens. This failure to provide what's called "exculpatory evidence" violated Senator Stevens's constitutional rights, influenced the outcome of his trial, and thus strongly influenced the outcome of his election.

While a federal court corrected the individual injustice and exonerated Stevens, it could not undo the results of the election, and it certainly couldn't undo the national consequences of the Democrats' unjustly gained sixty-seat majority in the Senate.

And that's just one example of prosecutorial misconduct and Department of Justice partisanship. There are many others that will be discussed later in the book, including instances where the Department of Justice made up crimes out of whole cloth, imprisoned Americans for crimes that did not exist, and circumvented Congress entirely to enrich its leftist activist friends and enact new laws without even the slightest pretense of a democratic process.

And that brings us to the next key truth:

Truth 2: There Is No Real Accountability

In 2011, *USA Today* published a review of federal agency disciplinary practices and came to a startling conclusion: "Federal employees' job security is so great that workers in many agencies are more likely to die of natural causes than get laid off or fired."[17]

This is true even when the "poor performance" includes gross abuse of power and reckless indifference to human life.

As of the writing of this book, here is the complete tally of IRS officials terminated in response to its systematic targeting of Tea Party and pro-life conservatives, targeting that included efforts to manufacture criminal convictions, targeted audits, and selective disclosures of confidential taxpayer information:

Zero.

That's right. Nobody. Not one person. No one fired.

As of the writing of this book, here is the complete list of VA officials terminated in response to the systematic and fraudulent manipulation of wait lists, manipulation that led to veterans waiting for weeks for life-sustaining treatment and sometimes cost American heroes their very lives:

Zero.[18]

Again. Nobody. Not one person.

I will outline scandal after scandal, and you will not only find that no one lost their jobs, but you'll sometimes find that wrong-doers are promoted (especially if their misconduct advanced the Left's ideological agenda), or the worst job action is a brief period of "administrative leave," which is bureaucrat language for "paid vacation."

In the private sector, an employee has two clear incentives to do their job well: First, if their employer can't succeed financially, then the business will close its doors, and the employee will be out of a job.

Second, even if the company is doing well, if the individual employee doesn't do their job well, they can be replaced relatively easily—the law protects them from discrimination, not incompetence.

In other words, private sector employees strive to do well because they want their employer to succeed and because they want successful employers to retain and promote them. People don't always respond the way they should, of course, so not all private sector employees work hard, but this incentive structure helps preserve our economy as still the most dynamic and innovative in the world.

These incentives simply do not exist in the federal government. As I'll show in my chapters regarding the IRS, an agency can engage in mass-scale incompetence and systematic corruption not only without suffering a threat to existence (ask Enron how easily private corporations can survive similar levels of corruption) but also without any real employee turnover. Immune from market forces, the IRS exists regardless of its performance, and its employees' jobs are safe despite their own misconduct.

Even the most incompetent employees are shielded from termination by a poorly named "merit" system that makes it extraordinarily difficult to fire the worst workers. An agency can spend hundreds of thousands of man-hours and still lose its case for termination on a technicality, a process so frustrating that federal managers often don't even bother to try.

And that brings us to the next truth. Our government refuses to be contained.

Truth 3: There Is Nowhere to Hide

If you think the explosive growth of government doesn't impact you, you're wrong.

Virtually every significant religious liberty challenge of the last thirty years has originated from unelected government officials.

Every single significant environmental regulation in response to "climate change" has originated not from Congress but from unelected government officials.

From the car you drive to the HVAC attached to your house to the Big Mac you eat, its cost, construction, or composition is impacted by unelected government officials.

Each visit to the doctor is deeply impacted by government regulations, even when you pay through private insurance or out of your own pocket.

It is one thing for America to vote for this level of government intrusion. If that is truly what the people want, then—barring constitutional violations—it is what they will have. It is another thing entirely, however, for Americans to simply drift into the hyperpartisan hyperregulation of every aspect of their lives.

It is one thing for America to vote for this level of government Intrusion. If that is truly what the people want, then—barring constitutional violations—it is what they will have. It is another thing entirely, however, for Americans to simply drift into the hyperpartisan hyperregulation of every aspect of their lives.

And we've been drifting for decades.

Partisan Bias

Entrenched bureaucracy is bad enough. It's worse when it is corrupt and incompetent. It's a threat to democracy when it is also thoroughly partisan, using its considerable power to advance the Left and punish conservatives.

During the now-notorious 2013 government shutdown, the National Park Service demonstrated bias in action, shutting the parks for the general public (including even World War II vets visiting the World War II Memorial, until a national outcry forced the Park Service to reverse course) while opening the National Mall for an amnesty rally, protecting the rights of a favored constituency—immigration activists—to peacefully assemble.[19]

Amnesty rallies are protected by the Constitution, but so is peaceful assembly at a war memorial. Yet the National Park Service played favorites.

Kevin Williamson, a *National Review* editor, has described this phenomenon as the party of government (the Democrats) merging with the government itself.[20] As Democrats take care of the government, the government takes care of Democrats. And in these increasingly polarized times, the result is a government that is not only openly hostile to conservative and Christian ideas and beliefs, it is increasingly isolated from the beliefs and values of millions of Americans.

The result is a government that is not only openly hostile to conservative and Christian ideas and beliefs, it is increasingly isolated from the beliefs and values of millions of Americans.

This uniformity and isolation creates its own social reality. Harvard Law School professor Cass Sunstein calls it the "law of group polarization," and describes it like this:

> In a striking empirical regularity, deliberation tends to move groups, and the individuals who compose them, toward a more extreme point in the direction indicated by their own predeliberation judgments.[21]

In plain English this means that when like-minded people gather together, they tend to grow more extreme over time. In other words, if everyone advocates for gun control, the group will tend to grow more committed to gun control. If everyone advocates for abortion, the group will grow more committed to abortion.

Within the bureaucracy, a more extreme government becomes a more activist government, driven by its own beliefs not only to advance what it believes to be true and good but to defeat those who disagree.

The stakes are high, the bias is obvious, and the drift away from democracy is real, but there is hope. Even as I describe in detail the threats to our democracy, as a Supreme Court lawyer I also think in terms of relief—of ways we can stop the drift, restore our democracy, and return the most important questions to the people.

As a lawyer who's served inside the federal bureaucracy — I started my career in the chief counsel's office of the IRS—I saw government work from the inside. As a lawyer who's argued a dozen times at the Supreme Court, I also know what it's like to challenge the government from the outside.

In short, I know what it takes to fight and win against a government intent on expanding its power and bringing ever more of your life and your work under its control.

In short, I know what it takes to fight and win against a government intent on expanding its power and bringing ever more of your life and your work under its control.

The solution will be easy to remember and easy to conceptualize, but challenging to execute. The other side will not relinquish power easily, and the Left knows it now controls key levers of national power even if it loses the presidency and both houses of Congress.

The solution begins with three R's.

First, **resist**.

Americans cannot consent to unlawful overreach. We must challenge federal lawlessness in courts of law and in the court of public opinion. And when you challenge, you can win. In this book I will describe how even the most unaccountable bureaucracies can back down in the face of public outcry, and I'll describe court victories against seemingly overwhelming odds.

Sometimes, you can tell the government, "No."

Next, **reform**.

Court battles and public resistance won't be enough to reform the system, to prevent abuse before it escalates to a court battle or public petition. Congress must reform our civil service to introduce real accountability, limit agencies' rulemaking authority, and strip public officials of their effective immunity from liability when they violate citizens' constitutional rights. Public officials will think twice before engaging in partisan witch hunts if they have to write personal checks for violating your First Amendment rights.

Finally, **restore**.

We must engage in a long-term effort to teach Americans the virtues of constitutional democracy. We are not a great nation because we always make the correct policy choices (indeed, we make many mistakes) but because a great people live under a great system of government. The "by any means necessary" system of the bureaucratic Left is ripping America from its foundations and transforming us into something different, something far more European than American.

Ultimately, this book is about empowering you, about teaching you exactly how our government is drifting, how it's upending America's exceptional place in this world, and then giving you the tools to fight back and protect your freedom.

In his legendary Gettysburg Address, President Abraham Lincoln famously declared our nation had a government "of the people, by the people, for the people." Yet a government divorced from electoral accountability is no longer "of the people" or "by the people." And a bureaucratic government that is dedicated not to serving impartially and fairly but to ruthlessly advancing a single ideology can no longer be "for the people."

Those are the stakes. The questions are profound. Do we still have a meaningful constitutional democracy? How much will presidents matter? How much will Congress matter?

And, critically, is America still exceptional?

As I answer these questions, let's first go back to the history of my family and the lessons of one family's journey as we ponder the nation we've been, the nation we are, and the nation we will be.

2

AMERICA, STILL EXCEPTIONAL?

My family name wasn't originally "Sekulow."

That's the Americanized version of Sokolov, or Sokolof—a Russian name that was difficult to translate into English. When my grandfather landed at Ellis Island, the intake officer heard his name and wrote "Sekulow," and we've been Sekulow ever since.

My grandfather fled Russia during the time of the Russian persecution of the Jews as the fires of repression and religious intolerance raged. The seeds of the Russian Revolution had been planted, which bloomed into the Soviet Union, a nation that continued the campaign of persecution. Europe has long been hostile to Jews (and, sadly, much of that hostility continues to this day), but Russia ramped up the persecution to an unprecedented level.

The story of the Russian Revolution is a story of death and war, with the Red Army cutting a swathe of destruction across Russia, enemies of the Soviet Union slaughtered in great numbers, and the larger world—exhausted by the devastation of World War I and struggling in the face of a horrific flu pandemic that killed millions—too distracted to prevent disaster.

Those who could flee, did. Fortunately, my grandfather's family had fled Russia in 1914, just three years before revolution took place.

So my grandfather wound up on Ellis Island, one young fourteen-year-old boy among millions who saw the Statue of Liberty, with its welcome to those who were "tired, poor," and "yearning to breathe free."

And like those millions, he immediately set to work becoming an American, to building a life in the land of the free.

He ran a fruit stand in Brooklyn, New York. His life wasn't easy, but he never stopped working, he never stopped striving, and he passed down his values—and his love of his adopted country—to his children and grandchildren.

Two generations later, one of those grandchildren of the fruit peddler was arguing cases at the Supreme Court of the United States.

I think of my grandfather every time I'm in the high court and I hear the words "Mr. Sekulow, we will now hear from you"—the grandson of Schmulik Sekulow arguing before the most powerful court in the world. You can call it many things, but I call it American exceptionalism.

America is an exceptional country, and my family's journey is a symbol of that exceptionalism. My family overcame the odds, moving from fruit peddling to the Supreme Court in just two generations. But we overcame the odds in part because we were in America, a land of unprecedented opportunity and liberty. And of course my family is not alone. Look far down virtually any American family tree and you'll find an immigrant family who came here against long odds and fought to build a better life.

And these families succeeded in building a free land that is the most powerful, most prosperous, and most secure in the history of the earth.

That is exceptional.

Sadly, however, when we speak today of "American exceptionalism," many on the Left will roll their eyes. They'll recount stories of America's past sins, or they'll do what President Barack Obama did and dismiss American exceptionalism by saying that of course we think we're exceptional, but so do the citizens of every country.[1] To these critics American exceptionalism is nothing but misguided parochial affection, no different than the pride sports fans feel in their local team.

But this is wrong. American exceptionalism isn't merely a garden-variety case of national pride. Nor is it a blind love of country. No one thinks America is sinless. After all, the phrase is American "exceptionalism," not American "perfection."

If American exceptionalism isn't American perfectionism, then what is it?

Was Thomas Paine, the great American patriot, right when he declared, "The cause of America is in a great measure the cause of all mankind"?

I believe he was.

Think about my grandfather. He was certainly not an American when his family fled Russia, where they faced certain persecution and possible death. But he was not without hope, because of America.

In every war or disturbance, there are refugees, and there are nations that take in refugees. But my grandfather was no refugee. He was fleeing, yes, but he was fleeing with his family to a fresh start—a place where he could reinvent himself and in a sense rewrite his family history. The course of my family's destiny for generations was impacted by the decision of my great-grandparents. They came to a place where they had a true hope for a new life. They came to America.

I have long believed that America's exceptional nature is a function of the symbiotic relationship between the nation's peoples and the nation's laws. I think of America as a nation with a great people matched with a great system of government. Note well that I did not say "great government." Sometimes we've been led by poor governments, but always the system—our constitutional system—has allowed us to persevere and, ultimately, prosper.

It may be apocryphal, but I love the story of Benjamin Franklin's admonition following the end of the Constitutional Convention, in 1787. As the tale goes, Dr. Franklin emerged from Philadelphia's Independence Hall and a woman asked him, "Well, Doctor, what have we got, a republic or a monarchy?"

His response?

"A republic, madam. If you can keep it."

The simple Webster's definition of a republic is "a government in which supreme power resides in a body of citizens entitled to vote and is exercised by elected officers and representatives responsible to them and governing according to law."[2]

But our government is not just a republic, but a "constitutional republic." The law that governs our nation is defined and limited by a constitution, and in our case the Constitution is designed primarily to guarantee the liberty of our citizens and limit the power of government over our lives.

In other words, Benjamin Franklin's short statement spoke volumes. We formed a government for a free people, for a people committed to liberty. And to keep that government the people had to be dedicated to preserving it.

For most of our history, Americans have not only been committed to "keeping" our republic, but to improving it—spreading freedom and liberty to those who weren't permitted to enjoy it fully at our nation's founding. And our republic has since allowed a free people to flourish, and the free people have continually pushed the government to protect their liberty and their primacy in our constitutional system.

By preserving in the Bill of Rights our rights to free speech, to religious liberty, and our right to petition the government for the redress of grievances, we put in motion the mechanisms for immense positive change. It's through the exercise of those rights that we were able to move past slavery and Jim Crow, grant women the right to vote, and preserve a host of American liberties through war and peace.

The system of checks and balances prevented our president from becoming a monarch, the Supreme Court from becoming an oligarchy of unelected judges, or the Congress from becoming—at worst—something like France's out-of-control National Convention, where mob rule brought ruin to a revolution.

It's a system I've dedicated my life to preserving and defending. As I said before, I began that defense as a public servant within the system, working for the Department of the Treasury, Office of Chief Counsel, for the Internal Revenue Service.

Yes, I worked for the same agency that is now best known in the conservative movement for launching a targeting campaign that has persecuted thousands of President Obama's political opponents.

But when I worked there, it was a very different time. I started in 1979, during the tail end of the Carter presidency, and left early in the Reagan administration. I remember those days well. We did our jobs, we enforced the tax code, and political discussions or considerations were simply not part of our job.

Even though the IRS was unpopular (when has a taxing agency ever been popular?), I was proud of the work that we did, honored to work with outstanding lawyers on both sides of the political aisle, and felt that I'd done at least some small part to work honestly and efficiently to support a constitutional structure that had done so much for me and my family.

After gaining that valuable experience, I left the IRS and launched out on my own, eventually doing more than I ever imagined I would to defend our Constitution, to defend that system that helps make our nation truly the "hope of the world."

In Supreme Court case after Supreme Court case, I defended individual liberty. I was honored, along with key partners, to found a law firm, the American Center for Law and Justice, that has by now filed hundreds of lawsuits and written thousands of briefs to defend our Constitution. Through victories large and small we've even been able to expand liberty in key areas, including in schools, in the workplace, and in our nation's public spaces.

But now that system that we've defended so vigorously is under threat. In fact, our very constitutional democracy is at stake.

I do not choose my words lightly. The threats emerging now, in 2015, dwarf anything I've seen in my long legal career, and the threats, while multifaceted in their legal character, tend to emanate not from our elected officials but instead from the emergent, vast additional branch of government, the fourth branch—the bureaucracy, a bureaucracy that increasingly circumvents the Founders' established checks and balances and imposes its will on the American people against their expressed wishes.

Have we prevented monarchy, oligarchy, and mob rule only to succumb to the dangers of a vast bureaucracy rendered invulnerable by its very complexity and size?

How could this possibly happen?

How a Bill Becomes a Law, and a Law, and a Law, and a Law . . .

When my sons were very young, Saturday morning featured not just normal kids' shows but also a series of extended educational cartoons set to music. Called *Schoolhouse Rock*, they featured catchy tunes and described the rules of grammar, narrated events in American history, and provided basic civics lessons.

My favorite was a short, three-minute episode called, simply enough, "How a Bill Becomes a Law."

I can still remember the lyrics: It began:

I'm just a bill
Yes, I'm only a bill [3]

And I can still see the singing "bill" (a rolled-up piece of paper with legs) sitting there on the steps of the Capitol, not far from where our ACLJ offices are today. (The singing bill made a national network comeback last year in a *Saturday Night Live* parody[4] of President Obama's expansive immigration executive order, a parody that made the same critique I make in this book, that the executive branch is simply making up its own laws.)

The original song took kids through all the basic steps.

First, the bill is written and presented to a committee in the House of Representatives or the Senate. If it survives in committee (with a majority vote of committee members), then it goes to the full House or Senate. If it passes with majority vote in both houses, it goes to the president for signature.

If the president signs the bill, it's a law, and it's headed for the statute books. If the president vetoes the bill, it goes back to the House and Senate, where it can still become law if the House and Senate override the veto with a two-thirds majority in each house.

Simple enough—even simpler when you tell the story in rhyme and song.

But the cartoon left out an important step, a final step that protects liberty from a Congress or president who disregards the Constitution. Most laws can be easily challenged in court by citizens who believe the law violates their rights. After all, in a constitutional republic, the supreme law of the land isn't represented by acts of Congress but instead by the text of the Constitution. Laws that conflict with the Constitution are (or should be) null and void.

So, for many laws, the journey from idea to reality is long and hard, involving committee hearings, votes in Congress, presidential evaluations, and—finally—judicial review. By the time a law is actually enforced—especially a law of true consequence—it's been debated, voted on, and challenged. The process has worked the way it is supposed to work.

But if you wish to expand the power of the government—and

believe the answer to society's ills is found far more in government action than in the workings of a private market or private charity—a process like that is simply too slow and inefficient to solve all the nation's problems.

So, enter the "rulemaking process." It sounds so benign. What could be wrong with making rules?

Plenty.

The bureaucracy creates thousands upon thousands of new laws—laws never voted on by Congress, rarely reviewed by judges, and enforced often by armed agents of the very agency that wrote the rule.

That's not separation of power, it's consolidation—apart from democracy.

Here's how the process works.

Federal statutes explicitly and sometimes implicitly not only create permanent federal agencies—agencies like the IRS, EPA, DOJ, NLRB, FCC, and many, many others—but also empower them to craft "rules" or "regulations" allegedly designed to help the agency enforce the law. Often, Congress fails to do its job and writes laws with deliberate gaps in meaning, directing or permitting federal agencies to write rules to fill in those gaps and "clarify" the meaning of the statute.

Notable recent examples include ObamaCare, where the law was so poorly drafted that it couldn't be understood without the Department of Health and Human Services (HHS), the IRS, and other agencies writing new rules and regulations. (We must be concerned that the IRS is now involved in our health-care decisions. The IRS has enforcement authority—through IRS agents—to mandate compliance. So now the IRS and HHS are supervising up to 20 percent of our nation's economy.)

Another example is the so-called Dodd-Frank legislation, written with the intent of tightening banking regulation so that crashes like the one that brought our economy to its knees in late 2008 and early 2009 won't ever happen again.

Dodd-Frank was passed and signed into law by President Obama in July 2010. Yet by the summer of 2014, the banking industry still wasn't sure what the law meant.[5] The law was intentionally incomplete, and instead of fully describing its provisions, Congress set 398 "rulemaking" deadlines so that unelected bureaucrats could fill in the gaps. In other words, it empowered federal agencies to make 398 separate regulations with the full force of law.[6]

By the summer of 2014, four full years after the law was passed, 208 rules had been finalized, but a whopping total of 96 hadn't even been proposed.[7]

"Pass the law to find out what's in it," indeed.

By comparison with federal statutes, federal regulations are thoroughly undemocratic. Whereas a bill can become a law only by vote of a popularly elected Congress, signed by the elected president, a proposed rule becomes a regulation through a process that vests virtually all the authority in the rulemaking agency and leaves the public with the ability to provide our opinion only.

Once an agency determines a rule is necessary, it publishes the proposed rule in a publication called the *Federal Register*, an enormously complex publication, thousands of pages that even few lawyers can truly understand or navigate.

The proposed rule is then subject to something called a "notice and comment" period, where you— members of the public—have an opportunity to support or critique the proposed rule. You do not vote. Nor do you vote on the people who are drafting or proposing the rule.

After receiving public comments, the agency will then once again take to the scintillating pages of the *Federal Register* to publish the rule, provide the specific date it will take effect, and describe how it responded to public comments.

That's it. That's the process.

And while the process is simple for bureaucrats, allowing them to write more than 13,000 new rules in the first years of President Obama's terms in office, it can be virtually impossible for the public to grasp.

The language alone is almost impossible to follow, with the *Federal Register* written not in plain English, but in a cryptic government-speak that requires a particular expertise to understand.

To get a sense of the bureaucratic language employed in the *Register*, here's the "summary" of a recent proposed rule called "Avocados Grown in South Florida and Imported Avocados; Clarification of the Avocado Grade Requirements":

> This proposed rule invites comments on changes to the minimum grade requirements currently prescribed under the Florida avocado marketing order (order) and a technical correction to the avocado import regulation. The order regulates the handling of avocados grown in South Florida, and is administered locally by the Avocado Administrative Committee (Committee). For South Florida–grown avocados, this proposed rule would align the regulations with current industry practice. It would remove language permitting the commingling of avocados with dissimilar characteristics in containers for shipment within the production area. All avocado shipments within the production area would need to meet the provisions of a U.S. No. 2 grade, as provided in the United States Standards for Grades of Florida Avocados. For imported avocados, this rule would also make a technical correction to the avocado import regulation to clarify that the minimum grade requirement for imported avocados remains unchanged at a U.S. No. 2.[8]

Clear enough? Got that? Good. Jobs are at stake.

As undemocratic as this process is, it's far more democratic than a process often used to regulate the environment, an area where millions of jobs, our national economy, and our public health are at stake.

As described in John Fund and Hans von Spakovsky's excellent book, *Obama's Enforcer*,[9] the environmental section of the Department of Justice has pioneered a process (called "sue and settle") where it will collude with a radical environmentalist organization to circumvent Congress and the *Federal Register* altogether.

This scandal will be described in greater detail later in the book, but here is the basic outline: The environmentalist group will sue, demanding a court order that would essentially act as a new environmental regulation on an industry. Rather than vigorously defend the law, the Department of Justice's own radical lawyers will actively collude with the outside environmentalists by intentionally "losing" the case through an agreed-upon settlement and then pay the environmental group sometimes millions in taxpayer dollars since they were the "prevailing party," meaning they had "won" the lawsuit.

This is a win-win for radical environmentalists and their bureaucratic friends. The environmentalists change the law and enrich themselves in the process while the bureaucrats are able to circumvent even the rudimentary democratic safeguards in the formal rulemaking process.

The loser, of course, is our republic, which slips steadily from a free people's grasp with each backroom deal.

Don't Even Think of Firing a Bureaucrat

Undemocratic rulemaking processes and backroom deals could be kept under control if elected officials had the power to fire out-of-control bureaucrats.

But thanks to an overreaction to a real historical problem, few Americans have greater job security than employees of the federal government. In fact, in many agencies an employee has a greater chance of dying in office than being fired or seriously disciplined.

How did this happen?

Going back to the founding of the nation, federal jobs were long considered to be plum prizes for political supporters of the winning party. Political wins often meant a veritable clean sweep of the federal government, as the employees from one party were ushered out in favor of the winners.

The phenomenon, this "spoils system," was so well-known and so crass that it was not unusual for political job seekers to stampede into Washington and line up outside offices looking for their place in the government, a process that could distract even the president of the United States.

Needless to say, the spoils system was not the best method for hiring an experienced, competent, and neutral civil service. Rather, it created instability and rewarded loyalty over competence.

So it was abolished, replaced over time by the "merit system" that governs federal employees today.

Most Americans don't realize that when a new president is elected, he has the power to hire and fire only the tiniest percentage of executive branch employees, the most senior leadership only. Beneath that senior leadership are hundreds of thousands of employees who can be fired—or even seriously disciplined—only after the agency works through a complex and exhausting legal process, a process so time-consuming and expensive that many managers simply learn to live with corruption and incompetence rather than even try to terminate an unmanageable employee.

How hard is it to fire a federal employee? The numbers are astonishing. In the introduction, I cited a *USA Today* survey that showed only 0.55 percent of federal employees were fired for cause. Other surveys show even more astounding numbers. As reported in *National Review*, "a CATO Institute survey showed that in one year, just 1 in 5,000 non-defense civilian federal employees was fired for cause." In the key legal positions, job security was virtually guaranteed, with only 27 of the government's 35,000 lawyers losing their jobs in 2011.[10]

The termination process itself requires managers to precisely document their reasons for firing employees and is so onerous that managers are often effectively prohibited from using any criterion that is subjective—like arguing the employee's work product is poor, the employee demonstrates bias, or the employee is difficult to manage. Rather, only the most clearly documented and objectively defined offenses lead to punishment, such as hitting a boss or stealing from your employer.

But in virtually every circumstance, the employee (once they're past their initial probationary period) is entitled to an appeal to the Merit Systems Protection Board. Again, here's *National Review*:

> Moreover, once an employee is fired, there is no guarantee he will *stay* fired. Each has the right to appeal to the Merit Systems Protection Board (MSPB), a Carter-era body created as part of an update to the civil-service reforms in the century-old Pendleton Act (a.k.a. the only reason you remember Chester A. Arthur's name). As a board spokesman told *Politico*, the initial appeal, before a regional administrative-law judge, takes an average of three months to process. A second appeal, to the D.C. board, could take another nine months or more. In the meantime, the terminated will usually have the full-throated advocacy of a union lawyer to go along with a set of MSPB guidelines that set a high bar for the terminators.[11]

What does all this mean? Don't even think about trying to fire a federal employee unless you're ready for a long legal battle where the employee has vigorous, free legal representation. In such circumstances, it's easier to transfer employees, muddle along, or simply shift their work to their overburdened, competent colleagues.

Don't even think about trying to fire a federal employee unless you're ready for a long legal battle where the employee has vigorous, free legal representation. In such circumstances, it's easier to transfer employees, muddle along, or simply shift their work to their overburdened, competent colleagues.

To be clear, I do not believe that federal employees should be fired merely at the whim of a manager. Like all working Americans, they should be protected from discrimination on the basis of race, gender, and religion. And they should also be protected from political discrimination. After all, the permanent bureaucracy should be strictly politically neutral.

But that protection should work the way it works for ordinary Americans: once the employee is fired, if they have evidence they've been discriminated against, they have the right to sue for damages, with no free lawyer provided at government expense.

That's the system that applies to the vast majority of Americans in the private sector, and it generally works. At least it works far better than the so-called merit system.

Exactly How Partisan Are Those Busy, Invulnerable Bureaucrats?

This is a key question, one that goes to the heart of democracy and fairness. It's bad enough that the bureaucracy can entirely circumvent the established constitutional process for passing new laws. It's bad enough that this bureaucracy is full of employees who—as a practical matter—can't be fired even for grotesque incompetence. But the problem reaches truly critical dimensions when those powerful, unaccountable bureaucrats act as partisans—as extensions of the Democratic Party.

Let's look at the National Treasury Employees Union, which represents 150,000 federal workers in thirty-one different federal agencies:

> The union endorsed Obama in both of his presidential runs and operates a political-action committee (PAC) that has donated $1.63 million to federal candidates and committees since 2008, more than 96 percent of it to help elect Democrats. During that period, IRS employees have contributed more than $67,000 to the PAC.
>
> Colleen Kelley, the union's president since 1999, worked as a revenue agent for the IRS for 14 years, and her political leanings are clear. She has given nearly $5,000 to the NTEU PAC since 2007, and she donated $500 to John Kerry's presidential campaign in 2004.[12]

Interestingly, Kelley has been to the White House at least eleven times during the Obama administration, meeting at least once with President Obama.[13] Access to the White House is a rare and precious gift, not given freely to Americans, even politically connected Americans. Kelley's frequent invitations demonstrate that she is no mere union boss, but rather a major player in national politics.

The problem is not confined to unions or to lawyers. To take just one agency, the IRS, its employees donated more than twice as much money to Barack Obama than to Mitt Romney in 2012 and an even greater percentage to Barack Obama over John McCain in 2008.[14]

And this disparity predates President Obama's two presidential races. Look at the numbers dating back to 1989:

> Overall, rank-and-file IRS employees donated more than $840,000 to federal candidates and committees from 1989

to 2012, according to [a Center for Responsive Politics] analysis. Democrats and liberal-leaning organizations received about two-thirds of this sum.[15]

As for government lawyers—key leaders in any federal bureaucracy—a more complete review of their giving, including even the Department of Defense, perhaps the most conservative federal agency, shows a staggering disparity. In some departments, such as the National Labor Relations Board and Department of Education, 100 percent of political gifts went to Barack Obama over Mitt Romney. Almost 84 percent of gifts from government lawyers in the Department of Justice went to President Obama. The most balanced department was the Department of Defense, with a disparity of 68 percent to President Obama.[16]

According to Gallup, government union members of all stripes—state and federal—preferred Barack Obama to Mitt Romney by a whopping 25 points.[17] By contrast, President Obama won reelection by a less than 4-point margin.[18]

These numbers are so far out of line with public preferences that—at best—they create a dangerous perception of bias. And, as the political giving numbers show, the bias becomes more pronounced the more a federal worker engages with politics.

No one is disputing federal workers' right to vote. No one is disputing their right to give money to the candidate of their choice. There is an unmistakable problem, however, with an entrenched bureaucracy that is so closely aligned with one side of our great political debates—and no longer accountable to the public.

Core executive functions are supposed to be strictly nonpartisan. Tax rates are not different for Democrats and Republicans. Criminal laws are not different for Democrats and Republicans. Environmental laws are not different for Democrats and Republicans. But when agencies are stacked with partisan employees, bias can creep into the process even if employees are well-meaning. And if employees aren't well-meaning but are instead biased and corrupt? Well, then there're fewer checks on their power.

The result is plain to see. The toxic combination of growing power, lifetime job security, and political bias is creating a federal bureaucracy that is corrupt, incompetent when it's not corrupt, and sometimes both corrupt and incompetent. Nonpartisan agencies should apply the law in a neutral manner.

And there are real consequences when an agency is implanting a political ideology and not fairly enforcing the law.

When my grandfather immigrated to the United States, he did not come to a perfect country, by no means. But he arrived at a country where he had a fair chance to succeed, where the government had little impact on his success or failure and helped mainly by staying out of his way.

True, the immigration law was complex in 1914 and still is today. The Constitution is clear, however. Congress passes the law, the president executes the law, and the judiciary interprets the law. Notice what is not in the Constitution—government by bureaucracy.

In the Russia he left, government was a suffocating everyday reality, where corrupt, ideological bureaucracies targeted political foes and microregulated the vibrancy and energy straight out of the economy.

That Russia was beyond brutal, of course, and soon set its sights on starving Ukraine into submission, but a bureaucracy does not have to be brutal to choke out liberty. It does not have to be violent to oppress its citizens. It need only be corrupt.

I fear for our American exceptionalism. Liberty cannot flourish when a vast government plays favorites.

Already we see signs that America is losing its title as the true land of liberty.

In 2012, the Fraser Institute issued a startling report: Canadian provinces were now more free than American states.[19] Yes, our neighbors to the north, with their monarchical tradition and only a recent history of true constitutional jurisprudence,[20] now grant greater protection to a host of individual rights, including property rights, than the "land of the free and home of the brave."

When my grandfather left Russia, he was certainly tired. He was certainly poor. He certainly "yearned to breathe free." Is the best destination for such men and women today New York? Or is it Alberta? Or Saskatchewan?

Only time will tell. In the meantime it is incumbent upon those of us who still "yearn to breathe free" to battle for our constitutional republic, to fight against a bureaucracy that can often combine corruption and incompetence as it suppresses dissent and discourages virtue. It's now time to take our country back and restore its constitutional framework.

Corruption and incompetence? No accountability? Abuse of power? Arrogance? All are hallmarks of our modern bureaucracy, and no bureaucracy embodies those characteristics more thoroughly than the IRS.

And that brings us to a truly sordid tale . . .

3

THE IRS

At War with Conservatives

By early 2010, two developments were shaking American liberals to their core. The first was the rise of the Tea Party; the second was a Supreme Court case that protected the right of free political speech.

Deeply troubled by multi-hundred-billion-dollar bailouts in the Bush and Obama presidencies, concerned by massive entitlements and looming national bankruptcy, and shocked at the vast reach of the expanding federal government, millions of Americans were mobilizing at the grass roots, showing energy and numbers that were already starting to thwart the Democrats' plan of a new, permanent majority—hopes that flared after President Obama's landslide 2008 election, a landslide that was already slipping away by 2010.

At the same time, the Supreme Court of the United States decided a critical First Amendment case, *Citizens United v. FEC*, or simply *Citizens United*.

In that case, decided January 21, 2010, the high court applied decades of First Amendment precedent to reach a rather common-sense holding: Corporations have the right to speak on political matters. Writing for the majority, Justice Anthony Kennedy affirmed that "if the First Amendment has any force, it prohibits Congress fining or jailing citizens, or associations of citizens, for simply engaging in political speech."[1]

It also cleared the way for anonymous donors to fund corporate political speech. While the Left cast this in sinister terms, in reality the decision did little more than reaffirm a core constitutional truth: Americans have the right to band together in associations and speak about political issues. We also have the right to anonymous speech. These two rather noncontroversial principles have been established since our nation's founding.

After all, anonymous speech helped propel the American Revolution. Anonymous speech, in the *Federalist Papers*, helped ratify the Constitution. Anonymous speech helped protect and advance the civil rights movement. When you speak, the government does not have a right to know who you are.

But to listen to the Left, the combination of *Citizens United* and the rise of the Tea Party represented the coming of the apocalypse, where shadowy "secret donors" would "Astroturf" (a term for a fake grassroots movement) a political movement to depose the Democratic majority and end its progressive experiments in health care, radical Keynesian economics, and abortion on demand.

On the day of the ruling, President Obama called it "a major victory for big oil, Wall Street, banks, health insurance companies, and other powerful interests that marshal their power every day in Washington to drown out the voices of everyday Americans."[2]

Obama later launched a direct attack on the decision in front of the Justices of the Supreme Court, Congress, and the nation, during his 2010 State of the Union address. He chastised the Justices:

Last week the Supreme Court reversed a century of law that I believe will open the floodgates for special interests— including foreign corporations—to spend without limit in our elections. Well I don't think American elections should be bankrolled by America's most powerful interests, and worse, by foreign entities. They should be decided by the American people, and that's why I'm urging Democrats and Republicans to pass a bill that helps to right this wrong.[3]

This comment was not only rated "mostly false" by even the liberal fact-checkers at PolitiFact; it was so at odds with the law and the text of the decision that it caused a visible reaction from Justice Samuel Alito, who simply said "not true."[4]

Justice Alito was correct. The president wasn't telling the truth. In reality, the decision empowered everyday Americans, allowing them to form grassroots associations, Tea Parties, pro-life groups, and others that magnified their voices and allowed them to impact debates not just about ObamaCare but also about the most local of issues, including the curriculum at the high school down the street.

And it was just this kind of power that the president and his allies at the IRS truly feared.

How do we know? Look at their actions.

In February 2010, the IRS responded to *Citizens United*, though not by targeting "big oil, Wall Street banks, health insurance, and other powerful interests." They did not take on Exxon or Goldman Sachs or Cigna health insurance. Instead they pulled every single application for tax exemption by groups whose names included the terms "Tea Party," "Patriots," or "9/12," or other conservative-sounding phrases like "We the People" or "Take Back the Country."

By March 2010, less than two months after the *Citizens United* decision, the IRS was coordinating this effort out of Washington, D.C., and referred to the cases internally as the "Tea Party cases."

Not the "big oil cases."

Not the "Wall Street cases."

The "Tea Party cases."

As 2010 dragged on, the targeting intensified, involving senior

IRS lawyers and—critically—the director of the Exempt Organizations Division of the IRS.

Lois Lerner was a known partisan. Previously at the Federal Election Commission (FEC), she had distinguished herself by her hyperaggressive pursuit of Christian or conservative organizations. Her attacks on the Christian Coalition, for example, were extreme.

I know. I was directly involved in that case, advising the founder of the Christian Coalition while the coalition endured Lois Lerner's unprecedented assault.

My friend and colleague James Bopp, one of the best constitutional litigators in America, also represented the Christian Coalition and described the scope of the investigation in testimony before Congress:

> The FEC conducted a large amount of paper discovery during the administrative investigation and then served four massive discovery requests during the litigation stage that included 127 document requests, 32 interrogatories, and 1,813 requests for admission. Three of the interrogatories required the Coalition to explain each request for admission that it did not admit in full, for a total of 481 additional written answers that had to be provided.
>
> The Coalition was required to produce tens of thousands of pages of documents, many of them containing sensitive and proprietary information about finances and donor information. Each of the 49 state affiliates were asked to provide documents and many states were individually subpoenaed. In all, the Coalition searched both its offices and warehouse, where millions of pages of documents are stored, in order to produce over 100,000 pages of documents.[5]

It's important to understand why Bopp emphasized the scope of this discovery. In litigation, it's a common (bad-faith) tactic to attempt to metaphorically bury your opponent in a flood of document requests, taxing their resources to the limits to answer information demands. To do this to a nonprofit as part of a massive fishing expedition was both chilling and unacceptable.

The FEC left no stone unturned:

> Furthermore, nearly every aspect of the Coalition's activities has been examined by FEC attorneys from seeking information regarding its donors to information about its legislative lobbying. The Commission, in its never-ending quest to find the non-existent "smoking gun," even served subpoenas upon the Coalition's accountants, its fundraising and direct mail vendors, and The Christian Broadcasting Network.[6]

But then it got much worse. The FEC turned its attention to the actual religious content of Christian Coalition activities:

> FEC attorneys continued their intrusion into religious activities by prying into what occurs at Coalition staff prayer meetings, and even who attends the prayer meetings held at the Coalition. This line of questioning was pursued several times. Deponents were also asked to explain what the positions of "intercessory prayer" and "prayer warrior" entailed, what churches specific people belonged to, and the church and its location at which a deponent met Dr. [Ralph] Reed.

The FEC put pastors under extreme scrutiny:

> One of the most shocking and startling examples of this irrelevant and intrusive questioning by FEC attorneys into private political associations of citizens occurred during the administrative depositions of three pastors from South Car-

olina. Each pastor, only one of whom had only the slightest connection with the Coalition, was asked not only about their federal, state and local political activities, including party affiliations, but about political activities that, as one FEC attorney described as "personal," and outside of the jurisdiction of the FECA [Federal Election Campaign Act]. They were also continually asked about the associations and activities of the members of their congregations, and even other pastors.[7]

At one point, the FEC even asked Oliver North what it meant when friends prayed for him, a line of questioning Lieutenant Colonel North rightly found offensive. Yet Lerner pressed on—far more focused on suppressing the Christian Coalition than respecting the First Amendment rights, including religious liberty rights, of American citizens.

And make no mistake, Lois Lerner was a biased, partisan liberal. Years after this investigation, she was caught using her official IRS email account to call conservatives "crazies" and "teRrorists" (yes, she used that spelling), and even used expletives to describe conservative groups.[8]

Speaking of conservatives she heard on radio, she said, "Maybe we are through if there are that many [expletive omitted]."[9]

Then she said, speaking again of conservatives, "So we don't need to worry about alien teRrorists. It's our own crazies that will take us down."[10]

In a bureaucracy governed by the Constitution, one that respects the rule of law, defends individual liberty, and is staffed by professionals, using official government email to slander an entire class of citizens would mean the end of a bureaucrat's career.

Likewise, in a bureaucracy governed by the Constitution, one that respects the rule of law, defends individual liberty, and is staffed by professionals, questioning American citizens about the content of their prayers would mean the end of a bureaucrat's career.

But when bureaucrats have immense power, enjoy near-absolute job security, and are brazen partisans, this kind of inquiry helps one rocket to the top. And so Lois Lerner found herself in a key position at the IRS, ready to choke off the Tea Party before it had even had the opportunity to fully form.

Lerner—and her numerous IRS colleagues—acted with an enthusiastic cheerleader in the White House, with President Obama even implying that conservative groups were receiving foreign funds.

In August 2010, just three months before the November 2010 midterms, President Obama warned about "attack ads run by shadowy groups with harmless-sounding names." He went on to say, "We don't know who's behind these ads and we don't know who's paying for them . . . you don't know if it's a foreign-controlled corporation . . . the only people who don't want to disclose the truth are people with something to hide." [11]

On September 16, 2010, President Obama was at it again, warning against a "foreign-controlled entity" that could be providing "millions of dollars" for "attack ads." [12] Less than a week later he complained that "nobody knows" who was supporting conservative groups. [13]

The campaign continued. On September 21, 2010, the White House tried to enlist the mainstream media. Sam Stein, writing in the *Huffington Post*, described how "a senior administration official . . . urged a small gathering of reporters to start writing on what he deemed the most insidious power grab that we have seen in a long time." [14]

Insidious power grab? That describes the IRS, not the pro-life and conservative groups they were at that very moment systematically targeting. It is the IRS that is on the power trip.

What do I mean by "targeting"?

First, a bit about legality and process. One of the best ways to engage in so-called issue advocacy is to form a nonprofit corporation under Section 501(c)(4) of the Internal Revenue Code. While donations to these corporations aren't tax-deductible, the corporation's income isn't taxed, and the donations to the corporation can be anonymous.

This protection—which prevents the government from controlling the message through the power to expose dissenters or to tax dissent—means that so-called (c)(4)s are nearly ideal vehicles for engaging in cultural and ideological argument, a fact the Left has long known.

Think of the most influential organizations on the Left—like Planned Parenthood, the ACLU, or the radical MoveOn.org. They all have affiliated 501(c)(4)s that enable them to fully engage the public. In short, nonprofit advocacy corporations have been around for a long time, the IRS has dealt with them for a long time, and conservatives had been behind the curve for an equally long time.

The Tea Party started to correct that imbalance, and the IRS was outraged. Normally, a 501(c)(4) application is a simple process: form the corporation, obtain an employer identification number, then complete and file IRS Form 1024, IRS Form 8718, and the appropriate fee.

Typically, the IRS will review the form and approve the application in a matter of months. On occasion, the IRS will respond with a few follow-up questions if the application is unclear or information is missing. Rarely does the process drag on. As I said, the IRS has been doing this for a long time.

But what happened when the Tea Party and other conservatives applied? How were they treated differently from the norm? This chart, from the House Ways and Means Committee, tells the story: [15]

IRS Targeting Statistics of Files Produced by IRS Through July 29, 2013

Organization Names*	Total	Questions Asked	Average Questions Asked	Approved	Approved %	Outstanding or Withdrawn
Conservative	8	100	12.5	3	38%	5
Tea Party	72	1012	14.1	33	46%	39
Patriot, 9/12	24	440	18.3	12	50%	12
Subtotal of Conservative Organizations	104	1552	14.9	48	46%	56
Progressive	7	33	4.7	7	100%	0

*One file In the enumerated categories has not been provided by the IRS despite numerous requests.

Let's translate: when evaluating progressive organizations, the IRS singled out only seven groups for additional scrutiny, asked an average of only 4.7 additional questions, and approved every single group.

By contrast, the IRS singled out 104 conservative groups, asked an average of 14.9 additional questions (some with multiple subparts), and ultimately approved fewer than half.

This chart was first published in July 2013, and some of the conservative groups waiting for approval were still waiting *as of the end of 2014.*

At the ACLJ, we are litigating on behalf of forty-one groups, some of which had been waiting for approval since 2009. That means they applied for a tax exemption before the iPad was invented, before LeBron James went to the Miami Heat and won two championships, before the most recent British royal wedding (much less the British royal baby). The list could go on.

And the entire time that the Tea Party groups waited for these tax-exemption determinations, they were losing donations, spending hours with lawyers, and answering voluminous questionnaires rather than organizing and advocating for conservative and pro-life ideas.

And what about those questions?

The IRS used the tax-exemption application process to attempt to conduct litigation-style investigations into the funding and operations of not just the Tea Party groups but also their individual volunteers and *their family members*. Here's a sampling of the questions the IRS asked:

> Do you directly or indirectly communicate with members of legislative bodies? If so, provide copies of the written communications and contents of other forms of communications.

And

> Please describe the associate group members and their role with your organization in further detail. (a) How does your organization solicit members? (b) What are the questions asked of potential members? (c) What are the selection criteria for approval? (d) Do you limit membership to other organizations exempt under 501(c)(4) of the Code? (e) Provide the name, employer identification number, and address of the organizations.

And

> Do you have a close relationship with any candidate for public office or political party? If so describe fully the nature of that relationship.
> List each past or present board member, officer, key employee and *members of their families* who:
> a) Has served on the board of another organization.
> b) Was, is or plans to be a candidate for public office. Indicate the nature of each candidacy.

c) Has previously conducted similar activities for another entity.

d) Has previously submitted an application for tax exempt status.[16]

These questions are illegal, pure and simple. They are outside the scope of legitimate inquiry and violate the First Amendment; it is none of the IRS's concern whether a Tea Party board member's father served on his church's board of deacons.

And, remember, these inquiries were not made after any allegation of wrongdoing—or part of any investigation of wrongdoing—but purely as a part of the IRS's "routine" examination of conservatives.

How did we know these kinds of inquiries are illegal?

Because the Supreme Court had considered cases like this before—decades ago, when state governments were using similar tactics to suppress the civil rights movement.

In 1958, in *NAACP v. Patterson*, the state of Alabama challenged the right of the National Association for the Advancement of Colored People (NAACP) to operate in the state unless it disclosed certain information to the state, including its membership lists. The Court, in a short but forceful opinion, denied Alabama's demand, noting:

> Effective advocacy of both public and private points of view, particularly controversial ones, is undeniably enhanced by group association, as this Court has more than once recognized by remarking upon the close nexus between the freedoms of speech and assembly. . . . Of course, it is immaterial whether the beliefs sought to be advanced by association pertain to political, economic, religious or cultural matters, and state action which may have the effect of curtailing the freedom to associate is subject to the closest scrutiny.[17]

The Court went on:

> It is hardly a novel perception that compelled disclosure
> of affiliation with groups engaged in advocacy may con-
> stitute as effective a restraint on freedom of association as
> the forms of governmental action in the cases above were
> thought likely to produce upon the particular constitutional
> rights there involved. This Court has recognized the vital
> relationship between freedom to associate and privacy in
> one's associations.[18]

In other words, when the government demands to know whom you
meet with or work with when you're engaging in political advocacy,
that may deter you from joining groups. Would you be more or less
likely to join a political organization if you knew that your name
and address would be immediately transmitted to the government?
Would you be more or less likely to join an advocacy organization
if you knew that you'd even have to disclose the activities of your
family members? It's simple common sense that Americans want
and demand a degree of privacy in their speech and activities. If
we're going to speak out, we want it to be on our own terms, not
when and how the government tells us to.

So, when comparing the cases, it's plain that the IRS's recent
demands of conservative groups went far beyond the state of Alabama's request for the NAACP's membership lists. After all, the
compelled disclosures included probing questions about donors and
even family members of group leaders—information that went even
beyond the information the state of Alabama wrongly demanded
from the NAACP.

Not only was the IRS's request for information unlawful—it was
also intimidating. Just as Alabama tried to intimidate the NAACP
in the 1950s, President Obama's IRS tried to intimidate conservatives throughout his first term and beyond. It is sad and ironic that

the Obama administration was using the old tools of segregationists against new political movements like the Tea Party.

At the ACLJ, we knew of Obama administration misconduct before Lois Lerner and the IRS issued their insincere confession and apology. In fact, in March 2012, we demanded answers, asking whether there was a "broad-based IRS assault on the Tea Party."[19]

In response, the IRS lied. Former IRS commissioner Douglas Shulman told Congress that the IRS prides itself on being non-political, and that its scrutiny of conservative groups was typical.[20]

In reality, based on our clients' experiences, it was clear the IRS conservative-targeting campaign was in full swing, was being conducted from IRS offices from coast to coast, and was discussed and monitored at the highest levels of the IRS.

In late May 2013, we'd seen enough. We filed a lawsuit, the largest in ACLJ history.[21] Ultimately including forty-one conservative and pro-life organizations in twenty-two states, it represented a comprehensive attack on the IRS targeting scheme and laid out in detail the consequences of the IRS's misconduct. The ACLJ filed its case with the following understanding:

> The IRS scheme had a dramatic impact on targeted groups, causing many to curtail lawful activities, expend considerable unnecessary funds, lose donor support, and devote countless hours of time responding to onerous and targeted IRS information requests that were outside the scope of legitimate inquiry.

Moreover:

> Unlawful IRS targeting, despite public apologies, is ongoing. Multiple conservative organizations still have not received final determinations on their applications, are still receiving intrusive requests for information, and are still

suffering financial harm. Some of these organizations, even after receiving tax-exempt status, have been subjected to continued monitoring by the IRS based on the same unlawful purposes for which their applications were originally targeted.[22]

As we filed our case—and used the full resources of the ACLJ to inform Congress and the American people—the scandal exploded.

There's an old Washington saying that the worst kinds of scandals are characterized by a "drip, drip, drip" of new information—with small new details emerging weekly or monthly until they slowly fill the news media with stories of wrongdoing.

But there was nothing "drip, drip, drip" about this scandal. It quickly became "flood, flood, flood."

In fact, as of the time of this writing, it is no longer appropriate to refer simply to "the IRS targeting scandal." The appropriate response is to ask, "Which IRS targeting scandal?"

They are legion.

The IRS Discloses Conservatives' Confidential Information

The IRS has a terrible habit of disclosing confidential taxpayer information about conservatives and conservative groups.

In 2012, at the height of the presidential election season, the IRS claimed it "inadvertently" sent a copy of confidential documents to a liberal group called the Human Rights Campaign showing that an organization affiliated with Republican presidential candidate Mitt Romney had donated to a prominent social conservative organization.[23]

This news—as well as the illegal disclosure—soon found its way onto the *Huffington Post*, where it was used to paint Romney as bigoted and further motivate President Obama's leftist base to turn out to vote.

The conservative organization sued, and in 2014 the IRS settled the case, agreeing to pay the group fifty thousand dollars in actual damages for the disclosure, but the real damage had already been done to the Romney campaign and—more important—the public trust.[24]

But even as the IRS settled it continued to maintain that the disclosure was a mistake.

A mistake? Really?

Here's the liberal news organization ProPublica:

The same IRS office that deliberately targeted conservative groups applying for tax-exempt status in the run-up to the 2012 election released nine pending confidential applications of conservative groups to ProPublica late last year.

How did this happen?

In response to a request for the applications for 67 different nonprofits last November, the Cincinnati office of the IRS sent ProPublica applications or documentation for 31 groups. Nine of those applications had not yet been approved—meaning they were not supposed to be made public. (We [ProPublica] made six of those public, after redacting their financial information, deeming that they were newsworthy.)[25]

Once again, it's important to emphasize the importance of these disclosures. Taxpayer confidentiality exists for a reason. Disclosure of confidential information leaves a taxpayer publicly exposed and vulnerable, and knowledge that their information is uniquely vulnerable to IRS "mistakes" can have a profound deterrent effect on the decision to even attempt to form a 501(c)(4) or to donate to a conservative nonprofit.

The IRS was following the rules with liberals, allowing their contributions to be secret. But with conservatives, the IRS was all too willing to break the rules, to expose conservative donations to the world. Their goal was obvious: to try to frighten conservatives into closing their wallets, depriving conservative groups of the money they needed to oppose the Left's agenda.

But that's not all, of course.

The IRS Audits Conservatives

Even as it emerged that the IRS systematically targeted conservative organizations for additional scrutiny in the nonprofit application process, many conservatives were reporting a much more up-close and personal encounter with the revenue agency:

> Despite [Lois Lerner's] assurances to the contrary, the IRS didn't destroy all of the donor lists scooped up in its tea party targeting [as they were ordered to do]—and a check of those lists reveals that the tax agency audited 10 percent of those donors, much higher than the audit rate for average Americans, House Republicans revealed Wednesday.[26]

Ten percent isn't just a "much higher" audit rate. It's astronomically higher. In fact, Tea Party donors were "1000% more likely to be audited" than your average taxpayer.[27]

And it wasn't just Tea Party donors; some of Republican nominee Mitt Romney's larger donors and other prominent conservatives faced their own IRS ordeals. Here's an ABC News report from May 2013:

> Now Frank VanderSloot, an Idaho businessman who donated more than $1 million to groups supporting Romney,

told ABC News he believes he may have been targeted for an audit after his opposition to the Obama administration. So did Hal Scherz, a physician who started the group Docs4PatientCare to lobby against President Obama's health care initiative, and became a vocal critic of the president on cable news programs. Franklin Graham, the son of the evangelist Billy Graham, said he believes his father was a target of unusual IRS scrutiny as well, according to published reports Wednesday.[28]

The IRS targeted not only Graham's evangelistic activities, but also Graham's humanitarian activities overseas, hitting Samaritan's Purse, a group known for—among other things—"Operation Christmas Child," a program that provides hope, gifts, and joy to desperately poor children around the globe.

Graham told Politico that groups founded by his famous father, the Billy Graham Evangelistic Association and the family's international humanitarian organization Samaritan's Purse, were both subjected to aggressive action by the IRS. In a letter to President Obama, which he shared with the news outlet, he wrote: "I do not believe that the IRS audit of our two organizations last year is a coincidence—or justifiable."[29]

And what about existing 501(c)(4)s, the organizations that made it through the IRS targeting and were granted exemptions?

Surprise, surprise: the IRS follow-up audits exclusively targeted conservative groups. Congressman Dave Camp, chairman of the powerful House Ways and Means Committee, said:

Additionally, we now know that the IRS targeted not only right-leaning applicants, but also right-leaning groups that were already operating as 501(c)(4)s. At Washington, DC's direction, dozens of groups operating as 501(c)(4)s were flagged for IRS surveillance, including monitoring of the groups' activities, websites and any other publicly available information. Of these groups, 83 percent were right-leaning. And of the groups the IRS selected for audit, 100 percent were right-leaning.[30]

So, in summary, Tea Party donors were 1,000 percent more likely to be audited, Mitt Romney's largest donors faced their own IRS ordeals, prominent Christian groups like Franklin Graham's Samaritan's Purse faced "aggressive" IRS action, and 100 percent of 501(c)(4)s selected for follow-on audits were conservative.

But that's not all, of course.

The IRS Targets a Conservative Senator

In December 2012, Lois Lerner took a break from targeting Tea Party groups to suggest a different target, Iowa Republican senator Chuck Grassley.[31]

Lois Lerner and Senator Grassley were apparently invited to speak at the same event, and their invitations were swapped, with Lerner receiving Senator Grassley's. The senator's invitation indicated that the group hosting the event was apparently offering to pay the senator's wife to attend, and Lerner pounced, suggesting this was improper and that the IRS "refer to exam."

Fortunately, cooler heads prevailed, and a highly inappropriate audit was avoided, but some context is required.

When Lerner targeted Senator Grassley, the target was hardly random. Senator Grassley had long monitored the IRS Exempt Organizations Division. He was doing what legislators should do, investigating whether the IRS was doing its job:

"'This isn't random," said Dean Zerbe, a tax lawyer who helped Grassley investigate tax-exempt groups and reform the law governing them. "This is going after the senator most active in conducting serious reviews of charitable organizations as well as the IRS work in this area."

And:

> Grassley was also one of a dozen senators who sent a letter to the IRS in March 2012 questioning whether Tea Party groups seeking tax-exempt status were being unfairly scrutinized.[32]

In other words, Grassley didn't view the IRS as his ideological partner, but rather as a federal agency that required oversight. This, apparently, made him an enemy of the IRS, one subject to audit at Lois Lerner's whim.

But that's not all, of course.

The IRS Loves Planned Parenthood and Hates the Pro-Life Movement

In 2009, the Coalition for Life of Iowa, a small pro-life group, sought IRS approval for a tax exemption under Section 501(c)(3) of the tax code.

And what was the IRS's response?

It wanted the group to promise that it wouldn't protest or picket Planned Parenthood, the nation's largest abortion provider.[33] Here's the congressional testimony of Susan Martinek, the group's president:

> "In June of 2009, Ms. Richards (no first name given) told me verbally that we needed to send in a letter with the entire

board's signatures stating that under penalty of perjury we would not picket/protest or organize groups to picket/protest outside of Planned Parenthood," Martinek said. "Upon receiving such a letter, she indicated that the IRS would allow our application to go through."[34]

But that wasn't all. The IRS was concerned with much more than Planned Parenthood picketing, and—pulling a page from Lois Lerner's playbook when she investigated the Christian Coalition—demanded details of the Iowa Coalition for Life's prayer activities. Again, here's Martinek's testimony:

> On June 22, 2009, IRS Agent Richards sent us additional written requests, as follows: "Please explain how all of your activities, including the prayer meetings held outside of Planned Parenthood are considered educational as defined under 501(c)(3). Organizations exempt under 501(c)(3) may present opinions with scientific or medical facts. Please explain in detail the activities at the prayer meetings. Also, please provide the percentage of time your organization spends on prayer groups as compared with the other activities of the organization. Please explain in detail the signs that are being held up outside of Planned Parenthood and explain how they are considered educational."[35]

These are extraordinarily intrusive inquiries, with an astounding level of detail demanded about "prayer meetings," and an extraordinary level of protectiveness toward Planned Parenthood. Why is the IRS concerned only about signs held up outside Planned Parenthood? If it's truly concerned about the group's educational purpose, the signs about Planned Parenthood are no more or less relevant than the signs the group uses elsewhere.

Yet the Iowa Coalition for Life's ordeal was not unique. The

IRS also targeted AMEN (short for "Abortion Must End Now"), an Arizona pro-life nonprofit, under Internal Revenue Procedure 86-43, an unconstitutionally vague procedure that allows biased IRS agents to subjectively determine whether an organization's educational materials are excessively "inflammatory" or "disparaging" or overly "emotional."[36]

In this case, the IRS targeted not just AMEN's pro-life materials, but also the name of the organization itself. Given the stunning level of vitriol and emotionalism that routinely pours forth from pro-abortion organizations, targeting a small pro-life group on these grounds was not only the height of irony, it was also unconstitutional viewpoint discrimination.

These attacks, where the IRS put its thumb on the scales of abortion—perhaps the most critical cultural, religious, and political argument of our time—demonstrates once again that employees of the IRS are less interested in impartial enforcement of tax laws than in using these tax laws to reward ideological friends and to punish ideological (and religious) foes.

But that's not all, of course.

The IRS Agrees to Monitor Free Speech in Churches

On July 21, 2014, the Freedom from Religion Foundation announced that it had reached a settlement with the IRS in response to a lawsuit filed in 2012. And what were the terms of the settlement?[37]

The IRS agreed to "monitor churches and other houses of worship for electioneering." (Electioneering is another word for taking an active part in a political campaign.)

In other words, the IRS—while under congressional investigation for its massive campaign of targeting, intimidation, and harassment of conservative groups—was at the same time *agreeing* with a radical atheist organization that it would step up its investigations of free speech in churches and other tax-exempt organizations.

The IRS—while fighting tooth and nail our ACLJ lawsuit brought on behalf of conservative and pro-life groups the IRS targeted—was *agreeing* with arguably the nation's most litigious atheists that it wasn't doing enough to keep Christians in line, that it needed to expose churches to even greater scrutiny.

It is well-known that churches and other nonprofits (which are typically 501(c)(3) organizations) cannot—consistent with IRS rules—officially endorse candidates. This is a relatively modest limitation on free speech that comes along with a tax exemption, but even that relatively modest limit has suspect origins—dating back to Lyndon Johnson's attempts to prevent churches from mobilizing opposition to his early political career.

Prior to the so-called Johnson Amendment, churches enjoyed the full range of free speech rights.

But the Freedom from Religion Foundation wants even *more* restrictions on religious speech, employing a very broad interpretation of IRS restrictions on political engagement that would essentially mean that religious officials not only couldn't endorse candidates, they couldn't even discuss key political issues from a biblical perspective from the pulpit, in Sunday school, on church websites, or through any other church resource.

Groups like the Freedom from Religion Foundation have advocated this view for so long that many churches and pastors are reluctant to discuss even the most basic of moral issues from the pulpit if they have political overtones. Let's take the fight for life, for example. Many Christians mistakenly believe that discussion of abortion from the pulpit is inherently "political" and thus unlawful. In reality, however, abortion is a moral issue, not just a political issue, and sharing a biblical perspective on that moral issue—and sharing truthful information about where individuals stand on life—is constitutionally protected speech.

But now that the IRS is required to "monitor" churches, temples, and houses of worship, will these institutions feel more or less free?

Should they trust the IRS to know the law and apply the law fairly?

And how, exactly, will it "monitor" them? By applying the same methods it applied to the Tea Party?

Once the congressional spotlight has shifted from the IRS scandals and the IRS once again feels a degree of freedom of action, I have little doubt that houses of worship will soon start to feel the presence of the tax man, through audits, investigations, subpoenas, and other forms of extraordinary scrutiny.

The IRS seems to be replacing "tax collection" with "oppression and censorship" as a key part of its agency mission statement.

But that's not all, of course.

The IRS Tried to Criminalize Conservative Speech

In perhaps the most ominous development of all, the IRS was not content with merely delaying and harassing Tea Parties and other conservative groups, not content with auditing conservative individuals, and certainly not content with investigating the prayer meetings of pro-life groups. To truly advance the Obama administration's agenda, the IRS needed to do more.

It needed criminal prosecutions—even if there was no evidence of a crime.

In early 2014, Judicial Watch uncovered a key email exchange between Lois Lerner and Nikole Flax, the former IRS commissioner's chief of staff.[38]

To be clear, the words you're about to read were written just days before Lois Lerner offered her insincere, misleading apology for targeting the Tea Party:

I got a call today from Richard Pilger Director Elections
Crimes Branch at DOJ. I know him from contacts from my
days there. He wanted to know who at IRS the DOJ folks
could talk to about [Rhode Island Democrat] Sen. Whitehouse idea at the hearing that DOJ could piece together
false statement cases about applicants who "lied" on their
1024s—saying they weren't planning on doing political activity, and then turning around and making large visible political expenditures. DOJ is feeling like it needs to respond,
but want to talk to the right folks at IRS to see whether there
are impediments from our side and what, if any damage this
might do to IRS programs.

I told him that sounded like we might need several folks
from IRS. I am out of town all next week, so wanted to reach
out and see who you think would be right for such a meeting and also hand this off to Nan as contact person if things
need to happen while I am gone—[39]

Here was Ms. Flax's response:

I think we should do it—also need to include CI, which we
can help coordinate. Also, we need to reach out to FEC.
Does it make sense to consider including them in this or
keep it separate?[40]

For those not familiar with the bureaucratic language of these
emails, Lerner is telling Flax that she spoke with the Department
of Justice about prosecuting conservative nonprofits, but not because there were any credible complaints of wrongdoing but only
because a liberal senator (Sheldon Whitehouse of Rhode Island) was
demanding IRS action.

The phrase "piece together" is government-speak for "make
up." They were going to make up cases against conservatives—send

people to jail because the IRS hated their speech. And rather than immediately condemn this idea, Flax endorsed it and even suggested expanding it to the Federal Election Commission. The earlier reference to "CI" is the Criminal Investigative Division. So there you have it: the real lawbreakers are the IRS and DOJ, which have conspired to deny our clients' constitutionally protected rights.

Simply put, this is the kind of behavior that one expects from the bad old days of East German politics or contemporary Cuba, where the government regime finds ways to concoct prosecutions against its opponents.

This was an unparalleled, unprecedented attempt to stifle political expression through the use of grand jury indictments and prosecutions without a shred of evidence. Fortunately, they were caught before they could bring any charges.

Lest anyone think this was simply an isolated exchange—just a few bureaucrats harmlessly brainstorming—it's clear that the IRS had long been committed to taking criminal action against the Tea Party.

In October 2010 the IRS sent a whopping total of 1.1 million pages of taxpayer files to the FBI in advance of a meeting to discuss potential criminal prosecutions against nonprofit groups.[41] According to *National Review*, many of these documents likely contained confidential taxpayer information. This means the IRS was not only attempting to prosecute dissent; it was violating its own governing statutes and regulations to do so.

It's hard to overstate the gravity of these revelations. Few things are more chilling than the prospect of federal criminal prosecution, and facing such a prospect for merely forming a group that, say, opposes ObamaCare or abortion is an unspeakable violation of the letter and spirit of the Constitution.

It's un-American.

But that's not all, of course.

The IRS "Loses" the Evidence

Imagine you approach a Hollywood executive with the following script idea: A powerful federal agency goes rogue. It targets political opponents with extraordinary investigations, targets opponents for audits, tries to throw opponents in jail, targets politicians who try to investigate its wrongdoing, and even attempts to monitor the prayers of the faithful. Then, just when investigators close in on the wrongdoers, they suddenly disclose that they've "lost" all the relevant evidence.

The movie would never be made. Why not? Because it's too cartoonish, too absurd to be believable.

But in the modern IRS, truth is truly stranger than fiction.

On Friday, June 13, 2014, the House Ways and Means Committee reported that the IRS "lost" emails from Lois Lerner, the top IRS official at the center of the targeting of conservative groups.[42]

Yes, "lost."

Incredibly, the supposedly "lost" emails are from "January 2009–April 2011"—the exact heart of the IRS targeting scandal, when hundreds of conservative groups applied for tax-exempt status and were intentionally slow-rolled as intrusive questionnaires were developed, when Lois Lerner was attempting to jump-start frivolous criminal investigations, when the IRS was working from top to bottom to crush the conservative movement.

Even more conveniently, all emails during the period "to and from" Lerner involving "outside agencies or groups, such as the White House, Treasury, Department of Justice, FEC, or Democrat offices" are gone—because of an alleged "computer crash."

A computer crash.

Never mind, of course, that government emails are not housed on individual hard drives but instead on the IRS exchange servers. Never mind that the exchange servers were backed up every six months. The emails were gone.

Vanished.

Even worse, the IRS discovered this alleged loss only weeks after promising Congress it would produce all of Lois Lerner's emails, even after it allegedly knew the emails were gone.

House Ways and Means chairman Dave Camp was justifiably outraged:

> The fact that I am just learning about this, over a year into the investigation, is completely unacceptable and now calls into question the credibility of the IRS's response to Congressional inquiries. There needs to be an immediate investigation and forensic audit by Department of Justice as well as the Inspector General.
>
> Just a short time ago, [IRS] Commissioner [John] Koskinen promised to produce all Lerner documents. It appears now that was an empty promise. Frankly, these are the critical years of the targeting of conservative groups that could explain who knew what when, and what, if any, coordination there was between agencies. Instead, because of this loss of documents, we are conveniently left to believe that Lois Lerner acted alone. This failure of the IRS requires the White House, which promised to get to the bottom of this, to do an Administration-wide search and production of any emails to or from Lois Lerner. The Administration has repeatedly referred us back to the IRS for production of materials. It is clear that is wholly insufficient when it comes to determining the full scope of the violation of taxpayer rights.[43]

Then it got worse. Much worse.

Days later, the IRS informed Congress that it lost emails from at least six more IRS officials, including Nikole Flax, the chief of staff to the former commissioner, and the very same individual who suggested roping the FEC into the IRS and DOJ's scheme to launch

made-up (excuse me, "pieced together") prosecutions of conservative nonprofits.[44]

Computers are crashing all over the IRS.

This was astounding behavior from an agency that demands
taxpayers—to paraphrase Comedy Central's Jon Stewart—to
become virtual "hoarders" of receipts and other records.

This from an agency that requires taxpayers to bear the burden
of proof of their own expenses when it launches an audit, a depar-
ture from the constitutional norm that typically requires the government to bear the burden of proof when it accuses citizens of
wrongdoing.

An ACLJ post from the week when this phase of the scandal
broke got it exactly right: "The IRS claims that it stores voluminous
amounts of email, yet just the important ones from what may be the
largest IRS scandal in history seem to disappear."[45]

In response, the IRS touted its data-keeping prowess:

> The IRS email system runs on Microsoft Outlook. Each of
> the Outlook email servers are located at one of three IRS data
> centers. Approximately 170 terabytes of email (178,000,000
> megabytes, representing *literally hundreds of millions of emails*)
> are currently stored on those servers. For disaster recovery
> purposes, the IRS does a daily back-up of its email servers.
> The daily back-up provides a snapshot of the contents of all
> email boxes as of the date and time of the backup.[46]

Somehow, out of "170 terabytes of email" stored on its servers, the
IRS managed to lose exactly the emails Congress most wanted to
see. How convenient.

On July 9, 2014, the scandal expanded from emails to "OCS"—
short for Microsoft Office Communications Server, the IRS's
internal instant messenger service. The House Oversight Committee released emails showing that a mere twelve days after the IRS

learned that the Treasury inspector general was going to blow the lid off the Tea Party targeting scandal, Lois Lerner emailed an IRS IT professional asking this:

> I had a question today about OCS [Microsoft Office Communications Server]. I was cautioning folks about email and how we have several occasions where Congress has asked for emails and there has been an electronic search for responsive emails—so we need to be cautious about what we say in emails. Someone asked if OCS conversations were also searchable—I don't know, but told them I would get back to them. Do you know? [47]

Here was the response:

> No, the IRS does not routinely save chat communications—unless employees intentionally take steps to preserve their conversation. These chat communications are not saved—and this is critical—despite the fact that "the functionality exists within the software." [48]

Let's be clear: This means that the IRS had the ability to save its internal "chat" communications, but chose not to do so. The "functionality" existed, but the IRS did not choose to use it.

Lois Lerner's reply?

"Perfect." [49]

Yes, for Lerner it was perfect—the exact answer she needed to hear. She could "caution" her team to be careful in emails, she could "crash" her computer, and then she could still—at least for the time being—speak internally on a communications system that the IRS was choosing not to save.

Keep in mind also that Lerner was urging "caution" in response to knowledge that Congress would be performing its constitutional oversight responsibility. Unelected bureaucrats should not be "cautious" in dealing with the American people's elected representatives; they should be transparent.

These revelations, taken together, provided a road map for other federal agencies to suppress or "lose" their own records of emails with Lois Lerner. And, yes, like clockwork the White House came forward days later to claim that it had done a comprehensive search of its own computer records and no one had ever emailed Lois Lerner.

So, here's the timeline: the IRS takes a year to tell Congress it "lost" the key Lerner emails, while it took the White House just days to report that no Lois Lerner emails exist.

But what about emails with chief of staff Nikole Flax? She visited the White House thirty-one times, and some segments of her emails were lost as well.[50] Did the White House thoroughly search for her communications?

During the Watergate scandal, the press went into a veritable feeding frenzy when the Nixon White House reported that slightly more than eighteen minutes of tape recordings of a key conversation between President Richard Nixon and his chief of staff, H. R. Haldeman, were erased.

The Nixon White House claimed it was an accident.

This erasure contributed immeasurably to the perception that the president was corrupt and helped bring down a presidency that only two years earlier had won reelection in a historic landslide.

(Ironically enough, one of the articles of impeachment[51] against Richard Nixon cited his attempts to use the IRS against his political enemies, attempts that were insignificant compared to the vast scope of actual IRS wrongdoing during the Obama administration.)

Fast-forward to 2014, with the IRS facing allegations of wrongdoing that absolutely dwarfed in scale and scope any of the allegations against the Nixon administration, and it "lost" far, far more evidence than a mere eighteen-minute conversation.

Yet aside from the indispensable conservative media, the mainstream media yawned, appearing to take at face value that, well, computers crash.

In 1974, dogged investigators hounded the president of the United States.

In 2014, aggrieved conservatives—victimized by a staggering amount of wrongdoing—could only turn to a Department of Justice so beset with its own partisan bias that it earns itself two entire chapters of this book, chapters that can expose only a small fraction of the department's recent wrongdoing.

And how did the Department of Justice respond to the IRS wrongdoing? By appointing a dedicated partisan and Obama donor to "lead" the DOJ's investigation of the IRS.[52]

Don't forget that this is the same DOJ that was trying—just days before the attorney general ordered it to "investigate" the IRS—to "piece together" prosecutions of conservatives.

The conflict of interest was obvious. And it was left obviously unaddressed, and it still has not been addressed as this book goes to print.

A single chapter in a book cannot possibly do justice to the full extent of IRS malice as it assaulted President Obama's political opponents. Those familiar with the scandal will read this book and immediately think of multiple additional incidents.

But the purpose of this book is not to provide the final word on the IRS's political corruption. Indeed, even as I write, litigation is ongoing—litigation that is revealing new facts every day. The purpose of this book is to show—agency by agency—how our federal bureaucracy is corrupting the rule of law, threatening our democracy, and acting with unchecked arrogance and malice.

And lest you think the arrogance and malice are confined to the government's treatment of conservatives, think again.

I'm not even finished talking about the IRS.

4

THE IRS

Auditing Adoption, Breaking the Law

A dopting a child is among the most meaningful, most important, and most loving acts that any person can take. Its consequences are profound, and its effects last a lifetime. Indeed, it impacts generations to come.

Children who are unwanted and abandoned become loved and cared for. Sometimes children are rescued from starvation abroad to join families that lavish them with attention and give them every advantage America has to offer—supplementing their love with nutrition, education, and opportunity.

One of the most rewarding aspects of my legal career has been the legal help I've been privileged to give adoptive families. Because of the ACLJ's extensive international work and sterling reputation with many foreign governments and foreign diplomats, I've been able to cut through red tape and help families work through immense challenges to bring their beloved children home.

On occasion, I've been blessed to see these kids in our offices, as the parents come by to thank our team and to show off their new families.

As a pro-life lawyer—one who's been fighting for kids for decades—I see adoption as especially crucial. It's heartbreaking to see families desperate to adopt and eager to raise a child unable to do so even while children die by the hundreds of thousands in Planned Parenthood "clinics."

But one doesn't have to be pro-life to support adoption. Indeed, there are many, many adoptive children of pro-choice parents, and those parents love their children with their whole hearts. In fact, one is hard-pressed to find anyone in the mainstream of American political and cultural life who's opposed to adoption.

Because of this broad support, Congress has long provided generous tax credits for adoptive families. The process can be crushingly expensive, often costing more than $30,000 even for relatively simple domestic adoptions, and adoptions of kids from overseas can easily run more than $50,000.

The process is not just expensive; it's also agonizingly complex, requiring families to endure extensive home studies, compile great masses of paperwork, and often run headlong into indifferent bureaucracies at every stage of the process. I've seen family adoption files that can rival law firm litigation files.

The adoption tax credit can make the difference between adding to your family or abandoning the adoption dream. It costs taxpayers very little but it means a tremendous amount to struggling middle-class families.

In fact, the adoption tax credit is one of the least controversial, most popular aspects of the Internal Revenue Code.

Except to the IRS.

The IRS apparently hates the adoption tax credit and sees no problem with inflicting mass-scale audits on adoptive families. In fact, during one two-year period adoptive families were more likely to be audited than any other significant category of taxpayers.

The statistics are staggering. In 2012, the IRS requested additional information from *90 percent* of returns claiming the adoption tax credit and went on to *actually audit 69 percent.*[1] This is a staggering number. Think about this: the IRS put as a top priority the auditing of parents who have adopted kids. The Taxpayer Advocate Service—which is part of the IRS—explained the gory details:

> During the 2012 filing season, 90 percent of returns claiming the refundable adoption credit were subject to additional review to determine if an examination was necessary. The most common reasons were income and a lack of documentation.
>
> Sixty-nine percent of all adoption credit claims during the 2012 filing season were selected for audit.
>
> . . . The average adoption credit correspondence audit currently takes 126 days, causing a lengthy delay for taxpayers waiting for refunds.[2]

Moreover, this massive audit campaign was utterly fruitless. Families faced the fear and uncertainty of an IRS audit for no good reason:

> Despite Congress' express intent to target the credit to low and middle income families, the IRS created income-based rules that were responsible for over one-third of all additional reviews in FY2012.
>
> Of the $668.1 million in adoption credit claims in tax year (TY) 2011 as a result of adoption credit audits, the IRS only disallowed $11 million—or one and one-half percent—in adoption credit claims. However, the IRS has also had to pay out $2.1 million in interest in TY 2011 to taxpayers whose refunds were held past the 45-day period allowed by law.[3]

It is difficult to construe this audit campaign as anything other than an IRS attack on adoption itself. Was there a logical reason to target such large numbers of adoptive families? Did the IRS expect considerable returns on its extended investment in time, energy, and money targeting adoptive families?

The audits received almost no media coverage. Instead, adoptive parents toiled in obscurity to regather their massive files, translate receipts from foreign languages, and otherwise prove that—yes— they adopted a child and—yes—the expense almost brought them to financial ruin. Here's how one adoptive family described the experience:

> It was early June when a letter arrived from IRS explaining that we (and lots of other adoptive parents, as it turns out) were being audited re: our adoption tax credit. The folks at IRS gave us 30 days to gather our receipts, invoices, cancelled checks, etc. to document our expenses and submit said documents to their tax examiner. If we couldn't comply within the time limit, they would set aside our request for a credit and we would be out of luck, meaning no more of our money would be refunded to us. If we got them the paperwork, then they would review our records and decide how much more of our money they would refund to us.[4]

Yet gathering paperwork is not so simple. As adoptive parents know, foreign adoptions often involve navigating cash economies, in foreign currencies, in foreign languages. In other words, a family may not know what a receipt says or even know if the document they're holding is truly a receipt. In other instances, receipts or other expense documents may not exist at all.

So, how does one document expenses in a cash economy— sometimes (in dealing with remote sections of Africa and Asia) working with people who do not have a written language? All the while, the IRS holds on to money that is due the family, money the family was counting on as part of its household budget:

Anyway, here we are, 30 days later. For the last several days, my dining room table has been covered with documents. I've been reliving my bad old times of adoption dossier preparation but in reverse this time. I finally got it all compiled, copies made, and the huge package of receipts, invoices, translations and conversions sent off to the IRS via Express mail. Now we wait for an answer . . . to see how much of our money the IRS will give us back. Let's see if they can turn it around in 30 days like I had to. Bitter??? Nooooo, not me.[5]

This adoptive family's story is hardly unique. In fact, one of my own ACLJ colleagues, a senior lawyer, faced exactly this kind of audit shortly after he returned home from Ethiopia with a beautiful two-year-old girl. At the very same time that they were working to overcome the worst side effects of her poverty and abandonment (she faced such extreme starvation that when she was two years old she weighed only fourteen pounds), the IRS launched an audit.

The audit was intrusive and difficult for an experienced lawyer, costing countless hours all for the sake of a minimal IRS adjustment, less than two hundred dollars, one that was likely smaller than the different fluctuations in value between American and Ethiopian currencies.

This is the kind of behavior that alienates citizens from their government. In an era of trillion-dollar deficits, allocating IRS resources to audit thousands of adoptive parents will not make the slightest bit of difference to the fiscal health of the nation. Instead, it demonstrates the IRS's lack of proportion and integrity, doing further damage to an agency whose reputation was already in tatters.

But the story gets worse. A closer look at the data shows that adoptive families are hardly taken from the ranks of the wealthy and privileged. People from a variety of economic backgrounds adopt. Once again, here's the Taxpayer Advocate Service:

With respect to the Adoption Credit, and in particular the credit for adoption of special needs children, the IRS has failed abysmally to take into account that over 45 percent of adopting families are at or below 200 percent federal poverty level, presenting particular communication and functional literacy challenges even as they are desperately in need of the funds which Congress has sought to deliver to them.[6]

Of course, not all the adoptive family returns were perfect. Human beings make mistakes. So the IRS did gather some additional revenue when it audited thousands upon thousands of middle-class families.

It gained an additional 1 percent from the adoptive taxpayers' tax refunds.

One percent. This represents a complete waste of government resources and taxpayer dollars.

I can't even imagine the amount of taxpayer dollars the IRS expended in these frivolous investigations (not to mention the heartache and concern of the families) to obtain that 1 percent return. And it's even more difficult to imagine that the IRS intentionally chose to carry on its adoption auditing program for a second consecutive year after the first year yielded insignificant returns and a finding that—yes—adoptive families are among our nation's most honest and conscientious, that their returns—in spite of all the financial complexity of international adoptions—were subject to corrections worth only 1 percent of their refund.

When our ACLJ attorneys first brought this scandal to public attention, causing a short-lived firestorm in conservative media, some IRS apologists came out of the woodwork with a simple explanation: the IRS was stamping out fraud.

But were adoptive families more likely to commit tax fraud? Were they going through the immense effort and expense of adoption—not to mention bringing a new child in their home, often with special needs, just to obtain a one-time tax refund?

Absolutely not. In fact, this question has been asked and answered by the Government Accountability Office. This 2011 GAO report is dispositive:

> Further, IRS officials also told us that they had not found any fraudulent adoption tax credit claims, and there had been no referrals of adoption tax credit claims to its Criminal Investigation unit.[7]

There was no fraud. None.

Even the rate of tax adjustments—where the IRS adjusts the amount of tax paid—was extraordinarily low. How low? Here's the GAO again:

> As of August 2011, 68 percent of the nearly 100,000 returns on which taxpayers claimed the adoption credit were sent to correspondence audit [an audit by mail]. However, of the approximately 35,000 returns on which audits have been completed as of August, the IRS only assessed additional tax about 17 percent of the time. The equivalent rate for all correspondence audits in 2010 was 86 percent.[8]

In other words, adopted families were five times *less likely* to make mistakes on their tax returns.

To demonstrate just how malicious the IRS was, remember that these are the 2011 numbers. Rather than retreat, chastened, into investigating taxpayers who are likely to commit actual crime, the IRS doubled down, hitting the adoption community yet again in 2012.

Some would attribute the IRS's attack on adoptive families to a bureaucratic snafu, but I know better. As demonstrated in the preceding chapter, the IRS is captured by one side of the political spectrum. Indeed, it's not just captured by the Left, but by a particular radical, lawless side of the Left. After all, there are many millions of good liberal citizens in the United States who would not dream of persecuting their fellow citizens—of abusing government power—just because they were on the other side of a political debate. The vast majority of Americans recoil from such behavior.

Could there have been an ideological explanation for the IRS's adoption audits?

Absolutely.

Little known to most Americans, there is a vibrant and virulent anti-adoption movement in the radical Left, one that expresses particular hatred for the evangelical adoption movement.[9] Here's a recent example of sheer anti-Christian bigotry from the prominent leftist online journal *Salon* as it reviewed an anti-adoption book by prominent leftist "journalist" Kathryn Joyce:

> When you think of adoption, what's the first thing that comes to your mind? Maybe it's the vague, rosy notion of a happy ending—of rescue, salvation or (more likely) some do-gooding Hollywood mouthpiece like Angelina Jolie adding kids of various ethnicities to her big, colorful brood.
>
> What probably doesn't automatically come to mind is coercion, racism and a conservative Christian agenda that extends beyond mere abortion prevention. . . . [Kathryn] Joyce details how the adoption industry has become overly enmeshed with the Christian right—how evangelical, pro-adoption church leaders have, in recent years, been creepily urging followers to adopt en masse, often internationally and from war-ravaged countries.[10]

And it wasn't that long ago that one radical social workers lobbying group actually called transracial adoption (many families adopt across racial lines) "cultural genocide." [11]

Genocide. For saving lives.

The IRS I knew and worked for is gone. Vanished. In its stead is an agency of unparalleled viciousness and malice, a lawless agency that sets its own policy priorities regardless of the rule of law and regardless of its impact on American families.

And lest you think that impact is limited to the relatively small numbers of Americans who actively engage in conservative politics or adopt children, I've got news for you: the IRS owes you money.

And lest you think that impact is limited to the relatively small numbers of Americans who actively engage in conservative politics or adopt children, I've got news for you: the IRS owes you money.

Lots of money.

Here's how.

The IRS's $132 Billion Illegal Welfare Scheme

For those who are aware of it, the Earned Income Tax Credit is one of America's more popular, more just programs designed to aid lower-income taxpayers. The tax credit itself is rather simple, providing tax credits based on income and family size, gradually phasing out as income grows.

It was originally enacted in 1975, then expanded by President Ronald Reagan as part of his 1986 tax reforms, then expanded and revised multiple times since, by Republican and Democratic presidents.

As a general matter, the tax credit is popular, is simple, and provides considerable help to low-income Americans.

It is also defined by statute as part of a political process where Congress fulfills its constitutional role by determining what America can afford to pay lower-income families as part of the tax credit and what's also in the best interests of taxpayers in other tax brackets. The process is messy and political, but it's also the one prescribed by law and binding on federal agencies.

Unless that federal agency is the IRS.

As noted earlier in this book, when the party of government begins to merge with the government itself, it's only natural that the government will take care of its core political constituencies.

And, make no mistake, lower-income Americans are a core Democratic constituency, as evidenced by the last presidential election.

In 2012, Mitt Romney won the popular vote among all voters who make between $50,000 and $100,000 per year by 6 percentage points. He won all voters who make more than $100,000 per year by 10 points.[12] Together, these two constituencies accounted for the large majority of the electorate, 59 percent.[13]

But Barack Obama won, mainly on the strength of voters who make less than $50,000 per year, winning the lower-income portion of the electorate by 22 points—Obama's 60 percent to Romney's 38 percent. Moreover, this lower-income section of the electorate was far larger in 2012, making up 41 percent of the total voters.[14] That same lower-income economic demographic was only 37 percent of the total vote in 2008, during the depths of a catastrophic recession.[15]

By now it should come as no surprise the left-leaning IRS is engaged in a massive transfer of wealth from wealthier Americans to this key leftist constituency.

After reading hundreds of documents about IRS lawlessness, I thought I couldn't get any more cynical about the IRS, until I read this report from an April 2013 edition of *The Hill*:

> The Internal Revenue Service (IRS) overpaid between $11.6 billion and $13.6 billion in tax credits designed to help

low-income families in fiscal 2012, the Treasury Department announced in a report released Monday.

The overpayments account for 21 percent to 25 percent of the tax credits issued under the Earned Income Tax Credit (EITC), the IRS estimated.

The report from the Treasury Inspector General for Tax Administration, the department's IRS watchdog, highlights the difficulties faced by the agency in properly issuing refunds and credits under the popular program.

Though the fiscal 2012 overpayment was among the agency's lowest in a decade, since 2003, as much as $132.6 billion has been improperly distributed as part of the EITC.[16]

It gets worse. The Treasury inspector general went on to say, "the annual EITC improper payment amount has consistently been one of the largest of all Federal programs."[17]

Read that again—an improper IRS payment scheme is so vast that it, by itself, is considered a "federal program."

This goes without saying, but $132 billion is a lot of money. In December 2013, the Tax Foundation reported (relying on IRS data) that there were 68,292,856 tax returns filed by individuals in the top 50 percent of income. These top 50 percent paid 97.1 percent of all federal income taxes.[18]

To give you some perspective on what this $132 billion overpayment means to the top 50 percent who actually pay the federal income tax, if you take 97.1 percent of that $132 billion (roughly $128 billion) and divide by the number of tax returns, then this IRS overpayment has cost each filing unit (which can include married couples as one filing unit) almost $2,000—money that many middle-class households desperately need. Yes, that means that the IRS misallocated $2,000 of your money to make unlawful payments.

And keep in mind, this overpayment is collected from you every time you file your taxes. It's wrong, and the IRS knows it.

No one doubts the plight of the poor. No one disputes that properly targeted and properly executed government aid programs can benefit our nation's most vulnerable citizens, but the United States of America is allegedly a nation of laws, and when one of its agencies can dramatically disregard the law and provide more than $130 billion in wrongful overpayments to a (conveniently) politically aligned constituency, then the rule of law itself is at risk.

Yet, as I said in the previous chapter, that's not all. If you want to know how the IRS unilaterally rewrote one of the most complex federal statutes of all time, imposed untold billions of dollars in costs on the American people, and "saved" President Obama's most unpopular reform, read on.

The IRS Rewrote ObamaCare

As originally passed, ObamaCare was structured to do a number of things:

- Mandate that individuals purchase insurance,
- Mandate that businesses provide insurance to employees,
- Provide incentives for states to shoulder as much of the administrative burden as possible by setting up insurance exchanges, and
- Require that states dramatically expand their Medicaid programs to make Medicaid available to families that were well above the poverty line.

To put the best spin on this structure, the goal was apparently to mandate coverage without creating a federal program so monstrously large as to be unmanageable. By delegating authority to the states, the program could—in theory—be more nimble and responsive to citizens' needs.

To make insurance affordable, the law required generous tax credits to subsidize the cost of insurance for most middle- and lower-middle-class families. To encourage the creation of state exchanges, the tax credits to individuals were available only if a state elected to set up its own exchange. Under the law as written, these tax credits were not available if the state declined to set up an exchange and instead referred its citizens to the federal exchange for insurance purchases. In a 2012 speech, one of the key architects of ObamaCare, Jonathan Gruber, explained the system. Here's the key portion of the transcript:

> Questioner: You mentioned the health-information Exchanges for the states, and it is my understanding that if states don't provide them, then the federal government will provide them for the states.
>
> Gruber: Yeah, so these health-insurance Exchanges . . . will be these new shopping places and they'll be the place that people go to get their subsidies for health insurance. In the law, it says if the states don't provide them, the federal backstop will. The federal government has been sort of slow in putting out its backstop, I think partly because they want to sort of squeeze the states to do it. *I think what's important to remember politically about this, is if you're a state and you don't set up an Exchange, that means your citizens don't get their tax credits.* But your citizens still pay the taxes that support this bill. So you're essentially saying to your citizens, you're going to pay all the taxes to help all the other states in the country. I hope that's a blatant enough political reality that states will get their act together and realize there are billions of dollars at

stake here in setting up these Exchanges, and that they'll do it. But you know, once again, the politics can get ugly around this.[19] (Emphasis added)

This is all quite simple. If the state does not set up an exchange, then—under the plain and unambiguous reading of the law—its citizens do not get insurance subsidies.

Critically, without the insurance subsidies, the first tenet of ObamaCare—required insurance—would be impossible to afford. Without the subsidies, insurance becomes costly enough that fail-safe ObamaCare provisions kick in that essentially kill the law's infamous individual mandate. Specifically, taxpayers are not supposed to pay more than set percentages of their income on health insurance. If the costs exceed the percentage, then they are exempt from the mandate. The *National Journal* explained it like this: "The mandate includes an exemption for people who can't afford coverage, and without subsidies, millions more people would qualify for that exemption."[20]

As a result, if a state did not want its citizens to be subject to the individual mandate, it could opt out of the exchanges and dramatically limit ObamaCare's application to their state. Opting out of an exchange meant opting out of much of Obamacare.

State after state made that choice. Ultimately, thirty-six states refused to establish an exchange, effectively telling the federal government that the individual mandate should not apply to their citizens. ObamaCare's viability was at stake.

So here came the IRS, riding to the rescue. Early on, the IRS wrote draft regulations that complied with the plain text of the law, providing tax credits for insurance purchased through state exchanges only. But then the IRS realized what was at stake. The *Wall Street Journal*'s Kimberley Strassel picks up the story:

An early draft of [the IRS] rule about subsidies explained that they were for "Exchanges established by the State."

Yet in March 2011, Emily McMahon, the acting assistant secretary for tax policy at the Treasury Department (a political hire), saw a news article that noted a growing legal focus on the meaning of that text. She forwarded it to the working group, which in turn decided to elevate the issue—according to Congress's report—to "senior IRS and Treasury officials." The office of the IRS chief counsel—one of two positions appointed by the president—drafted a memo telling the group that it should read the text to mean that everyone, in every exchange, got subsidies. At some point between March 10 and March 15, 2011, the reference to "Exchanges established by the State" disappeared from the draft rule.[21]

In other words, the IRS made a political decision to rewrite the law and to provide subsidies to insurance purchased through either the state or federal exchanges—a change that unilaterally imposed massive new financial burdens on taxpayers by opting them into a system their state governments had opted out of.

The story gets worse. As Strassel reports, career civil servants were "worried they were breaking the law" as they responded to pressure to revise IRS regulations to contradict the ObamaCare statute itself. In a functioning bureaucracy, lawyers would exercise basic oversight functions to make sure that regulations implemented the clear language of the statute. Here, government lawyers decided to implement not the law, but a "political goal":

Yet rather than engage in a basic legal analysis—a core duty of an agency charged with tax laws—the IRS instead set about obtaining cover for its predetermined political goal. A March 27, 2011, email has IRS employees asking Health and Human Services (HHS) political hires to cover the tax agency's backside by issuing its own rule deeming HHS-run exchanges to be state-run exchanges. HHS did so in July 2011. One month later the IRS rushed out its own rule—providing subsidies for state and federally run exchanges.[22]

The IRS passed this new rule to save ObamaCare, to preserve the viability of the individual mandate, not to enforce the law as written. And it was immediately challenged in court.

Faced with disaster, leftist defenders of ObamaCare lapsed into hysterical language, claiming that the provision limiting subsidies to insurance purchased through state exchanges only was a mere "typo" or "drafting error."

On July 22, 2014, two federal courts of appeal handed down conflicting rulings on the legality of the IRS's unilateral change. The Fourth Circuit Court of Appeals, based in Richmond, Virginia, held that, while the question was close, the IRS rule should be upheld.

The Court of Appeals for the District of Columbia Circuit, however, disagreed, holding that the statute means what it says, and the IRS's subsidy expansion was unlawful. In its ruling, the Court of Appeals explicitly recognized the stakes:

> We reach this conclusion, frankly, with reluctance. At least until states that wish to can set up Exchanges, our ruling will likely have significant consequences both for the millions of individuals receiving tax credits through federal Exchanges and for health insurance markets more broadly. But, high as those stakes are, the principle of legislative supremacy that guides us is higher still. Within constitutional limits, Congress is supreme in matters of policy, and the consequence of that supremacy is that our duty when interpreting a statute is to ascertain the meaning of the words of the statute duly enacted through the formal legislative process. This limited role serves democratic interests by en-

suring that policy is made by elected, politically accountable representatives, not by appointed, life-tenured judges.[23]

With conflicting court rulings, the matter will now be decided by the Supreme Court. Indeed, a decision may be issued by the time this book arrives in bookstores. But a judicial ruling on the technical legality (or illegality) of IRS action will not change the fundamental facts: the IRS—acting on its own—rewrote the law.

That's not the only time the IRS has intervened decisively to put its own ideological imprint on a hot-button political issue.

Let's turn now to immigration, where the IRS is a law unto itself.

The IRS's Unilateral Immigration Reform

Immigration reform is undoubtedly one of America's central political challenges, with deep feelings on all sides of the debate. Certainly, there is enormous sympathy for struggling immigrants who left desperate circumstances in their own country to seek a better life in the United States. After all—as I described in the second chapter—that's my own family's story. (In fact, in late 2014 I testified before the House Judiciary Committee regarding the unilateral action to, as President Obama said, "change the law" regarding immigration.)

At the same time, there are real victims when border controls aren't enforced. National security is at risk with porous borders, a flood of low-skill workers can depress and stagnate wages and increase unemployment, and public services can be strained to the breaking point—with schools, emergency rooms, and other state services left to deal with populations who often have little money, face linguistic challenges, and often bring with them the economic and health struggles of the nations they left.

Seeking to control the border isn't "racist," it's common sense.

At the same time, welcoming immigrants isn't foolish or irresponsible, it's the American way. Any lasting immigration deal will have to balance our very real national needs and limits with our equally real desire to welcome new citizens and continue America's robust immigrant tradition. In other words, it's not easy.

Unless, of course, you work at the IRS, where you can unilaterally give away billions of dollars to illegal aliens.

In October 2013, the Center for Immigration Studies released a report showing that "midlevel bureaucrats" implemented a policy change that funneled $4.2 billion in "additional child tax credits" to illegal aliens without congressional permission and even without the approval of senior IRS leadership. The *Washington Times* explains:

> The "additional child tax credit" was created to help out those who make too little to qualify for the full child tax credit. The ACTC is refundable, meaning that even if the taxpayer doesn't owe income tax, he or she could get a payout from the IRS.
>
> That becomes an avenue for fraud, particularly when combined with illegal immigrant workers, whose use of the tax credit has jumped from 796,000 filers in 2005 to 1.5 million in 2008 and 2.3 million in 2010, according to the IRS's official auditor.[24]

In fact, the markers for fraud were obvious:

> Investigators identified one address in Atlanta where 23,994 (Individual Tax Identification Number) ITIN-related tax refunds were sent—including 8,393 refunds deposited to a single bank account.[25]

I suppose when an agency is busy auditing tens of thousands of adoptive families, engaging in a nationwide targeting campaign against conservative speech, or handing out tens of billions of dollars in improper Earned Income Tax Credit payments, it's stretched too thin to find real fraud.

The story gets worse. The IRS made a "policy decision" to—in the words of the Treasury inspector general—essentially "'legalize' illegal aliens." In July 2013, CNS News told the complex story.[26]

First, Congress passed the Illegal Immigration Reform and Immigration Responsibility Act, a law that required interagency cooperation in identifying illegal immigrants:

> Section 642 of this law said that no other law or official could bar any agency or official from providing information about illegal aliens to the Immigration and Naturalization Service (INS)—the agency then responsible for enforcing immigration law.

It didn't take long, however, for the IRS to essentially overrule a congressional statute through its own regulation:

> This regulation said the IRS would grant what it called Individual Taxpayer Identification Numbers (ITINs) to aliens who did not qualify to work in the United States and did not qualify for Social Security Numbers. The IRS had three basic requirements for people receiving these numbers: 1) they had to be an alien, 2) they could not be qualified to work in the United States or have a Social Security Number, and 3) they owed taxes in the United States. Additionally, as with all Americans, the IRS must keep tax information confidential and, with a few exceptions, may not share that information with other government agencies.[27]

The inspector general, however, did not agree with this reasoning.

In September 1999, the Treasury Inspector General for Tax Administration, which has oversight of the IRS, published an audit report on the ITIN regulation. It was titled "The Internal Revenue Service's Individual Taxpayer Identification Number Program Was Not Implemented in Accordance with Internal Revenue Code Regulations."[28]

The inspector general essentially said keeping aliens' tax information confidential was in direct conflict with a federal statute.

"The Internal Revenue Service (IRS) made a policy decision to issue IRS Individual Taxpayer Identification Numbers (ITINs) to illegal aliens so tax filing obligations could be met," said the IG. "This IRS policy, to 'legalize' illegal aliens, seems counter-productive to the Immigration and Naturalization Service (INS) mission to identify illegal aliens and prevent unlawful alien entry."[29]

This is the modern bureaucracy in action. Now, you may read this section and sympathize with the IRS. How should it collect taxes from illegal immigrants? After all, if they're working in the United States, they should pay taxes on their earnings, just like anyone else. You may even think the IRS made the right "policy" decision.

But that's beside the point. A bureaucracy does not exist to overrule the elected legislature. It is not the role of unelected bureaucrats to make "policy decisions" that contradict federal law. If the federal law creates issues for tax collection, then that is a matter for Congress to decide, not a matter for the IRS to determine—especially when its determinations so frequently help core Democratic constituencies or so neatly dovetail with Democratic Party priorities.

The IRS scandals go on and on, but the sake of brevity, I'll address one more:

The IRS goes to space.

Bureaucrats Gone Wild: The IRS Conference Scandal

In 2013, less than a month into the IRS Tea Party targeting scandal, word broke of IRS misconduct that was far less consequential but far more amusing. In this scandal, the IRS didn't target dissenting taxpayers, it didn't wrongly distribute billions of dollars in taxpayer funds, nor did it rewrite and contradict federal statutes.

Instead, the IRS leadership decided to dance. You heard me—dance.

In a June 2013 video of the IRS's frivolous "training videos," one of them a *Star Trek* parody and another a *Gilligan's Island* parody, the other—the best one—was a video of a line dancing lesson in the "cupid shuffle."[30]

It's a shame that books can't yet embed video, because the reader is missing out on the sheer absurdity of the productions. Their cost ($60,000 of your money) doesn't do justice to the absurdity and poor judgment.

No one begrudges workers in the private or public sector blowing off steam on their own time, even if that does involve poorly produced videos. The problem is an agency so devoid of accountability, so immune from political oversight, that large numbers of employees can enthusiastically participate in wasteful frivolities at public expense.

The problem, put simply, is a culture of excess.

If $60,000 of taxpayer funding for parody videos seems like a nonscandal, let's talk about real money. According to the *Washington Post*, the IRS spent $49 million on 220 conferences.[31]

It's worth repeating that all of that money is taxpayer money—money spent during a time of unprecedented budget deficits with much of it borrowed from China.

The IRS is an agency out of control, with scandals raging from top to bottom, scandals that hurt Americans, unlawfully redistribute wealth, and contradict our constitutional structure.

This is an agency that is incapable of reforming itself. Simply put, the IRS is incapable of self-correcting.

In later chapters I will go into much greater detail about potential solutions, from short-term legislative fixes that can dramatically increase accountability, bringing federal workers more on par with private sector workers, to longer-term, structural fixes that will limit the power of the federal government to maintain or expand the bureaucracy.

But one solution should be mentioned now—a drastic but necessary step.

Abolish the IRS as We Know It

While it is undoubtedly true that the United States needs a stable and just method of collecting revenue, it is equally true that it does not need the IRS. Indeed, the nation needs to rid itself of the IRS's systematic corruption.

The purpose of this book is not to set tax policy, but at least two proposals show great promise for drastically limiting federal favoritism and corruption in tax collection: the flat tax and the so-called fair tax, really a national sales tax.

A flat tax—a tax that imposes the same tax rate on all forms of income at all levels and either eliminates or largely eliminates all deductions—wouldn't eliminate the need for a tax collection agency, but it would eliminate the need for the vast bulk of the tax collection bureaucracy. In fact, implementing a flat tax would require so few workers relative to the current monstrous IRS that it could be implemented in connection with a wind-down of the agency itself, to be replaced by a new entity, with new personnel operating under a much tighter regulatory scheme.

Implement the tax, eliminate the regulatory discretion, then revise the tax rate as economic and revenue needs dictate.

The fair tax, a sales tax, would be an even more fundamental reform, requiring an even smaller revenue collection agency. Multiple states—like Tennessee, Texas, and others—depend on sales taxes for revenue, and many of these states (especially Texas) lead the nation in economic growth even while accommodating vast and growing populations.

Again, this is not a tax policy book, but the virtue of either a flat tax or national sales tax is that such tax reform would not require Congress to dive into the labyrinth of existing tax law, to unwind a tax code so complex that precious few Americans can even begin to understand it.

It has been said that the "power to tax is the power to destroy." But the contemporary IRS enjoys much more than the mere power to tax. As you've read, it has the power to investigate, to harass, to target, and to at least attempt to imprison. Similarly, for its friends, it has the power to reward, to enrich, and to provide safe harbor even from other federal agencies.

The IRS has too much power. It is corrupt, hurting Americans it dislikes while rewarding its friends. It will not reform itself.

It must be abolished.

5

THE VA

When Incompetence Kills

Sometimes corruption begins with incompetence, not malice.

There are few federal departments with a more noble mission than the Department of Veterans Affairs. With its Abraham Lincoln–inspired motto, "To care for him who shall have borne the battle and for his widow, and his orphan," the VA speaks to the highest ideals of our constitutional republic.[1]

If men and women are willing to lay down their lives for us, shouldn't we be willing to do all we can to care for them? Whether the government drafts men to fight, as millions were drafted in World War II, Korea, or Vietnam, or whether men and women volunteer to serve, as in our more recent conflicts in Iraq and Afghanistan, we owe them the same debt.

That debt only grows when they suffer wounds, whether physical or psychological, in that service.

As a civilian, I can barely grasp the intensity and fear of combat. Movies, books, and even the stories of veterans can't do justice to the reality. Several colleagues at the ACLJ have served in combat and shared what they saw and experienced, and while we can't understand combat, we can and should fund the care that veterans need.

In fact, this sentiment is so widely shared that veteran care may be one of the few truly nonpartisan, unifying causes in American public life. Rare is the American who begrudges taking care of veterans. Rarer still is the American who tolerates inefficiency or—worse—corruption in the administration of those services.

But even with bipartisan support, public agreement, and billions of dollars in funding (including a more than 30 percent increase during the Obama administration),[2] the VA is now so incompetently and corruptly managed that American veterans are dying of neglect.

How did this happen?

It's a long and tangled story, but here's the short version, from the *Arizona Republic*'s excellent reporting: In early 2012, a VA whistle-blower, Dr. Katherine Mitchell, sounded the alarm that the Phoenix VA's emergency room was "overwhelmed and dangerous." Rather than deal with the problem, Dr. Mitchell alleged, the VA immediately punished her.[3]

Later that same year, the VA ordered "implementation of electronic wait-time tracking [and making] improved patient access a top priority." In December, the Government Accountability Office (GAO) told the VA that its "reporting of outpatient medical appointment wait times is 'unreliable' and that 'improvements are needed.'"[4]

In March 2013, a GAO representative told Congress, "Although access to timely medical appointments is critical to ensuring that veterans obtain needed medical care, long wait times and inadequate scheduling processes [at VA medical centers] have been persistent problems."[5]

VA employees, under renewed pressure to report shorter wait times for employees, began a deceptive scheduling practice where they would in essence create two wait lists: a long list to schedule an appointment, then a much shorter list once the appointment was made. In the words of one VA whistle-blower, the second appointment may be "14 days out" from seeing the medical provider, "but we're making them wait 6–20 weeks to create that appointment. That is unethical and a disservice to our veterans."[6]

By the fall of 2013, at least two separate Phoenix VA employees complained to the VA inspector general, claiming that "purported successes in reducing wait times stem from manipulation of data, not improved service, and that vets are dying while awaiting appointments for medical care."[7]

In December one of the complaining VA employees took his claims to the *Arizona Republic*. By April 2014, the allegations started to hit the national media and Congress, with a public rally in Phoenix that drew attention to the scandal.[8]

The first concrete disciplinary actions weren't taken until May, when the then secretary of veterans affairs, Eric Shinseki, placed a total of three employees on "administrative leave" as the inspector general completed his investigation. Shinseki also ordered an audit of all VA facilities.[9]

"Administrative leave" is paid leave under federal civil service rules. In other words, after abundant evidence of wrongdoing—wrongdoing that may have cost sick veterans their lives—the secretary's response was to put three employees on leave.

But this is not the private sector, and, as previously mentioned, it is extraordinarily difficult to fire a federal worker.

So, in lieu of termination, the offending managers received a paid vacation while they waited on the outcome of a lengthy investigation.

On May 8, Shinseki ordered an audit of all VA health-care facilities around the United States. On May 15, the VA inspector general revealed that criminal investigators were probing the Arizona VA.[10]

On May 21, President Obama addressed the nation in a televised press briefing, where he expressed outrage and promised a thorough investigation. On May 30, Secretary Shinseki resigned, ending an illustrious career in public service—one that included a long army career and brilliant service record in combat.[11]

General Shinseki could defeat America's enemies in combat, but Secretary Shinseki couldn't defeat the VA bureaucracy.

The direct cause of Shinseki's resignation was an audit report that, in CNN's words, cast the VA's problems in the "starkest terms."[12]

The findings, as outlined by CNN, were sobering:

- Efforts to meet the needs of veterans and clinicians led to an "overly complicated scheduling process that resulted in high potential to create confusion among scheduling clerks and front-line supervisors."[13]
- Meeting a fourteen-day wait-time performance target for new appointments was "simply not attainable given the ongoing challenge of finding sufficient provider slots to accommodate a growing demand for services. Imposing this expectation on the field before ascertaining required resources . . . represent[s] an organizational leadership failure."[14]
- Of scheduling staff surveyed, 13 percent said they received instruction to enter in the "Desired Date" field a date different from the one requested. The survey did not determine whether this was done "through lack of understanding or mal-intent unless it was clearly apparent."[15]
- In some cases, "pressures were placed on schedulers to utilize inappropriate practices in order to make Waiting Times appear more favorable. Such practices are sufficiently pervasive to require VA [to] re-examine its entire Performance Management system and, in particular, whether current measures and targets for access are realistic or sufficient."[16]

The *Washington Post* chronicled the human cost in cities across the nation:

- In Phoenix, Arizona, an unspecified number of veterans (potentially "dozens") died while on "secret" wait lists maintained to conceal the true wait times for provider appointments.[17]
- In Fort Collins, Colorado, clerks were apparently instructed to falsify records to create the illusion that doctors were seeing 14 patients per day.[18]
- In Miami, Florida, a VA police officer complained of widespread cover-ups and illegal drug trafficking.[19]
- In Columbia, South Carolina, six deaths were tied to delays of care, 52 patients with cancer suffered "delays in diagnosis and treatment," and the program had "3,800 backlogged appointments."[20]
- In Pittsburgh, Pennsylvania, six veterans died after an outbreak of Legionnaires' disease, and the VA not only covered up the outbreak, it falsely informed Congress that the cause was faulty equipment instead of human error.[21]

As you read this sad tale, keep in mind that this is coming from one of our most popular federal agencies, an agency that has received lavish federal funding, has been led by honorable warriors like General Shinseki, and has no discernible partisan bias.

But it's still incompetent. And corrupt.

But the incompetence and corruption don't stop with the VA scheduling scandal or the associated scandals outlined above. According to the *Economist*, the failure extends to disability claims.

Nearly 1 [million] veterans are now waiting. On average it takes the VA about nine months to complete a claim. In

some big cities the average delay is over 600 days. Those
who appeal against a refusal usually wait two years for a
resolution. Mr Obama entered the White House with a
promise to fix the system, but waiting-times have increased
considerably on his watch. Even the navy SEAL who shot
Osama bin Laden says he is waiting for his claim to be pro-
cessed.[22]

These delays have real costs. Disabled veterans can struggle to find
full-time work, and many thousands can't work at all.

There's no doubt that claims have increased as a result of war,
but so too has the VA's budget. And the war is now more than a
decade old. In other words, there's been ample time for the VA to
adjust—so much time, in fact, that private companies facing similar
circumstances would have already adjusted . . . or they would be out
of business.

The incompetence and corruption keep piling up. Just as with
the IRS, the VA failures could merit a book all their own. But rather
than dissect all of the VA's failings, let's just look at a few remaining
low points.

On June 24, 2014, retiring senator Tom Coburn published his
own top-ten list of VA scandals, a list that should shock the conscience of any American taxpayer. Below are some of the worst:

- If you think the VA can restrain its employees from
  committing acts of sexual abuse, consider this story
  from Kansas:
  "A male neurologist at the Colmery-O'Neil VA
  Medical Center in Kansas violated at least five female
  patients by conducting unnecessary 'breast examina-
  tions' and at least one unnecessary 'pelvic examination.'
  He received a 32-month suspended sentence and is now
  a registered sex offender."[23]

- In Massachusetts, a VA employee essentially ran a drug ring from his facility:

  "A VA employee in Massachusetts sold cocaine to patients receiving treatment for substance abuse. Patrick McNulty, 28, sold cocaine, marijuana and ecstasy to the veterans he was treating on VA property. He was also recorded talking about his drug sales, once stating 'I can get coke like it's nothing. I can get more coke all day.' He was sentenced to three months community confinement in a halfway house, followed by three months of home confinement and three years of probation."[24]

- And if you think the VA always treats even dying veterans with the respect they deserve, think again:

  "A nurses' aide at a VA medical facility in Pennsylvania was arrested for stealing a 14-carat gold chain with a crucifix off the neck of a female veteran in hospice care. He attempted to sell the valuable necklace at a jewelry store; the veteran died the next day."[25]

- "The chief of police of the Bedford VA Medical Center in Massachusetts was arrested by the FBI and convicted of federal conspiracy for two plots to kidnap, rape and murder women and children. He pleaded guilty in January 2014 and 'now stands convicted of serious federal crimes.'"[26]

Of course anecdotes don't paint the whole picture. Let's take a look at the statistics that go beyond the wait list scandals:

According to [Senator] Tom Coburn, the VA had the most security incidents of any government agency last year, reporting 11,368 in 2013. "Security incidents" include anything from a stolen laptop to a computer virus download to the mishandling of documents. In one instance, a VA employee was sentenced to six years in federal prison for aggravated identity theft. VA employee David Lewis accessed veterans' personal information "in exchange for crack cocaine," allowing this identifying information to be used to file fraudulent tax returns and apply for fraudulent lines of credit.[27]

These systemic problems include the most basic responsibilities of employment, responsibilities like showing up for work. As the VA demanded ever-greater funding, it turns out that many of its employees saw work as essentially optional. I doubt, however, they saw their paychecks as optional:

> VA employees fail to show up for work unexcused—termed "absent without leave"—at a rate exceeding every other federal department and agency. AWOL can include anything from being late to work to disappearing from the office for months at a time. In one instance, lack of supervision enabled a VA employee to be absent without leave on more than 25 separate occasions. This employee took advantage of the "unlimited freedom" allowed by his supervisors and "admitted that his misconduct negatively affected his performance."[28]

Sadly, the stories just keep getting worse. While I was writing this book, two more abuses were revealed. The first involved the VA in Philadelphia. After responding to complaints of falsifying data and whistle-blower retaliation in Philadelphia, congressional investigators discovered that they were working in an office that was "bugged" with audio recorders and video cameras. In other words, the Philadelphia VA was spying on them.[29]

Just as bad, the investigators discovered evidence of written instructions from VA officials to "ignore their requests for information."[30]

The arrogance is astonishing, and—as of this book's publication—no one had been fired for this outrage.

The second abuse was revealed when the liberal *Huffington Post* discovered that the VA had been massively, systematically overpaying its employees:

The jobs of some 13,000 VA support staff have been flagged by auditors as potentially misclassified, in many cases resulting in inflated salaries that have gone uncorrected for as long as 14 years.

Rather than moving quickly to correct these costly errors, VA officials two years ago halted a broad internal review mandated by federal law. As a result, the overpayments continue.

Perhaps the worst news is that the department's ability to quickly stop this financial outflow is limited. Even if the improper pay grades are eventually downgraded, VA officials said that employees will be able by law to keep their higher salaries, meaning the VA will be saddled with these excessive costs for years.[31]

That's quite a racket. Overpay employees, do it intentionally, halt the investigation of wrongdoing, and then lock in the employee gains through the abuse of federal law.

If the federal bureaucracy's complexity and lack of accountability can lead to corruption at the VA, then it can corrupt anything. It is, quite simply, a law of human nature that zero accountability leads inevitably to abuse. Not everyone will be incompetent or corrupt, of course, and there are many thousands of good workers in the VA, but even a minority of bad employees can create massive problems—especially when lives are on the line.

Given this reality and given the VA's systematic misconduct, it was distressing to see General Shinseki's immediate replacement at the VA, Acting Secretary Sloan Gibson, begin his tenure with a full-throated defense of VA employees: "This idea that 'let's fire everybody, let's pull everybody's bonus away'—that's a bunch of crap. . . . I'm not going to see people sit there and say that we got 350,000 people that aren't worth a crap."[32]

No one claimed every VA employee was incompetent, but hundreds and perhaps thousands are. Many of those are corrupt. And we know now that up to 13,000 are being paid more than they're worth, siphoning away dollars that could be used to hire more doctors and nurses.

VA reforms will make it easier to fire senior executives, but the idea that bureaucratic incompetence can be cured by cleaning out the very small layer of top executives is inexcusably naïve. After all, cleaning out the top slice of management won't do anything to adjust inflated salaries. It won't do anything to make life easier for whistle-blowers, nor will it impact the employees who bugged and watched congressional investigators.

In many ways, taking out the top management—as necessary as that may be—smacks of scapegoating if that's all that changes. Wrongdoing at the VA is top to bottom, and no one should be safe. Real accountability means accountability at every level, from the best-paid political appointees to the worst-paid custodians or administrative assistants. Everyone has to do their job. Our veterans—our citizens—deserve no less.

The VA scandal is bad enough on its own terms, representing an outrageous breach of faith with veterans and a grotesque abuse of the public trust. But in many ways, even the scandals outlined above barely scratch the surface of the true danger.

What happened with the VA should serve as fair warning, a foreshadowing of what happens when the government assumes control of our health care. Which brings us back to ObamaCare.

The ObamaCare Challenge

There is a constant tug-of-war in this country between those who believe health care is best administered in private hands, through largely free-market mechanisms, and those who believe the government should take the lead role, not just in payment but also in providing the health care itself.

There's much debate about "single-payer" health care—where the government in essence acts as the insurance company—but the VA represents something more than single payer. It is socialized medicine in the true sense of the term, when the government not only pays for the services, but also builds and owns the hospitals and health-care facilities.

If a liberal could point to a socialized medicine success story like the VA, who could fear ObamaCare? After all, ObamaCare doesn't represent true socialized medicine. It isn't even true single-payer health care (because citizens are still responsible for some of the medical costs).

To those liberals who wanted socialized medicine, the VA became the poster child, not just when defending ObamaCare, but also as a potential destination for American medicine. After all, if the VA "worked" for our nation's veterans, why couldn't it work for the rest of us? Some activists spoke of "Medicare for all," but what about a "VA for all"?

Writing in the *Washington Post*, prominent "policy wonk" Ezra Klein said that "expanding the Veterans Health Administration to non-veterans" was "one of his favorite ideas."[33]

He went even further, arguing that the VA functioned the "best" of all the American health systems, with the private individual health insurance market the "worst-functioning."[34]

He wasn't alone in his opinion. Columnist Nicholas Kristof wrote in the *New York Times* in 2009:

Take the hospital system run by the Department of Veterans Affairs, the largest integrated health system in the United States. It is fully government run, much more "socialized medicine" than is Canadian health care with its private doctors and hospitals. And the system for veterans is by all accounts one of the best-performing and most cost-effective elements in the American medical establishment.[35]

Citing a study by the RAND Corporation, he said:

Americans treated in veterans hospitals "received consistently better care across the board, including screening, diagnosis, treatment and follow-up." The difference was particularly large in preventive medicine: veterans were nearly 50 percent more likely to receive recommended care than Americans as a whole.[36]

Should the VA model be extended? "Yes," said Kristof (and RAND): "'If other health care providers followed the V.A.'s lead, it would be a major step toward improving the quality of care across the U.S. health care system.'"[37]

This kind of opinion persisted in the *New York Times* even after ObamaCare passed and even as problems with government health care were becoming increasingly obvious. In 2011, Paul Krugman, arguably the nation's most influential leftist pundit and a *New York Times* columnist, attacked a Mitt Romney plan to reform the VA:

What Mr. Romney and everyone else should know is that the V.H.A. is a huge policy success story, which offers important lessons for future health reform.

Many people still have an image of veterans' health care based on the terrible state of the system two decades ago. Under the Clinton administration, however, the V.H.A. was overhauled, and achieved a remarkable combination of rising quality and successful cost control. Multiple surveys have found the V.H.A. providing better care than most Americans receive, even as the agency has held cost increases well below those facing Medicare and private insurers. Furthermore, the V.H.A. has led the way in cost-saving innovation, especially the use of electronic medical records.[38]

Those words ring hollow today, as veterans die waiting for care.

If and when ObamaCare is fully implemented, it will expand the federal government's reach into virtually every area of American health care, supplementing already extensive regulations of private insurance and private hospitals and doctors with its already existing private insurance subsidies.

Republicans estimate that ObamaCare alone will cost $2.6 trillion in the first decade after 2014. Democrats dispute these figures, but no one—not even the president—sees costs lower than $900 billion.[39]

To be clear, we're overlaying those vast federal expenditures and complex regulations onto the same bureaucratic and employment system that produced the VA scandal, a system that has proven utterly incapable of disciplining employee misconduct and generates corruption far more efficiently than it provides health care.

Does anyone think this will turn out well?

How Bureaucracies Fail

Bureaucracies tend to fail.

Now, they don't necessarily fail *completely* or *totally*—they can limp along for quite some time—but they do fail at efficiency, they fail at fairness, and they do generally fail compared to the vast majority of private alternatives.

True, there are some government bureaucracies that are simply unavoidable. Running a military is a complex operation that cannot be privatized, for example. It's impossible to move tens of thousands (and sometimes millions) of men and women, provide them with weapons and training, equip them in the field, and deploy them for combat without creating government systems (a bureaucracy) that make this happen.

But even in the military context, if you ask officers why they leave our armed services, or what they hate the most about the military, they answer in overwhelming numbers: the bureaucracy. In one key survey, when asked the top reason why they left the military, a whopping 82 percent of veterans said "frustration with the military bureaucracy."[40]

And that's the military bureaucracy, the one bureaucracy that most Americans would agree we must have, and it's staffed and led by our most respected professionals: our men and women in uniform.

Yet it is a source of constant frustration and sometimes even despair in the ranks.

Talk to any member of the military and they can tell you horror stories.

I've heard of young soldiers who lost their homes before the military could process disability claims.

I've heard of separation packets that reach the hundreds of pages and take months to process just to kick out of the service soldiers who are in the midst of serving lengthy prison sentences in civilian jails.

I've talked to vets who tell stories of supply nightmares in Iraq and Afghanistan where units get flooded with gear they don't need (such as dozens of flat-screen high-definition televisions), while they have to write home to get relatives to send them the gear the army can't provide.

I bring up these stories not to attack the military but to illustrate reality: a bureaucracy is a problematic method of delivering government services, and the bigger the bureaucracy, the more problematic it generally becomes.

But why?

Writing in the *American Thinker*, J. R. Dunn provided an excellent summary of the role of human nature in bureaucratic processes. Relying on anthropologist Robin Fox for much of his analysis, he summarizes that bureaucracies fail "because they are, in some sense, inhuman."[41] By this he doesn't mean that they are vicious or cruel (although they can be), but that they are, by their very nature, at odds with human nature as it exists. He goes on to say it's because bureaucracies attempt to function through fixed procedures, while human beings invariably do not:

> Bureaucracies . . . are an attempt—heroic or otherwise—to force the world to conform to a rational system. But human beings, much as we pride ourselves on our rational thinking, are actually a grab-bag of instincts, intuition, and habit, with a handful of rationality thrown in to pull everything else together. This serves us well because it matches how the universe actually works, but it also means that there will always be a conflict between bureaucracies and human beings. The relationship starts out on the wrong foot and gets worse as it goes along.[42]

This is exactly right. Human beings have an extraordinarily poor track record in conforming to systems. If they can hide their incompetence or corruption in the midst of that system, the track record is even worse.

In 1967, James Q. Wilson wrote in *National Affairs* of the "Bureaucracy Problem," and his words are timeless. Addressing the persistent hope that the appropriate government system can address society's ills, he concluded: "It is ironic that among today's members of the 'New Left,' the 'Leninist problem'—i.e., the problem of over-organization and of self-perpetuating administrative power—should become a major preoccupation."[43] In other words, bureaucracies have been problematic for a very long time. Self-perpetuating and self-interested, they will easily lose sight of their mission.

There is no easy fix to the problem of bureaucracy, but one can't even begin to fix a problem if the constant answer from one side of the political aisle is "more." More money. More bureaucrats. More systems that inevitably manifest the same problems.

At the same time that the Left creates a larger bureaucracy, it helps create its own powerful political constituency. The party of government creates more government, and that government inevitably embraces the party that creates and sustains it. With livelihoods directly dependent on taxpayer funding, public workers can often be among the most motivated campaign volunteers and the most avid and reliable voters.

Even so, the liberal elite shuns bureaucracy even as it embraces it for the rest of us. Wealthy liberals routinely seek the best private doctors and send their kids to the best private schools—thus opting out of the very public-run systems they relentlessly support.

I don't resent anyone for seeking the best medical care or seeking the best education for their kids, but there is something more than a little unseemly in telling Americans they should be content or even happy with the government services that they're so quick to shun.

So why do bureaucracies fail?

Because people fail. And yes, people fail at corporations also, but intrinsic to the free market is the concept of "creative destruction," where the process of failure clears the way for success, as companies that fail to adapt give way to companies that innovate.

The most obvious recent example of "creative destruction" comes from the world of consumer technology. Companies that dominated the markets—like Nokia did with cell phones[44]—lost to companies, like Apple or Samsung, that innovated faster and reached the consumer with superior technology. The process of creative destruction can be painful in the short term, but it ultimately drives economic progress, incentivizes innovation, and enriches our lives in ways we constantly take for granted.

The bureaucracy, by contrast, specializes in the process of "destructive creation," where inefficiency or failure results not in fundamental reform or the destruction of the failing entity but rather the creation of new processes, new departments, and new rules. Failure creates more red tape, and more red tape creates more failure.

How many times have you heard bureaucrats under fire cry out for more funding? It seems to be the catch-all explanation for every conceivable failure. Computers wouldn't crash if there were more funding. Auditors would be more fair and more competent if there were more funding. The VA wouldn't have wait times if there were more funding.

In other words, bureaucrats beg Congress to essentially reward their failures with vast sums of additional money.

In other words, bureaucrats beg Congress to essentially reward their failures with vast sums of additional money.

All too often our elected representatives fall for this trick, throwing even more money at federal agencies until they are bloated beyond recognition. The number of rules explodes, the complexity increases, and more money is then needed to hire more bureaucrats to manage the ever-greater number of regulations that then require more money to enforce.

And it is never, ever enough.

6

THE DEPARTMENT OF JUSTICE— MAKING IT UP AS THEY GO ALONG

There are few more heroic figures in pop culture than the federal prosecutor. Countless movies and TV shows present the same image—the heroic government lawyer, standing on the courthouse steps, surrounded by swarms of reporters, as he celebrates the conviction of mafia bosses, drug kingpins, or corrupt politicians.

Prosecutors are the good guys. Most of us remember the opening lines of the legendary television show *Law & Order*: "In the criminal justice system, the people are represented by two separate yet equally important groups: the police, who investigate crime; and the district attorneys, who prosecute the offenders. These are their stories."

The music sounds, and the show begins. And we're hooked.

The prosecutor's power over the popular imagination is matched only by his power over our liberties. In fact, prosecutors are arguably our most powerful civilian public officials, possessing the sole, unappealable discretion to decide whether a citizen will be prosecuted and perhaps lose their liberty and, sometimes, their life.

In our system of government, a prosecutor has the discretion to decide whether to prosecute any given crime. As a practical matter, that discretion often extends beyond the decision to prosecute to the question of whether to even investigate.

If a prosecutor chooses to prosecute a drug dealer on one street and not another, or to charge them differently, that's his or her decision. If a prosecutor chooses to expend resources investigating tax cheats and not someone who writes a bad check, that's his or her decision.

In other words, not all crimes are investigated or prosecuted with equal vigor. And—under governing law—prosecutors are not required to pursue or prosecute them equally.

This discretion makes a high degree of sense. After all, we want our public officials to prioritize, to place "first things first" and pursue major crimes even if it means occasionally neglecting to prosecute minor, nonviolent offenses.

Moreover, a prosecutor enjoys near-absolute immunity from the civil liability of aggrieved citizens. When you pair prosecutorial discretion with prosecutorial immunity (which grants absolute immunity to prosecutors doing their job), there are few effective restrictions on a prosecutor's power.

As a consequence, our most basic and vital government responsibilities—our ability to dispense justice—utterly depend on the integrity of the relevant officials, with little recourse if those officials prove to be dishonest or corrupt.

Yet are federal prosecutors inherently more honest than other lawyers? Are they less likely to suffer from political bias or less likely to violate citizens' rights?

To be clear, I've had the privilege of knowing and working with dozens of federal prosecutors and found most of them to be men and women of sterling character, striving to fulfill the highest ideals of the legal profession. In fact, I served on the legal faculty for the Department of Justice, working with U.S. attorneys from across the country. I've had the privilege to work with U.S. attorneys general and several state attorneys general.

Unfortunately, not all prosecutors meet these high standards.

And few people can do more damage to the rule of law, to the fabric of our democracy itself, than a rogue prosecutor. And that's not just my theory.

It's a fact.

ObamaCare: Brought to You by the Department of Justice

A key message you *must* take away from this book is that problems with the federal bureaucracy go far beyond any given presidency. While most Americans blame the presidency for America's problems, there is a vast mechanism of government that the president doesn't directly control, and this mechanism can go awry and profoundly damage our nation.

How do we know? An abusive prosecution during the Bush administration helped bring us ObamaCare.

Former Alaska senator Ted Stevens's prosecution is that case. After all, by 2008, he was a long-serving Republican senator, one of the most powerful men on Capitol Hill. Unlike poor or middle-class Americans who often simply don't have the resources to effectively fight for their legal rights, Senator Stevens had it all: connections, power, and access to financial resources.

He was not a soft target.

So that meant, when federal prosecutors brought public corruption charges against him, most Americans likely thought the charges were legitimate. After all, most people don't trust politicians to begin with and believe they constantly rig the system in their favor, so Americans tend to stand up and cheer when a politician is finally called to account.

Moreover, the claims against Stevens, that he "failed to report that an oil services firm remodeled his house,"[1] seemed to represent the classic kind of corruption the public hates—using your influence to gain petty personal favors. Alaska, after all, is an oil-producing state, so *of course* an oil service firm would want to curry favor with the state's senior senator.

Right?

A federal jury seemed to think so, convicting Senator Stevens on ethics charges less than two weeks before the 2008 election.

Republicans and Democrats alike called for Senator Stevens to step aside, but he refused. He continued to proclaim his innocence and claimed that prosecutors had violated his rights. Very few Americans believed him. Indeed, very few members of his own party thought he was telling the truth.

Stevens was so popular in Alaska that not even a federal conviction could deter all his supporters, but enough deserted him that he lost a close race to Democrat Mark Begich.

Mark Begich became the sixtieth Democratic senator in that U.S. Senate, the sixtieth vote for ObamaCare, and the man who made a filibuster—a procedure that as a practical matter means that legislation needs a sixty-vote majority to pass the Senate—impossible.

Of course, if Senator Stevens was, in fact, guilty of the charges against him, then his loss was his own fault, and Bush-era federal prosecutors can't be blamed for ObamaCare. There are, after all, consequences to corruption, and if that means losing a formerly popular Republican senator, then so be it.

However, it turns out Ted Stevens wasn't guilty.

Roughly three months after his conviction, a federal whistle-blower came forward with a sordid tale. Federal prosecutors had knowingly and willfully withheld evidence in violation of the Constitution and the Federal Rules of Criminal Procedure that would have helped exonerate Senator Stevens (a criminal defendant has a constitutional right to what's called "exculpatory evidence") and may have even knowingly elicited perjury in their zeal to throw Senator Stevens in jail.

Senator Stevens's conviction was promptly thrown out, but by then incalculable damage had been done.

The federal judge on the case was so outraged that he appointed an outside lawyer to investigate DOJ misconduct, declaring: "In 25 years on the bench, I have never seen anything approaching the mishandling and misconduct that I have seen in this case."[2]

What, exactly, did federal prosecutors do?

The independent investigator, Henry F. Schuelke, ultimately issued a 524-page report that, among other things:

> Paint[ed] a picture of a prosecution team so hampered by in-fighting that disgruntled attorneys cut corners by assigning document-review duties to FBI and IRS agents who were left largely unsupervised. Crucial information—including the fact that trial witness Bill Allen had once bribed a child prostitute, whom he'd had a relationship with, to commit perjury, and that the home repairs in question were worth hundreds of thousands of dollars less than originally alleged—was never given to Stevens' defense team.[3]

Worse, the investigator believed prosecutors were not forthcoming in their accounts of DOJ wrongdoing:

> The Senator's defense rested on notes he had sent his friend Allen, then the top executive of the Alaskan oil pipeline service and construction company VECO Corp., which had performed the repairs on his home. In the notes, Stevens requested a bill for the work and referenced his need to comply with ethics rules. Defense attorneys had the notes but didn't know Allen had been inconsistent with prosecutors about whether he thought Stevens was really asking for a bill or whether he was "just covering his [expletive]."[4]

DOJ prosecutors apparently had a collective memory failure that they'd never tolerate in a criminal defendant. Apparently "none" of them could remember key facts about their own wrongdoing.

Schuelke asked prosecutors about Allen's back-and-forth view of Stevens' notes, but none of the DOJ lawyers could recall when Allen first told them the notes were disingenuous. Schuelke wrote that the prosecution team's "collective memory failure strains credulity."[5]

So, what happened to these rogue prosecutors—government officials whose misconduct shocked the conscience of a sitting federal judge? Were they fired? Were they prosecuted? How much jail time did they receive?

If you think any of these things happened, think again. I don't want you to miss the point of this book.

In May 2012 the *New York Times* reported:

The Justice Department has found that two prosecutors involved in the botched 2008 corruption trial of Senator Ted Stevens engaged in "reckless professional misconduct," but it stopped short of firing the men, saying their mistakes were not intentional.

In a cover letter to a 672-page report provided to Congress on Thursday, alongside additional attachments and findings, the Justice Department said the two prosecutors would be suspended without pay—Joseph Bottini for 40 days, and James Goeke for 15 days.[6]

Sadly, Senator Stevens did not live to see these suspensions—meager though they were. He died in a plane crash on August 9, 2010.

Failing Up: Abusing Power as a Path to Power

The Ted Stevens prosecution is not an aberration. It's not a rare failure within an otherwise sterling department.

Chief Judge Alex Kozinski of the Ninth Circuit Court of Appeals has described prosecutorial misconduct as "an epidemic."[7]

He's right, and the mainstream media is starting to take notice. The *New York Times* editorial board called it "rampant."[8] *USA Today* was concerned enough to launch its own comprehensive investigation, and the findings were startling:

> Federal prosecutors are supposed to seek justice, not merely score convictions. But a *USA Today* investigation found that prosecutors repeatedly have violated that duty in courtrooms across the nation. The abuses have put innocent people in prison, set guilty people free and cost taxpayers millions of dollars in legal fees and sanctions.
>
> Judges have warned for decades that misconduct by prosecutors threatens the Constitution's promise of a fair trial. Congress in 1997 enacted a law aimed at ending such abuses.
>
> Yet *USA Today* documented 201 criminal cases in the years that followed in which judges determined that Justice Department prosecutors—the nation's most elite and powerful law enforcement officials—themselves violated laws or ethics rules.[9]

Is it any wonder the misconduct doesn't stop? The incentive isn't there. After all, a high-profile prosecution can turn a prosecutor into a local celebrity, spin off into books and movies, or launch a political career. Even something as serious as "reckless professional misconduct" merits little more than a short suspension.

Sometimes, however, misconduct merits a promotion.

On June 13, 2014, the *New York Observer* published an article that should profoundly disturb anyone who values the rule of law and governmental accountability. Called "All the President's Muses: Obama and Prosecutorial Misconduct," it features a photograph of President Obama meeting with three key advisers "strategizing" after the 2012 attack on the U.S. diplomatic compound in Benghazi, Libya.[10]

Those advisers are Kathryn Ruemmler, Lisa Monaco, and Susan Rice.

Susan Rice's name should be familiar to most readers. She's the Obama administration official most identified with the narrative about the Benghazi attacks, taking to the Sunday talk shows to deliver misleading talking points and blaming a YouTube video for the deadly attack. The truth, of course, was quite different. The compound was attacked as part of a preplanned terrorist operation— launched even as President Obama was bragging on the campaign trail about his success in stopping terrorism.[11]

That's not Susan Rice's only public failure, but it is certainly her most prominent. Less well-known but more consequentially, she helped bungle the American response to Rwandan genocide, declaring during an interagency conference as the violence raged: "If we use the word 'genocide' and are seen as doing nothing, what will be the effect on the November [congressional] election?"[12]

Susan Rice, we know, but what about Kathryn Ruemmler? She served as President Obama's "longest serving White House Counsel" and reportedly is "one of his closest and most trusted advisors." President Obama has called her an "an outstanding lawyer with impeccable judgment."[13]

Is she really that "outstanding"? Perhaps not. It turns out that she prosecuted and sent to prison Americans for "crimes" that were essentially concocted as a prosecutor's legal theory. Describing one of her more famous prosecutions—as part of the Enron task force, charged with prosecuting individuals responsible for Enron's spectacular decline and fall—former DOJ prosecutor Sidney Powell, writing in the *New York Observer*, said this:

> The conduct the prosecutors alleged was not criminal. At the same time, she deliberately hid exculpatory evidence—

that is, evidence she was constitutionally compelled to hand over to the defense. Indeed, the prosecutors not only acknowledged the evidence as exculpatory, they yellow-highlighted it as such—then buried it.[14]

The alleged misconduct was comprehensive, including lying to opposing counsel and obtaining testimony that she almost certainly knew to be false.[15] A federal court of appeals tried to right most of the wrongs, but by that point the damage was done. Again, here's Ms. Powell:

> The Fifth Circuit Court of Appeals ultimately reversed 12 out of 14 counts of conviction against the executives, acquitting one entirely. All the defendants were released, after having spent up to a year in prison on a sham indictment, while Ms. Ruemmler and her cronies continued both to hide the evidence that defeated the government's case and to demand that the Merrill executives be prosecuted a second time on the same indictment.[16]

But surely Lisa Monaco has a better record than her two colleagues, right?

Not so fast. It turns out that Ms. Monaco was also deeply involved in the failed Enron prosecutions, part of the same team that not only failed to secure the convictions they sought but was also plagued with allegations of misconduct, including eliciting false testimony and threatening witnesses.[17]

Misconduct in the Enron cases brings up an important point about our Constitution: it doesn't just protect the unpopular, it *especially* protects the unpopular. In many ways—and as politicians know better than anyone—popularity can be its own protection. Just ask Bill Clinton, who survived impeachment with an approval rating at the end of his second term that President Obama would envy, even though President Clinton was guilty of lying under oath.

But if you're unpopular? Heaven help you. At the time of the Enron prosecutions, it would have been hard to find a company or senior executives with a worse public reputation. The name "Enron" had become synonymous with exploitation and fraud, and ambitious prosecutors looking to make a name for themselves smelled blood in the water and circled Enron leaders like hungry sharks.

And when those sharks attacked, they did not always play by the rules. In their zeal to catch their prey, they ruined lives.

Unjustly ruining lives should be a career ender for federal prosecutors. Instead, it appears to have been a positive qualification for their next jobs, as they soon found themselves in the White House serving as key advisers to the president.

But Monaco and Ruemmler were not the only rogue prosecutors who rose ever higher in Justice Department ranks. Would you believe that the head of the Criminal Division of the DOJ, Leslie Caldwell, destroyed a multinational corporation through a frivolous prosecution before being promoted to her position at the DOJ?

Once again, what should have been career-ending misconduct was barely even a speed bump on the road to power. Obama chose Monaco to be his counterterrorism adviser. Perhaps it was because of Monaco's experience with the "terror of a prosecutor" Leslie Caldwell, also from the Enron Task Force, who now heads the Criminal Division of the Department of Justice.[18] Caldwell spearheaded the destruction of accounting giant Arthur Andersen LLP and its 85,000 jobs, only to have it reversed 9–0 by the Supreme Court because of the flawed indictment and the absence of criminal intent.[19]

Of course, these are just a few examples. One could fill a book with stories of prosecutorial abuse, and indeed, many writers have. But every story begs the question, was anyone held accountable?

With President Obama's close advisers Lisa Monaco and Kathryn Ruemmler it seems clear their abuse of power only helped them climb to the top. After all, the appeals and judicial outrage occurred well after these rogue prosecutors secured their convictions and seized the headlines. They collected their legal scalps and moved on.

In the meantime, ordinary Americans were left to pick up the pieces.

But it's not just the stories of failed prosecutions that are outrageous. Some of the Justice Department's "success stories" demonstrate a department intoxicated with its own power. A department lacking any sort of proportion, willing to abuse private citizens for the sake of purely ideological agendas.

Just ask Gibson Guitars.

Do You Have Legal Wood on Your Guitar?

A couple of years ago I was in a guitar shop in Virginia shopping for a new guitar. (I've long loved music, and even now I play guitar and drums in a band.) I came looking for a specific brand: a guitar from the world-famous Gibson Guitar Corporation, maker of the Les Paul.

When I asked the salesman to show me the Gibsons, he surprisingly said, "You don't want to buy a Gibson." Of course it's a bit unusual for a salesperson to discourage sales of his or her own store's product, so I asked him why.

"Because Gibson's been indicted for selling illegal wood," he answered.

"That's precisely why I want to buy a Gibson," I responded.

It was my own small rebellion against a government that was careening out of control.

On August 24, 2011—for the second time in two years—armed federal agents descended on Gibson Guitar Corporation in Nashville, Tennessee. They stopped production, cleared employees out of the factory, and confiscated suspected contraband.

What, exactly, were they searching for? Drugs? Weapons?
Wood.

Yes, wood.

The Department of Justice was investigating a possible violation
of the Lacey Act, a federal law protecting endangered species that
had been recently amended to include plants. Under the Lacey Act,
the government can impose criminal penalties if a person imports
wood that was logged not in violation of U.S. law, but in violation of
the law of the originating country.[20]

For example, if a company purchases wood from India, it's responsible under penalty of U.S. criminal law "to certify the legality
of their supply chain all the way to the trees."

Moreover, the law—absurdly enough—is retroactive. In
other words, you can be liable for the wood on a guitar purchased
years ago:

> Nashville's George Gruhn is one of the world's top dealers of
> old guitars, banjos and other rare stringed instruments. "It's
> a nightmare," he says. "I can't help it if they used Brazilian
> rosewood on almost every guitar made prior to 1970. I'm not
> contributing to cutting down Brazilian rosewood today."[21]

Let's presume for the moment that the Lacey Act—however silly—
is constitutional and enforceable in U.S. courts. Does that justify
the use of armed agents to shut down production and confiscate
wood, and cost a corporation millions of dollars on the mere suspicion of wrongdoing?

Does it justify this scene, as described to Bill Frezza, at *Forbes*?

> "Henry. A SWAT team from Homeland Security just raided
> our factory!"
> *"What? This must be a joke."*
> "No this is really serious. We got guys with guns, they

put all our people out in the parking lot and won't let us go into the plant."

"Whoa."

"What is happening?" asks Gibson Guitar CEO Henry Juszkiewicz when he arrives at his Nashville factory to question the officers. "We can't tell you." *"What are you talking about, you can't tell me, you can't just come in and . . ."* "We have a warrant!" *"Well, lemme see the warrant."*

"We can't show that to you because it's sealed."[22]

Remember, this level of force, this level of coercion, was all to make sure the wood on Gibson's guitars was logged in accordance with foreign law.

Facing years of legal uncertainty, threats of jail time, and millions of dollars of losses, Gibson settled with the federal government, agreeing to pay $300,000 plus a payment of $50,000 to an environmental group, the National Fish and Wildlife Foundation.[23]

Congratulations, federal government. Your years-long investigation and your dangerous armed raids netted you a few hundred thousand dollars.

Gibson Guitars, however, is not without a sense of humor. When the government returned to Gibson its "contraband" wood, Gibson immediately created the "Government Series" Les Paul guitar, selling for slightly more than one thousand dollars.[24]

Gibson said it was their way of "fighting the establishment."

Be Careful What You Fish For

The armed agents of the federal government don't just protect guitars from contraband wood; they also can get involved when your fish are too small.

I'm not making this up.

In the fall of 2014, the Supreme Court heard arguments in a case about a fisherman and his grouper, and tried to determine whether a federal law designed to prevent large-scale financial fraud applied to his decision to throw a few fish back into the sea.

The case dates back to 2007, when Florida officials stopped a fisherman named John Yates while he was still on board his boat. These officials inspected his catch, and determined that a number of the grouper were smaller than the mandated twenty-inch minimum.

The state officials told Yates to save the fish, but Yates had other ideas. He allegedly tossed the grouper overboard, allowing the incriminating evidence to swim away, to live again to be fished another day.

Here's where the story gets strange. Nothing meaningful happens, but then—in Yates's words: "Three years later, all of a sudden they come with bulletproof vests and guns. They put me in handcuffs and they took me to jail."[25]

His alleged crime? A violation of provisions of the Sarbanes-Oxley Act of 2002,[26] specifically of provisions prohibiting destruction of documentary evidence. In fact, the title of the section of the statute that he allegedly violated was "Destruction and Alteration of Records."[27] Is a fish a "record"? Can financial fraud statutes be stretched to cover fish? And why are bulletproof vests and guns involved in the matter at all? Are fishermen considered just as dangerous as guitar makers?

When the U.S. Supreme Court heard the case, the Justices and lawyers laughed[28] at some of the obvious humor of hearing a case about grouper, or comparing fish to documents, but federal offenses are ultimately no laughing matter, nor is the degree of force used to enforce those same statutes. It is the disturbing practice of the Department of Justice to read criminal statutes as broadly as it can—and then bring down the full, armed force of the federal government on those they deem lawbreakers.

Enough is enough.

You Might Be a Criminal

The Gibson case, in addition to highlighting the government's remarkable use of excessive force, also illustrates the very dark side of the expanding regulatory state. Just as regulations proliferate, so do criminal laws—to the point where it is now actually difficult for corporations to *avoid* violating the law.

In 2009, noted civil libertarian Harvey Silverglate published *Three Felonies a Day: How the Feds Target the Innocent*,[29] a book that demonstrated how vague and expansive legal regimes can make felons of us all—especially as laws are abandoning the requirement that prosecutors have to prove criminal intent. The *Wall Street Journal* highlighted one such case:

> In 2001, a man named Bradford Councilman was charged in Massachusetts with violating the wiretap laws. He worked at a company that offered an online book-listing service and also acted as an Internet Service Provider (ISP) to book dealers. As an ISP, the company routinely intercepted and copied emails as part of the process of shuttling them through the Web to recipients.
>
> The federal wiretap laws, Mr. Silverglate writes, were "written before the dawn of the Internet, often amended, not always clear, and frequently lagging behind the whip-crack speed of technological change." Prosecutors interpreted the ISP's role of momentarily copying messages as they made their way through the system akin to impermissibly listening in on communications. The case went through several rounds of litigation, with no judge making the obvious point that this is how ISPs operate. After six years, a jury found Mr. Councilman not guilty.[30]

Imagine six years of uncertainty, fear, and stress—as the government pursued criminal convictions over the use of technology it apparently didn't understand, all without evidence of criminal intent or even real harm to a real victim.

Regulation increases criminal prosecution in subtle but important ways. For example, under our common-law traditions, to commit a crime one must possess the intent to commit a crime, the mens rea. As Silverglate outlines in his book, the way our DOJ works now, many crimes require no proof of intent at all.

Moreover, as Silverglate explains, "Since the New Deal era, Congress has delegated to the various administrative agencies the task of writing the regulations." At the same time, "Congress has demonstrated a growing dysfunction in crafting legislation that can in fact be understood." The result is complexity and confusion that can trap citizens into committing crimes without intent, under laws they can't understand.[31]

And this brings us full circle. Recall from earlier in this book that the IRS and DOJ conspired to "piece together" prosecutions of conservative nonprofits, without any evidence that the nonprofits had broken laws. They had "identified defendants to go after" and were using a vast regulatory system to give them the leverage they needed.

As laws proliferate, the DOJ is both unable to—because of limited resources—and unwilling to—because of concern for public outrage—prosecute every single federal crime in the United States. Prosecutions even of white-collar, nonviolent criminals often trigger federal mandatory sentencing laws, and thus can lead directly to lengthy prison sentences. Flooding our jails with inadvertent, confused "criminals" is not the way to endear the federal government to the American people.

Yet this very proliferation increases the potential for politically motivated targeting. After all, if a prosecutor has to choose from among many, many potential targets, how will he or she choose? In the case of the IRS scandal, prosecutors were apparently letting a partisan IRS help make the call, as conservative nonprofits were put under a microscope and liberal nonprofits continued their years-long pattern of operation with minimal oversight.

In July 2014, the House Judiciary Committee heard testimony about the DOJ's "Operation Choke Point," an effort to target banks that facilitate and provide financial services to fraudulent businesses.[32]

Sounds simple and benign, right?

Not exactly. It turns out that the DOJ, rather than locating fraudulent businesses first and then investigating their links with banks, began targeting banks that provided services for a long list of disfavored—though perfectly legal—industries, including "ammunitions sales," "fireworks companies," and twenty-two other business categories.

The evidence of DOJ overreach was startling:

> Letters have poured in from company owners in support of these suspicions [that the DOJ was targeting them], noting startling cases where the DOJ reportedly has directly strong-armed banks into dropping [legal] clients not engaging in fraud.
>
> Virginia Republican Rep. Robert Goodlatte revealed that one of the more egregious examples sent in to the committee was a meeting between the DOJ and a bank regarding the continued provision of financial services to a payday loan company.
>
> The DOJ official reportedly told the banker, "I don't like this product, and I don't believe it should have a place in our financial system. And if you don't agree, there will be an immediate, unplanned audit of your entire bank."[33]

Needless to say, threats like this—coming from a virtually unfireable but powerful government official—represent an abuse of power, an abuse of power that is all too common in the Department of Justice.

Injustice Demands a Response

It's time to impose real sanctions for prosecutorial misconduct. A finding of wrongdoing by a federal court should—at the very least—end the prosecutor's career and strip that prosecutor of any immunity from private lawsuit. Any prosecutor who would break the law to deprive an American citizen of his constitutional rights and indeed his very life or liberty should no longer work for the government.

And we need to carefully consider whether the explosive growth of criminal sanctions, including potential jail time, is good for American liberty and American democracy. Do we really want to throw a man in jail, separate him from his family, and ruin his life and career because the government believes he should have known that wood he purchased was illegally logged under the law of, say, Madagascar?

The best cure for abuses of prosecutorial discretion is to limit the number of prosecutable laws. Prison shouldn't offer mass confinement for the confused, unlucky, or unpopular but rather for the violent and dangerous.

The bottom line, however, is that nothing will change without accountability, without federal employees, including prosecutors, knowing that they'll likely face penalties when they violate their oath to defend the Constitution and instead use their power to violate the Constitution.

As the saying goes, with great power comes great responsibility. And thus those who abuse their power must be held responsible.

7

THE DEPARTMENT OF JUSTICE— PERMANENTLY RIGGING THE GAME

At this point in the book, I want you to notice something important. While I've spent much of the last six years fighting President Obama's agenda in federal court, on Capitol Hill, and across the globe, this book is *not* about his administration.

It's about the permanent executive branch, the government that stays as presidents come and go.

In January 2017, Barack Obama will make the same flight so many presidents before him have. As helicopter Marine One lifts off from the White House lawn, he'll be cheered and booed by the crowd of supporters and protestors at the White House gates, and his successor will walk into the Oval Office.

Many Americans will think everything has changed.

In reality, less will change than you think.

The new president will lead the same federal workforce as the old president. Certainly, he or she will be able to pick their appointees, and those appointees will have influence, but they will stand at the top of a legion of federal employees who are pursuing agency initiatives that many cabinet secretaries will never know about.

At the grassroots level, these federal employees will make countless thousands of decisions that impact Americans' lives without any input at all from presidential appointees. They will pursue departmental and ideological programs that can last for decades, programs that can slowly but surely transform America. Regardless of the president's party, these federal employees keep their jobs, advance their ideologies, and trample on the rights of citizens. The president doesn't choose the vast majority of federal employees: the permanent bureaucracy does—a permanent bureaucracy that is partisan and often corrupt.

Few departments of the United States government are better at this long, slow march through American political and cultural life than the Department of Justice.

The previous chapter's stories dealt with criminal law—the power of the government to deprive a citizen of his or her liberty, and sometimes even their life.

This chapter, however, deals with civil law—the power of the government to define your rights, regulate our economy, and control citizens and corporations with fines and court orders.

And in civil law, the Department of Justice is rigging the game.

To be more specific, career officials at the DOJ are collaborating with ideological allies to wage regulatory warfare to entirely circumvent the democratic process and impose new rules and regulations on the American people. They're conspiring with interest groups to give away vast sums of money to key liberal constituencies, and—to help make sure that the department's leftist slant is permanent—they're actively campaigning to intimidate and sometimes even threaten conservative employees.

In at least one key DOJ Department—Civil Rights—career employees are conspiring to create a conservative-free zone, a department that will willingly pursue a Democratic president's agenda while waging a form of low-intensity legal warfare against a conservative president.

It's difficult to overstate the consequences for our system of justice and the rule of law. When citizens realize that the system is rigged in favor of one side of the debate—sometimes to the extent that the federal government is forcing taxpayers to fund radical activists—then the system loses its legitimacy. The DOJ's short-term gains will come at the expense of its long-term credibility, and democracy itself will suffer.

Even in the short term, as abuses accumulate largely outside the public eye, the cost is great.

If you doubt me, read on . . . and learn about the Department of Justice racket known as "sue and settle."

Regulation by Litigation: The DOJ Colludes with Radicals

In my career, I have sued the government countless times. And in virtually every case, the pattern is the same.

Immediately the federal government will file what's called a "motion to dismiss," claiming that my lawsuit has absolutely no legal merit. Just filing that motion often results in substantial delays—months—as the trial court determines whether my case has merit.

In fact, this is exactly what happened when I filed suit against the IRS on behalf of forty-one conservative groups in twenty-two states. All of those groups had been targeted by the IRS, subject to unconstitutional delays and unconstitutional questions merely because they were identified as "Tea Party" or "Patriot" groups. The IRS wrongdoing was so obvious that the agency has issued a public apology.

But still it fought back against our lawsuit, ferociously. The government, at taxpayer expense, hired two of the nation's highest-priced law firms to defend IRS officials, and the DOJ represented the government. All three entities, the two law firms and the DOJ, filed a motion to dismiss, a motion that immediately brought our case to a halt while the judge considered their arguments. In that case, we waited several months for a judge to issue an order, and for each one of those months, the case was essentially frozen, held in suspended animation, while the judge considered his ruling. As of the date of this writing, the case is now on appeal, a process that can take years.

After a motion to dismiss is denied there comes a long period of discovery, in which the parties exchange documents relevant to the case and take depositions—sworn testimony under oath—of the key witnesses.

In my experience this is yet another contentious phase, with the government fighting to hold back documents, fighting to limit questions, and generally doing everything it can to make the process longer, more difficult, and more expensive.

Next, the government files something called a motion for summary judgment—yet another attempt to dismiss the case. The government will argue that even after discovery there is not enough proof to support our claims.

It is usually only at this point—late in the case, after years of litigation—that the government will seriously think about settling the case. A settlement is simply another word for an agreement between the parties that ends a lawsuit. Usually the plaintiff will agree to drop the case and in exchange the government will give the plaintiff something of value—sometimes money, sometimes a policy change.

Often even the settlements are hard fought, agreed to only after lengthy and contentious mediation sessions. The government will settle mainly for one reason and one reason only: the risks of litigation outweigh the costs of settlement.

Critically, a settlement creates a *legally binding* obligation on the government. So even a settlement is subject to constitutional limitations on federal power. In other words, the government cannot agree to violate the Constitution. It cannot agree to spend money in violation of federal appropriations. It cannot agree to create rules without proper regulatory authority.

At least, that's the way settlements are supposed to work.

To be clear, I don't believe the government is doing anything inherently wrong when it fights back against litigation. Indeed, I'd be concerned if the government simply rolled over whenever citizens sued. Not every citizen suit is constitutionally sound or legally proper. I don't mind a hard legal fight. No lawyer should.

And we're certainly in a hard legal fight in our IRS cases. The judge in those cases granted the government's motion to dismiss, and we're now appealing to the federal court of appeals in Washington, D.C. The case could continue for years longer.

But what if the Department of Justice doesn't always fight back? What if it not only fails to contest lawsuits, but actively cooperates with outside activists to create "settlements" that yield new and burdensome rules that send millions of dollars to those same outside activists?

That wouldn't be a lawsuit, that would be a racket.

In May 2013, the U.S. Chamber of Commerce blew the lid off just such a scam, issuing a forty-nine-page report called "Sue and Settle: Regulating Behind Closed Doors."[1] The scheme it described should outrage every American who believes in democracy, the constitutional separation of powers, and fundamental fairness.

Here's how the scheme works:

First, an outside advocacy group—Earthjustice, for example—will file a lawsuit under the nation's extraordinarily expansive environmental regulations demanding that the Environmental Protection Agency take certain actions or issue certain regulations.

Ordinarily, as I just outlined, the Department of Justice will vigorously defend against lawsuits, but in the "sue and settle scheme," the DOJ and the agency (typically the EPA) decide not to defend the government. Instead, they immediately enter into settlement talks. Critically, these talks take place behind closed doors, with *zero* public input.

The DOJ, EPA, and outside environmental group then agree

(among themselves) to specific new environmental rules and then spell out those rules in documents called "consent decrees" or "agreed orders." These consent decrees are then filed with a federal court and soon signed by a federal judge, giving them the force of law.

Taxpayers, who've just been cheated out of a fair and vigorous defense by their own Department of Justice, will also have to support the consent decrees that often contain provisions entitling the outside environmental group to substantial legal fees, fees that can add up to millions of dollars. Here's Larry Bell, writing in *Forbes*:

> [W]e taxpayers, including those impacted regulatory victims, are put on the hook for legal fees of both colluding parties. According to a 2011 GAO report, this amounted to millions of dollars awarded to environmental organizations for EPA litigations between 1995 and 2010. Three "Big Green" groups received 41% of this payback: Earthjustice, $4,655,425 (30%); the Sierra Club, $966,687; and the Natural Resources Defense Council, $252,004. Most of this was paid to environmental attorneys in connection to lawsuits filed under the Clean Air Act, followed next by the Clean Water Act.
>
> In addition, the Department of Justice forked over at least $43 million of our money defending EPA in court between 1998 and 2010. This didn't include money spent by EPA for their legal costs in connection with those rip-offs, since EPA doesn't keep track of their attorney's time on a case-by-case basis.[2]

On at least one occasion, the collusion between the environmental group, the DOJ, and EPA was so blindingly obvious that the lawsuit and the corresponding settlement documents were filed on the very same day.[3] To be very clear, the lawsuit, the settlement, and the new regulations were a simultaneous injustice to the American people, who footed the bill for all of these expenses.

Even though it's a left-leaning technique, the Obama administration did not invent this practice. It's been embedded in our bureaucracy for years. Career "litigators" (I hate to call any lawyer who colludes with his opposition and fails to zealously represent his client a true litigator) have been doing this for decades. True, the trend accelerated under President Obama, but not by much.

The Chamber of Commerce has traced the number of Clean Air Act sue-and-settle cases since the second Clinton term and found a distressing number since the Clinton administration, with a startling rise under President Obama. In Clinton's second term there were 27 sue-and-settle cases, 38 in President George W. Bush's first term (so the number increased under a Republican president), 28 in President Bush's second term, and a whopping 60 in President Obama's first term.[4]

In addition to paying the legal fees of the activist lawyers (not to mention the salaries of the DOJ staff that are busy waving the white flag), the rules that result from sue-and-settle cases can be extraordinarily costly to our economy. The Chamber of Commerce's list of top ten most costly sue-and-settle regulations includes rules that cost $9.6 billion annually and one rule that would have cost a whopping $90 billion every year.[5]

Fortunately public outcry prevented the most costly of these from full implementation, but just one of the new rules, called the "Utility MACT Rule," costs almost as much annually as the IRS Earned Income Tax Credit scheme covered in chapter 3.

Bureaucratic partisanship has real costs. And those costs extend beyond dollars and cents. Sue-and-settle contributes to the perception that there are two systems of justice, one for the bureaucracy's favorites—usually activists representing just the right sort of interest groups—and another, far more adversarial system for the rest of us.

And in no "case" is that bias more evident than in the massive, multibillion-dollar DOJ giveaway known as the *Pigford* scandal.

Co-Conspirators in Fraud: The DOJ's *Pigford* Giveaway

In chapter 3 of this book I outlined how the IRS took the Earned Income Tax Credit—a broadly supported program that benefits the working poor—and transformed it into a $130 billion program that goes far beyond Congress's intent, a program that directly benefits key Democratic constituencies.

But for sheer audacity, that scandal is amateur hour compared to the Department of Justice's *Pigford* fraud.

Like the Earned Income Tax Credit scandal, the DOJ's *Pigford* fraud has legitimate legal roots. In 1997, ninety one African-American farmers filed suit against officials from the U.S. Department of Agriculture (USDA), alleging they'd been discriminatorily denied farm loans. There is little doubt—and no meaningful dispute—that a number of these plaintiffs did, in fact, face discrimination and those plaintiffs should be compensated.

But the case soon morphed from a rather straightforward race discrimination case into something else entirely: a billion-dollar slush fund available not only to African-American farmers who were victims of discrimination but also to Hispanics, Native Americans, and women—most of whom had never farmed in their lives.

The Department of Justice agreed to settle the *Pigford* case, creating a settlement fund that made $50,000 payments available to claimants with little requirement for documentation.[6] As word of the payments spread, the Department of Justice, members of Congress, and others worked to expand the pool of available funds, as well as expand the pool of eligible claimants—all of them favored Democratic constituencies.

In a lengthy exposé, the *New York Times* charted the scandal's growth:

> The compensation effort sprang from a desire to redress what the government and a federal judge agreed was a painful legacy of bias against African-Americans by the Agriculture Department. But an examination by the *New York Times* shows that it became a runaway train, driven by racial politics, pressure from influential members of Congress and law firms that stand to gain more than $130 million in fees. In the past five years, it has grown to encompass a second group of African-Americans as well as Hispanic, female and Native American farmers. In all, more than 90,000 people have filed claims. The total cost could top $4.4 billion.[7]

The money was made so widely available that claimants didn't even have to prove they were farmers:

> From the start, the claims process prompted allegations of widespread fraud and criticism that its very design encouraged people to lie: because relatively few records remained to verify accusations, claimants were not required to present documentary evidence that they had been unfairly treated or had even tried to farm. Agriculture Department reviewers found reams of suspicious claims, from nursery-school-age children and pockets of urban dwellers, sometimes in the same handwriting with nearly identical accounts of discrimination.[8]

To their credit, some career lawyers and career bureaucrats did object to this utterly absurd legal result, but they were overruled by a toxic combination of self-interested politicians, greedy trial lawyers, and sympathetic peers in the bureaucracy.

How prevalent was the fraud? This prevalent:

> In 16 ZIP codes in Alabama, Arkansas, Mississippi and North Carolina, the number of successful claimants exceeded the total number of farms operated by people of any race in 1997, the year the lawsuit was filed. Those applicants received nearly $100 million.[9]

The extent of the fraud staggers the imagination, becoming so blatant and obvious that the DOJ essentially became co-conspirators in an effort to defraud the taxpayers and drain the Treasury:

> In Maple Hill, a struggling town in southeastern North Carolina, the number of people paid was nearly four times the total number of farms. More than one in nine African-American adults there received checks. In Little Rock, Ark., a confidential list of payments shows, 10 members of one extended family collected a total of $500,000, and dozens of other successful claimants shared addresses, phone numbers or close family connections.[10]

And did you know there were "farms" in the city? According to the DOJ there were:

> Thirty percent of all payments, totaling $290 million, went to predominantly urban counties—a phenomenon that supporters of the settlement say reflects black farmers' migration during the 15 years covered by the lawsuit. Only 11 percent, or $107 million, went to what the Agriculture Department classifies as "completely rural" counties.

According to the *American Thinker*, "every apartment in a *New York City building* received a settlement of at least $50,000."[11]

Let me emphasize, if an African-American farmer (or Hispanic, or Native American, or female) ever faced unlawful discrimination, and they have, they deserve all the compensation the law allows, but the decision to use the discrimination suffered by a few as a pretext to invite fraud and simply hand out billions in taxpayer dollars is inexcusable.

And yet that's the Department of Justice.

Conservatives Need Not Apply: Enforcing Ideological Purity

I've saved what is quite possibly the worst of the DOJ scandals for the last. I don't claim this book provides an exhaustive accounting of the DOJ's flaws—for that I highly recommend John Fund and Hans Von Spakovsky's *Obama's Enforcer: Eric Holder's Justice Department*—but I have chosen select scandals to illustrate the breadth and depth of the problems in America's most vital and powerful law enforcement agency.

These scandals share certain characteristics: they have dramatic impact on American life, they are unjust, and they are difficult to correct in large part because they are rooted in or sustained by the enormously powerful, unaccountable federal bureaucracy.

However, there is one hopeful sign among story after story of government abuse. At the IRS, at the VA, at the DOJ, and elsewhere, many if not most of the worst scandals have been exposed by whistle-blowers, other bureaucrats with the integrity and courage to come forward and expose wrongdoing.

In other words, there are good people in the federal government. Lots of good people. And it's vital not only to protect them but also to preserve a hiring process that leads to a key, overlooked element of diversity—diversity of viewpoint.

When I worked for the IRS, politics rarely came up. In fact, I don't think I remember a single explicitly political conversation while on the job. To this day I don't know the political leanings of many of my former colleagues. We just had a thirty-fifth-year reunion from my old IRS chief counsel office. We had a great time, sharing the "war stories" of cases from more than three decades ago. We talked about a lot of things--family, health, grandkids, careers. You know what we did not discuss? Politics. We didn't discuss it last summer, and we didn't discuss it thirty-five years ago. In such an environment, partisanship would have raised a red flag, and I have little doubt that a number of us would have immediately acted to stop any bias before it could do real harm. Things have changed with the agency today.

But what if the workplace in many agencies is now fundamentally different? What if the political leanings of your colleagues are not only well-known but almost universal? Would you feel like risking your own job to stop abuse?

What if that political bias was so open and notorious that dissenters either couldn't get a job or found working conditions so intolerable that they had to leave? There would be no whistle-blowers, and abuses could rage on, unchecked, for years until—perhaps by chance—a reporter or member of the public could bring them to light.

In a key division of today's Department of Justice, this intolerant ideological uniformity is quickly becoming a reality.

There are few divisions in the Department of Justice more important than the Civil Rights Division. While U.S. attorneys are on the front lines, prosecuting criminals and maintaining law and order, attorneys in the Civil Rights division ideally make sure that all American citizens enjoy their most basic constitutional and statutory rights. And given our nation's fraught and violent racial history, its key role is enforcing civil rights laws. The DOJ describes its mission like this:

> The Division enforces the Civil Rights Acts; the Voting
> Rights Act; the Equal Credit Opportunity Act; the Ameri-

cans with Disabilities Act; the National Voter Registration Act; the Uniformed and Overseas Citizens Absentee Voting Act; the Voting Accessibility for the Elderly and Handicapped Act; and additional civil rights provisions contained in other laws and regulations. These laws prohibit discrimination in education, employment, credit, housing, public accommodations and facilities, voting, and certain federally funded and conducted programs.[12]

Given this key role, nonpartisanship—vital for every federal agency—is absolutely imperative. The politics of race and gender are among the most contentious and potentially explosive in the United States, and before the full weight of the federal government is brought to bear, citizens expect, and deserve, careful, neutral consideration of the merits of cases and the merits of any given legal position.

Unfortunately, however, key personnel in the Civil Rights Division are doing their absolute best to shred any last remnants of neutrality and fairness in division decision-making, even to the point of hounding and threatening conservative employees and hiring almost exclusively from organizations with a radical leftist bias.

In March 2013, in response to numerous congressional complaints, the Department of Justice inspector general released a lengthy report on the operations of the Civil Rights Division's key Voting Section, the section charged with protecting the right to vote, obviously a key constitutional right and a foundation of our democracy.[13]

The findings were startling.

Many of those individuals told the (Office of the Inspector General) OIG that they believed that the reason the voting rights laws were enacted was to protect historic victims of discrimination and therefore the Section should prioritize its resources accordingly. Additionally, some of these individuals, including one current manager, admitted to us that, while they believed that the text of the Voting Rights Act is race-neutral and applied to all races, they did not believe the Voting Section should pursue cases on behalf of White victims.[14]

Moreover, the treatment of conservative employees was startling. The inspector general said it was "surprised and dismayed at the amount of blatantly partisan political commentary that we found in e-mails sent by some Voting Section employees on Department computers."[15] The report went on to detail the abuses that were nothing short of astonishing:

> Karen Lorrie, [not her real name] a non-attorney employee in the Voting Section, initially denied under oath to us that she had posted comments to websites concerning Voting Section personnel or matters. Later in her second OIG interview she admitted that she had posted such comments, identified several of the statements that she had posted, and acknowledged that she had lied under oath in her first OIG interview. She also told the OIG that she understood that the comments she had posted would remain on the Internet and follow the targets in the future. Lorrie told the OIG that she posted comments online as a way of "relieving the never-ending stress on the job."[16]

In other words, not only did a career bureaucrat attack colleagues online, but she lied under oath about those attacks. But that's not all. Career employees kept using the Internet as a weapon against their own colleagues, resorting to language that was both unprofessional and "juvenile." Again, here's the inspector general:

During this period, at least three career Voting Section employees posted comments on widely read liberal websites concerning Voting Section work and personnel. The three employees who we were able to identify with certainty included three non-attorney employees. Many of the postings, which generally appeared in the Comments section following blog entries related to the Department, included a wide array of inappropriate remarks, ranging from petty and juvenile personal attacks to highly offensive and potentially threatening statements. The comments were directed at fellow career Voting Section employees because of their conservative political views, their willingness to carry out the policies of the CRT division leadership, or their views on the Voting Rights Act. The highly offensive comments included suggestions that the parents of one former career Section attorney were Nazis, [and] disparaging a career manager's physical appearance . . . speculation that another career manager was watching pornography in her office, and references to "Yellow Fever," in connection with allusions to marital infidelity involving two career Voting Section employees, one of whom was described as "look[ing] Asian." [17]

It just keeps getting worse. Threats of physical violence were not out of bounds, with indications that the threats were backed up by actions, like monitoring individuals' movements in the office— monitoring that was "disturbing" in context:

We found other postings by career Voting Section employees that contained intimidating comments and statements that arguably raised the potential threat of physical violence. For instance, one of the employees wrote the following comment to an article concerning an internal Department investigation of potential misconduct by a Section manager: "Geez, reading this just makes me want to go out and choke somebody. At this point, I'd seriously consider going in tomorrow and hanging a noose in someone's office to get myself fired, but they'd probably applaud the gesture and give me a promotion for doing it. . . ." Some postings by Section employees contained statements that could be viewed as disturbing, such as comments that monitored managers' movements in the office and described their actions.[18]

Keep in mind, the choking threat came from a "Section manager," not a low-level intern or a temporary employee on a work-release program from prison.

Now back to the "sue and settle" discussion in the first part of this chapter. There was evidence that DOJ attorneys cooperated with sympathetic liberal groups so completely that they would share confidential legal information:

> We also found incidents in which Voting Section career staff shared confidential Section information with outside civil rights attorneys, some of whom were working on matters where they were adverse to the Department.[19]

Abuses in the Civil Rights Division were not unique to the Obama administration. Indeed, the inspector general found problems during the Bush administration as well, but that's hardly a surprise. The problem of government is not a problem with a particular administration but rather systemic, where a lack of accountability combines with partisan rancor and pervasive incompetence to create a crisis of justice.

There's an old saying in the law: "A good lawyer knows the law, but a *great* lawyer knows the judge." This saying harks back to old-school local justice when lawyers and judges would often cut deals based on personal and sometimes financial relationships—a way of legal life that is fortunately largely vanishing from the American scene. I've practiced in federal courts across the nation and have been uniformly impressed with the professionalism of judges and their staffs.

But, sadly, that does not mean our system is healthy. When it comes to legal practice against the United States of America, when the DOJ is acting as its law firm, perhaps there should be a new saying: "A good lawyer knows the law, but a *great* lawyer works for a liberal law firm."

Backroom deals with sympathetic legal organizations, sharing confidential information, revolving-door hiring relationships, open hostility against conservatives—all of these things add up once again to the merger of the party of government with the government.

Every American who shares my belief in the rule of law and the impartial administration of justice should be infuriated. My clients in the IRS Tea Party–targeting cases are confronting *admitted* government wrongdoing, yet face a ferocious and well-funded DOJ defense. Yet American taxpayers pick up the tab when the DOJ "confronts" its liberal allies, negotiating backroom deals that advance leftist goals and enrich leftist lawyers.

This approach to justice is intolerable. And yet until there's meaningful civil service reform, it's virtually unstoppable. No political appointee can exercise comprehensive oversight over thousands of lawyers practicing tens of thousands of cases. No political appointee can clean house when "cleaning house" means confronting massive resistance in endless proceedings before the Merit Systems Protection Board.

I've said it before, and I'll say it again: it's time to introduce private sector rationality to public sector employment, and nowhere is it more vital than in the Department of Justice, where entrenched corruption means that you can not only lose your rights, you can even lose your most basic liberties.

Protect employees from political discrimination, as well as discrimination on the basis of race, gender, religion, and other protected characteristics, yes—but render them otherwise "at will" employees like you. Like me.

But lawyers—because of their unique power—should be held to an even higher standard. In the previous chapter, I urged reforms that required automatic termination for any prosecutor who commits an act of prosecutorial misconduct. In fact, this standard should be extended to cover *any* unethical act, including sharing confidential information with opposing attorneys. Government attorneys who violate ethics rules should lose their jobs.

There will be no reform without accountability. There will be no justice without reform.

8

THE EPA

The World's Least Democratic Agency

It's hard to imagine a federal agency more perfectly suited for trampling on democracy and shredding our Constitution than the Environmental Protection Agency.

The EPA deals with a subject matter that is almost impossibly complex. The relationship between the environment, human actions, public health, and weather (just to name a few factors) is multifaceted and ever changing. Scientific conventional wisdom rises and falls, sometimes within the same generation, and seemingly simple questions—like whether a given pesticide causes cancer—can be hotly disputed for decades.

Given the complexity, it's hardly surprising that EPA issues come laden with scientific jargon and are rarely presented in plain English (unless that plain English is artificially contrived to create fear or alarm). To take just one example, here is the Chamber of Commerce's description of an EPA issue in its "sue and settle" report I discussed in the previous chapter. And as you read it, keep in mind that the Chamber wrote this with the goal of simplicity and clarity:

On May 23, 2008, environmental groups sued EPA to challenge the final revised ozone NAAQS, which the agency had published on March 27, 2008. The 2008 rule had lowered the eight-hour primary ground-level ozone standard from 84 parts per billion (ppb) to 75 ppb. On March 10, 2009, EPA filed a motion requesting that the court hold the cases in abeyance to allow time for officials from the new administration to review the 2008 standards and determine whether they should be reconsidered. On January 19, 2010, EPA announced that it had decided to reconsider the 2008 ozone NAAQS. Although EPA did not enter into a settlement agreement or consent decree with the environmental group, it readily accepted the legal arguments put forth by the group despite available legal defenses. The agency announced its intention to propose a reconsidered standard ranging between 70 ppb and 65 ppb. Although the reconsidered ozone NAAQS was not published—and was withdrawn by the administration on September 2, 2011— EPA had estimated that the reconsidered standard would impose up to $90 billion of new costs per year on the U.S. economy.[1]

Can you understand that? If so, congratulations, you're one of a select few Americans. Here's how most of us read this paragraph:

The EPA wants to change something I don't really understand for reasons I don't really understand, and it will cost the economy $90 BILLION PER YEAR.

In other words, issues we don't understand carry with them enormous potential costs.

But here's the way the EPA uses this complexity to its advantage, and it's another reason why the EPA is an almost perfect engine of democracy destruction.

The EPA is always telling us the stakes are very, very high. You may not understand the science, it says, but—trust us—if you don't do what we say, people will die.

Lots of people.

The EPA's partners in alarmism include the government and its allies in the mainstream media. For example, here's how one reporter in the respected British newspaper the *Guardian* described the stakes of climate change: "Now we are living through a man-made mass extinction event."[2]

Yes, mass extinction. And, yes, that claim was published in a major newspaper.

Let me stop for a moment and state very clearly: I am not a scientist. So don't read this chapter and expect a scientific argument about whether the earth is warming or cooling or whether man is causing any warming or cooling.

But while I'm not a scientist, I've spent enough time in courtrooms and our team has cross-examined enough Ph.D.s to know that scientists are often wrong—sometimes embarrassingly so. I also know that scientists are human, and as human beings they are subject to the same kinds of biases and prejudices as any other person. In other words, they often see and hear what they want to see and hear.

Or, as *National Review*'s Kevin Williamson said, "The problem with science is scientists."[3]

It's not hard to find examples of environmental scientists making spectacularly wrong predictions. In April 2014, Mark Perry from the American Enterprise Institute compiled a list of "18 spectacularly wrong apocalyptic predictions" made in 1970, the year of the first Earth Day.[4] Here are some of my favorites:

> Harvard biologist George Wald estimated that "civilization will end within 15 or 30 years unless immediate action is taken against problems facing mankind."[5]

We're still here.

"Population will inevitably and completely outstrip whatever small increases in food supplies we make," Paul Ehrlich confidently declared in the April 1970 *Mademoiselle*. "The death rate will increase until at least 100–200 million people per year will be starving to death during the next ten years."[6]

Ehrlich missed that prediction by 100–200 million. At present, true starvation occurs only in the most "extreme" circumstances, such as during "recent famine in [war-torn] Somalia."[7]

Ehrlich sketched out his most alarmist scenario for the 1970 Earth Day issue of *The Progressive*, assuring readers that between 1980 and 1989, some 4 billion people, including 65 million Americans, would perish in the "Great Die-Off."[8]

Ehrlich missed that prediction by even more—by about 4 billion.

"It is already too late to avoid mass starvation," declared Denis Hayes, the chief organizer for Earth Day, in the Spring 1970 issue of *The Living Wilderness*.[9]

No, it wasn't too late.

In January 1970, *Life* reported, "Scientists have solid experimental and theoretical evidence to support . . . the following predictions: In a decade, urban dwellers will have to wear gas masks to survive air pollution . . . by 1985 air pollution will have reduced the amount of sunlight reaching earth by one half. . . ."[10]

Wrong. The sun shines brightly even over New York City.

> Ecologist Kenneth Watt declared, "By the year 2000, if present trends continue, we will be using up crude oil at such a rate . . . that there won't be any more crude oil. You'll drive up to the pump and say, 'Fill 'er up, buddy,' and he'll say, 'I am very sorry, there isn't any.' "[11]

Not only is that wrong, but the world is producing more oil than we produced even thirty years ago,[12] and America is now, some say, the world's largest oil producer.[13]

Finally, here's one of my favorites given the current "consensus" on global warming:

> Kenneth Watt warned about a pending Ice Age in a speech. "The world has been chilling sharply for about twenty years," he declared. "If present trends continue, the world will be about four degrees colder for the global mean temperature in 1990, but eleven degrees colder in the year 2000. This is about twice what it would take to put us into an ice age."[14]

The world hasn't gone into an ice age, nor has it heated up appreciably. In fact, during the last sixteen years temperatures haven't changed much at all.[15]

And lest anyone think that it's unfair to judge science by predictions made forty-five years ago, here is one of the more entertaining recent claims of looming disaster:

> "Some of the models suggest that there is a 75 percent chance that the entire north polar ice cap, during some of the summer months, could be completely ice-free within the next five to seven years," [former vice president Al] Gore said in 2008.

Gore was echoing the predictions made by American scientist Wieslaw Maslowski in 2007, who said that "you can argue that may be our projection of [an ice-free Arctic by 2013] is already too conservative."[16]

I could go on, but you get the point. We simply can't accept scientific predictions as fact and react accordingly. That doesn't mean that all scientific predictions are wrong. Of course many have proven true, but *all* scientific predictions are suspect—and by that I mean they should be subject to rigorous inquiry and testing.

The environmentalist Left and its allies in Congress and the EPA are fond of arguing that the stakes are too high to wait, that "something must be done." But what if the cure is worse than the disease? What if helping hurts?

The EPA's Own War on Science: The Lessons of Banning DDT

Before I deal with the modern EPA, let me go back a bit—back to World War II and the introduction of a "miracle pesticide" called DDT.

Although it was first synthesized in 1874, DDT wasn't used on a mass scale until the latter days of World War II.[17] While medicine had advanced greatly by the 1940s, the U.S. Army still faced prohibitive casualties from disease. In fact, disease is traditionally a more deadly killer in wartime than combating the enemy. In the Civil War, for example, far more Confederate and Union soldiers fell to diseases like typhoid and dysentery than they did to bullets—in even the war's bloodiest battles.

In World War II, malaria was still a profound threat to American forces, claiming lives and health, as soldiers faced long, debilitating illnesses that sapped their strength and American fighting power. DDT, by killing the mosquitoes that carried malaria, promised relief.

But DDT—developed for American troops—also proved its worth helping civilians.

Italy surrendered to the Allies in September 1943, more than a year before the Allies finally conquered Nazi Germany, but that surrender hardly meant that Italy was out of the war. The German army occupied most of the Italian peninsula and—for the rest of the war—fought a fierce and savage defensive battle as it slowly retreated north toward the Italian Alps.

All along the way, the Germans brutalized the Italian population, in some cases engaging in what amounted to deliberate biological warfare by blowing up dikes and destroying public utilities—causing public sanitation to degrade, swarms of mosquitoes to descend, and triggering lice epidemics, with all the disease that follows.

The American army responded as it always has—by rushing to rescue the vulnerable and defenseless. Vast quantities of the new pesticide were shipped forward, citizens were dusted, newly created marshes were sprayed, and disaster was averted. Writing in the *New Atlantis*, here's how Robert Zubrin described the reaction:

> From now on, "DDT marches with the troops," declared the Allied high command. The order could not have come at a better time. As British and American forces advanced in Europe, they encountered millions of victims of Nazi oppression—civilians under occupation, slave laborers, prisoners of war, concentration camp inmates—dying in droves from insect-borne diseases. But with the armies of liberation came squads spraying DDT, and with it life for millions otherwise doomed to destruction. The same story was repeated in the Philippines, Burma, China, and elsewhere in the Asia-Pacific theater. Never before in history had a single chemical saved so many lives in such a short amount of time.[18]

DDT was so successful that Paul Müller, the chemist most responsible for its public use, was awarded the Nobel Prize for Medicine in 1948, with the Nobel committee declaring that he was responsible for preserving "the life and health of hundreds of thousands." [19]

When DDT went into widespread civilian use after World War II, the number of lives saved climbed from the hundreds of thousands to the millions.

Cheap and easy to produce, it could be shipped and used in vast quantities in the Third World, and it was utterly deadly to malaria-carrying mosquitoes. But it wasn't just the Third World that benefited. Few Americans remember, but we used to have a malaria problem in our own country. DDT wiped it out. [20]

As important as American successes were, they were even more important in the Third World, which had a much worse public health infrastructure than the United States. And in the Third World the results were beyond dramatic. Europe, which used to have a malaria problem, "virtually eradicated" the disease, while "South African cases of malaria quickly dropped by 80%." In Sri Lanka, the results were beyond dramatic, with cases of malaria dropping "from 2.8 million in 1946 to 17 in 1963." Other nations saw similar results, where DDT use "soon cut malaria rates in numerous countries in Latin America and Asia by 99 percent or better." [21]

No one seriously disputes DDT's effectiveness as a pesticide, not even radical environmentalists, though in a manner that adopts the typical glass-half-empty approach of radicals who see people as a problem. As Zubrin reminds us, Alexander King from the liberal environmentalist think tank the Club of Rome said this in 1990:

> My own doubts came when DDT was introduced for civilian use. In Guyana, within two years it had almost eliminated malaria, but at the same time the birth rate had doubled. So my chief quarrel with DDT in hindsight is that it has greatly added to the population problem.

By the late 1950s and early 1960s, DDT was an unqualified public health success.

Then along came a book called *Silent Spring*, by environmentalist heroine Rachel Carson.[22]

Zubrin's critique is telling: "While excellent literature, however, *Silent Spring* was very poor science."[23]

Carson painted a vivid picture of a silent world, one where birds were driven to extinction because they could no longer feed on insects, and described insecticides as "elixirs of death." Specifically, she turned her sights on DDT, claiming that it was a "chemical carcinogen."

This claim was false.

The book, despite its flaws, was wildly successful and is credited with essentially creating the modern environmentalist movement. And it triggered a public health panic, one that had immediate and deadly consequences. Nations across the world stopped spraying with DDT, and people suffered immediately and profoundly. To go back to the example of Sri Lanka, the number of malaria victims soared from 17 in 1963 to "half a million victims per year by 1969."[24]

While Carson's book was popular, many scientists were unpersuaded, even alarmed. They knew the high human stakes of this scientific argument. The National Academy of Sciences tried to head off disaster, writing in 1970:

> To only a few chemicals does man owe as great a debt as to DDT. It has contributed to the great increase in agricultural productivity, while sparing countless humanity from a host of diseases, most notably, perhaps, scrub typhus and malaria. Indeed, it is estimated that, in little more than two decades, DDT has prevented 500 million deaths due to malaria that would otherwise have been inevitable. Abandonment of this valuable insecticide should be undertaken only at such time

and in such places as it is evident that the prospective gain to humanity exceeds the consequent losses. At this writing, all available substitutes for DDT are both more expensive per crop-year and decidedly more hazardous.[25]

But the environmentalist movement was unimpressed. And they had a new and powerful ally, the Environmental Protection Agency, established in 1970. In 1971, the EPA investigated. Zubrin recounts what followed:

> Lasting seven months, the investigative hearings led by Judge Edmund Sweeney gathered testimony from 125 expert witnesses with 365 exhibits. The conclusion of the inquest, however, was exactly the opposite of what the environmentalists had hoped for. After assessing all the evidence, Judge Sweeney found: "The uses of DDT under the registration involved here do not have a deleterious effect on freshwater fish, estuarine organisms, wild birds, or other wildlife. . . . DDT is not a carcinogenic hazard to man. . . . DDT is not a mutagenic or teratogenic hazard to man." Accordingly, Judge Sweeney ruled that DDT should remain available for use.[26]

But why let a little thing called "science" get in the way of a leftist agenda. Remember what happened next when you hear an apologist for the EPA accuse conservatives of waging a "war on science." The EPA administrator, William D. Ruckelshaus, "did not attend a single hour of the investigative hearing" and allegedly "did not even read Judge Sweeney's report."[27] Yet the EPA banned DDT anyway.

While the EPA could ban DDT only within the United States, its action had long-lasting and far-reaching consequences, impacting countries dependent on American aid. The human suffering has been staggering:

As a result, insect-borne diseases returned to the tropics with a vengeance. By some estimates, the death toll in Africa alone from unnecessary malaria resulting from the restrictions on DDT has exceeded 100 million people.[28]

It's obvious that environmental science is fallible. The EPA can make profound mistakes, and it does not in any way, shape, or form deserve to be exempted from American democratic processes. "We the people" have to hold the EPA accountable, yet its power only grows . . . thanks largely to "climate change."

When Fighting Climate Change, Democracy Is Optional

I think most of us can agree that air pollution is bad.

During my legal career I've been blessed to travel around the world, defending liberty in places as far-flung as China, Israel, and Europe. And in those travels I've visited cities that seem almost besieged with smog, so much so that citizens frequently go outside wearing surgical masks just to keep from coughing and choking.

I'm old enough to remember a different era in this country as well, when one could drive toward a city—particularly a city with an unfavorable geography—and even from miles away see the smog hovering, dark and ominous, a visibly unhealthy sign of pollution.

So I'm for clean air. I've never met anyone who isn't for clean air.

And it was in response to sights like those smog-covered cities that our democratic system worked. Congress debated and passed—and the president (Lyndon Johnson) signed—the Clean Air Act, a law that (broadly speaking) gave the federal government broad powers to limit "air pollutants" in the United States.

And what is an "air pollutant"? The definition is broad:

The term "air pollutant" means any air pollution agent or combination of such agents, including any physical, chemical, biological, radioactive (including source material, special nuclear material, and byproduct material) substance or matter which is emitted into or otherwise enters the ambient air. . . .[29]

Moreover, under the act, the EPA is obligated to publish a list of air pollutants, giving citizens and industries fair warning of incoming limitations and regulations. In other words, if you're manufacturing a product, and in the process your plant is emitting a defined and listed "air pollutant," be prepared to face tough regulations.

But here's where it gets interesting.

As concerns about global warming grew, the EPA realized it had a problem on its hands. Faced with terrifying predictions of global disaster, activists, the mainstream media, and many (mainly Democratic members of Congress) were crying out for the EPA to "do something."

These cries only grew more urgent as the democratic process "failed" (at least as many activists defined failure) to "solve" the problem. After all, the U.S. Senate resoundingly rejected the Kyoto Protocol, an international agreement that would have bound thirty-seven industrial nations (including the United States) to reduce greenhouse gas emissions.[30]

There were many reasons why the Senate rejected the Kyoto treaty. It would have damaged the U.S. economy, it might not have reduced greenhouse gases overall since developing countries would have continued to increase emissions, and it would have placed much of America's economy under the thumb of international controls, thereby harming American sovereignty.

Having failed in Congress, activists—now including states—petitioned the EPA to act, to issue a so-called endangerment finding and begin the process of regulating carbon dioxide as an "air pollutant." When the EPA—to its credit—refused, Massachusetts and a coalition of states, local governments, and activist groups sued, and won.

The Supreme Court held, in a 5–4 decision, that EPA had "offered no reasoned explanation for its refusal to decide whether greenhouse gases cause or contribute to climate change. Its action was therefore 'arbitrary, capricious, . . . or otherwise not in accordance with law.'" The Court went on to say that it was not ordering "endangerment finding," but by that time, the outcome was a foregone conclusion.[31]

On December 7, 2009, the EPA administrator "signed two distinct findings regarding greenhouse gases":

- **Endangerment Finding:** The Administrator finds that the current and projected concentrations of the six key well-mixed greenhouse gases—carbon dioxide (CO_2), methane (CH_4), nitrous oxide (N_2O), hydrofluorocarbons (HFCs), perfluorocarbons (PFCs), and sulfur hexafluoride (SF_6)—in the atmosphere threaten the public health and welfare of current and future generations.
- **Cause or Contribute Finding:** The Administrator finds that the combined emissions of these well-mixed greenhouse gases from new motor vehicles and new motor vehicle engines contribute to the greenhouse gas pollution which threatens public health and welfare.[32]

And with that, the EPA was off to the regulatory races. The "finding" helped prime the pump, enabling the EPA to write rule after rule. The "finding" was legally necessary to empower the rulemaking, and once the "finding" was issued, the EPA had all the justification it needed to begin to transform the American economy. What follows is a partial list of EPA regulatory activities, all of which were enacted without congressional approval, and all of which have had profound economic effects that exceed the impact of most congressional acts.

- New fuel standards:

  EPA and the National Highway Traffic Safety Administration (NHTSA) are taking coordinated steps to enable the production of a new generation of clean vehicles—from the smallest cars to the largest trucks—through reduced greenhouse gas emissions and improved fuel use.[33]
- New renewable fuel programs.

  EPA is also responsible for developing and implementing regulations to ensure that transportation fuel sold in the United States contains a minimum volume of renewable fuel. By 2022, the Renewable Fuel Standard (RFS) program will reduce greenhouse gas emissions by 138 million metric tons, about the annual emissions of 27 million passenger vehicles, replacing about seven percent of expected annual diesel consumption and decreasing oil imports by $41.5 billion.[34]
- New emissions standards for power plants:

  On June 2, 2014, the EPA issued a proposal to cut carbon pollution from existing power plants, the largest source of greenhouse gas emissions in the United States.[35]
- New oil and gas pollution standards:

  On April 18, 2012, EPA finalized cost-effective regulations to reduce harmful air pollution from the oil and natural gas industry, while allowing continued, responsible growth in U.S. oil and natural gas production.

That's a partial list, but it's enough. These regulations impact only the cars we drive, the nation's entire energy production industry, and the nation's entire power-generating industry.

In fact, the Obama administration pushed through regulations that would mandate a whopping 54.5-mpg standard for cars and light trucks by 2025, only ten years from the publication of this book.[36] As of now, only a few cars sold in the United States can meet that standard, and those cars are very small and fragile compared to larger, less fuel-efficient cars and light trucks. At least one think tank estimates mandatory fuel efficiency standards have "caused between 1,300 and 2,600 traffic deaths every year since they were established in 1975."[37]

Not only does this new standard essentially mandate smaller cars, but it will increase the cost of new cars by an average of $3,000 per vehicle and—according to a car dealer association—"shuts almost 7 million people out of the new-car market entirely and prevents many millions more from being able to afford new vehicles that meet their needs."[38]

Is fuel efficiency worth that cost—in blood and treasure? Shouldn't the American people's elected representatives decide?

It's important to remember that none of these regulations ever saw a ballot, because regulations are not decided by a popular vote. They are simply passed by the agency in charge, in this case the EPA. If there were a vote, it's doubtful that a single one of the EPA's major climate change regulations could make its way through Congress. As Ramesh Ponnuru, writing for Bloomberg, pointed out:

> In 2010, when Democrats held a filibuster-proof majority in the Senate and a large majority in the House, they failed to get a major climate-change law to the president's desk. That legislation probably had a better cost-benefit ratio than today's regulations do.[39]

But don't mistake that failure to act for gridlock. By no means. Rationally, why would the Left politically risk voters' wrath through highly public, fiercely debated bills when they can get even more draconian regulations through the EPA with minimal public attention and— even more important—no real opportunity for the democratic process to work?

Remember, our government is not in gridlock. Instead, when it comes to the vast regulatory apparatus of the federal government, our government actually has one-party rule. The Left doesn't need to win a congressional vote when it owns the bureaucracy.

The Left doesn't need to win a congressional vote when it owns the bureaucracy.

In fact, to slow down or stop the bureaucracy—which can churn out regulations by the tens of thousands, even regulations that can remake our industries and economy (like the EPA standards)—Congress has to go through the difficult process of actually passing a law.

In July 2014, the House of Representatives approved a spending bill that would, if passed, block a number of the EPA's most expansive regulations.[10] Yet when the House passed the bill, leaders knew it had no chance to pass in the Senate. Indeed it likely wouldn't even be brought to a vote, and indeed—it wasn't. The bill went nowhere.

This leaves the EPA with a free hand to pass regulations, subject only to the limits imposed by federal courts—courts that are often loath to interfere with agency discretion unless it clearly, unmistakably exceeds its very wide regulatory mandate.

But is the EPA content with this enormous power? Does it stay within its vast territory, or does it abuse that power? Does it constantly grasp for more?

You already know the answer.

The EPA Goes Rogue

If you ask Americans to provide a list of powerful public officials, they'll likely start with President Obama, move to Vice President Joe Biden, and then name perhaps three or four more elected officials before they exhaust their full knowledge of America's "public servants."

You'd probably have to survey a hundred thousand Americans before you could find one who named Al Armendariz as either powerful or dangerous.

But he's both. Or at least he was.

Appointed by President Obama in 2009 to run the EPA's "Region 6" office in Dallas, Armendariz had his fifteen minutes of fame (more like fifteen seconds) when he was caught on video saying:

> The Romans used to conquer little villages in the Mediterranean. They'd go into a little Turkish town somewhere, they'd find the first five guys they saw and they would crucify them. And then you know that town was really easy to manage for the next few years.[41]

He was speaking, of course, not about literal crucifixion but instead about wielding the EPA's enforcement power, about making examples of companies in order to deter alleged misconduct.

The problem is that it was his job to enforce the law fairly and evenhandedly, not to "hit [people] as hard as you can"[42]—especially not when you're known as an ideological zealot.

And what does it mean to "hit . . . as hard as you can"? Sometimes it means making things up, at great cost to American industries.

In April 2012, *Forbes* writer Christopher Helman highlighted how Armendariz chooses his "examples":

[N]ot only has Armendariz talked about crucifying oil companies, he's tried to do it. In 2010 his office targeted Range Resources, a Fort Worth–based driller that was among the first to discover the potential of the Marcellus Shale gas field of Pennsylvania—the biggest gas field in America and one of the biggest in the world. Armendariz's office declared in an emergency order that Range's drilling activity had contaminated groundwater in Parker County, Texas. Armendariz's office insisted that Range's hydraulic fracking activity had caused the pollution and ordered Range to remediate the water.[43]

And what was the conclusion of Armendariz's assault on Range? He overreached. Here's Helman again:

Nevermind that he couldn't prove jack against Range. For a year and a half EPA bickered over the issue, both with Range and with the Texas Railroad Commission, which regulates oil and gas drilling and did its own scientific study of Range's wells and found no evidence that they polluted anything. In recent months a federal judge slapped the EPA, decreeing that the agency was required to actually do some scientific investigation of wells before penalizing the companies that drilled them. Finally in March the EPA withdrew its emergency order and a federal court dismissed the EPA's case.[44]

Do you recognize the pattern by now? Does this sound like the IRS or the Department of Justice? Tough-talking bureaucrats speak loudly about pursuing lawbreakers, carry the very big stick of the full power of the federal government, yet are all too often simply making things up. Worse, they're making things up to advance a specific and intolerant political agenda.

Make no mistake, there are real costs to these attacks. While Range Resources no doubt spent vast amounts of money defending itself from baseless charges, these attacks deter further growth and development in America's vital energy sector. To environmentalists this is of course a good outcome, but for most Americans it is very bad indeed.

Deterring growth in America's energy sector doesn't just cost jobs. It goes beyond simply making America more strategically vulnerable as we continue to import vast amounts of foreign oil. It actively empowers some of the worst regimes in the world, including regimes—like Iran's—that are violently hostile to the United States of America.

Deterring growth in America's energy sector doesn't just cost jobs. It goes beyond simply making America more strategically vulnerable as we continue to import vast amounts of foreign oil. It actively empowers some of the worst regimes in the world, including regimes—like Iran's—that are violently hostile to the United States of America.

True polluters should be liable for damages they cause, but no federal agency should declare an entire American industry (or class of citizens) worthy of extraordinary government harassment merely because they are disfavored by the partisan ideologues who populate our vast federal bureaucracy.

There was a happy ending to this controversy, as Armendariz not only lost in court, he was forced to resign.[45] But his is just one fight in a very long war.

And when I say long, I mean long. At the beginning of this chapter, I introduced you to the EPA by recounting its shameful history with DDT, including its decision to ban a lifesaving chemical—a decision that cost countless lives.

But the EPA—like most federal bureaucracies—refuses to learn its lessons. A brief history of EPA misconduct spans every modern

American presidential administration (so, no, it is not all President Obama's fault).

Grove City College's Mark Hendrickson has collected a considerable number of stories of EPA misconduct, tracing its abuse of power through the 1970s up through the present. Some key incidents:

- In 1978, the EPA tried to suppress research showing the cost of proposed air pollution standards. If Pennsylvania's two senators at the time (John Heinz and Richard Schweiker) hadn't intervened, the EPA would have imposed standards stringent enough to effectively shut down the U.S. steel industry.[46]
- In 1991, a panel of outside scientists brought in to review EPA practices concluded (among other things) that the EPA often tailors its science to justify what it wants to do and shields key research from peer review. EPA Administrator William Reilly acknowledged that "scientific data have not always been featured prominently in environmental efforts and have sometimes been ignored even when available."[47]

Moreover, for the sake of the "greater good," the EPA is often just plain lawless, defying court orders and destroying evidence:

- In the 1990s, under the leadership of Carol Browner, the EPA refused to divulge how it calculated cost-benefit analyses. Indeed, in 1997 Browner admitted that new research would be required to set a "scientifically defensible" standard for air-quality issues that would "fill obvious and critical voids in our knowledge." The Browner-led EPA also blatantly broke federal law by actively lobbying against legislation designed to curb some of EPA's abuses. Browner herself defied a federal judge's orders and oversaw the erasure of the hard drives and the destruction of backup email tapes that she had used as administrator.[48]

And, by the way, if you ever feel intimidated by the EPA's alleged expertise on all things environmental, sometimes the things it does quite simply violate the most basic forms of common sense:

• One of the most amazing rulings to come out of Browner's EPA was a letter sent to the city of San Diego, ordering them to stop treating the sewage pouring into the Tijuana River Valley on the grounds that human actions were disturbing the "sewage-based ecology" of the affected estuary—ignoring the fact that the sewage posed a health threat to human beings (whose "ecology" obviously wasn't considered as important by the EPA).[49]

Fed up with the EPA's propensity for taking action on the basis of "science" it won't disclose, House Republicans proposed the "Secret Science Reform Act of 2014," which would prohibit the EPA from enacting new environmental regulations unless the scientific basis for those regulations is fully disclosed.[50]

It's difficult to think of a more commonsense proposal. In a democratic society, where the default position (except for matters of urgent national security) is that the government's actions are open, transparent, and subject to public critique, it should already be the EPA's practice to open up its scientific information. After all, the environment is at stake, public health is at stake, jobs are at stake, and our economy is at stake.

But since the bill is about increased accountability, key members of the environmentalist Left[51]—which has the coziest of relationships with the ideologues in the EPA—are utterly opposed.[52] To them, "peer review" by ideological fellow travelers is all the review that's needed, and the public's right to know is trumped by the Left's desire to give the EPA a free hand.

And just as the EPA refuses to learn its lessons, it also—like most federal bureaucracies—works hard to evade accountability.

The EPA's former administrator Lisa Jackson was among the worst offenders, going to creative and exhausting lengths to conceal her collaboration with ideologically sympathetic radical environmentalists.

According to federal law, most federal records—including emails from official accounts—are subject to production under the federal Freedom of Information Act, which requires the federal government to produce documents to citizens upon request. FOIA requests (as they're called) can be invaluable for uncovering public corruption and keeping government officials honest.

In fact, many of the documents I've discussed in this book—especially documents uncovered in the IRS scandals—were first made public under FOIA requests. At the ACLJ we frequently file FOIA requests and have gained extremely valuable information that has helped us defend constitutional liberty.

But FOIA requests are considerably less useful if bureaucrats are willing to game the system and break the law. Lisa Jackson was just such a bureaucrat.

In 2013, Americans learned that Jackson created an email alias named "Richard Windsor" to help her communicate with outside environmentalist groups without worry that her emails would be read by concerned citizens.[53] Since no outside groups knew to ask for the fictional "Richard Windsor's" email, the EPA kept them in-house, and Jackson kept using the address to communicate.

How often did she speak as "Richard Windsor"? When the scandal was finally discovered, she produced more than twelve thousand "Richard Windsor" emails.[54]

Jackson resigned from the EPA shortly thereafter.

Yet the EPA's email scandal didn't end there. In July 2012, reports emerged that the EPA was "slow-walking" new environmental regulations so they wouldn't become an election-year issue.[55] Conservative critics were concerned, seeing "a crass political calculation at play: Don't give [Mitt] Romney any more ammunition before the election—and then open the floodgates after the polls close."

I'm left to wonder, was the EPA helping the Obama administration obscure its true agenda before the 2012 elections? After all, in a supposedly nonpartisan agency, political considerations should be irrelevant to the regulatory timetable. If the need to protect the environment means new regulations are necessary, those regulations shouldn't be proposed based on their presumed impact on electoral politics.

The scandal continued when on August 17, 2012, the Landmark Legal Foundation—a conservative legal organization headed by my friend Mark Levin—filed a Freedom of Information Act request for EPA communications "relating to all proposed rules or regulations that have not been finalized" between January 1, 2012, and the date of the request.[56]

In response, the EPA waged a campaign of evasion and deception that necessitated not only a Landmark Legal lawsuit, but multiple motions in federal court to require the EPA to fulfill its most basic responsibilities under federal law. In fact, as of the date of this writing, the EPA had still not provided Landmark Legal with a straightforward, legally appropriate response to its rather simple initial request.

In an absurd postscript to the story, a postscript so ridiculous that it's hard to believe, the fictional "Richard Windsor" was prolific enough online that "he" received an award. An ethics award.

I'm not making this up. The EPA declared him a "scholar of ethical behavior" for his numerous accomplishments in information technologies compliance.[57]

And that's your federal bureaucracy at work: using all its ingenuity to evade its transparency obligations under federal law while being simultaneously so incompetent it can't even distinguish real and fictional employees.

But while the EPA uses secret science to publish industry-killing regulations, abuses its power to go after disfavored industries, and then tries to hide it all from the public, at least it doesn't suffer from some of the excesses of the IRS, right?

At least it doesn't misuse government funds for lavish personal benefits for employees, right?

Wrong:

> In a huge Environmental Protection Agency warehouse in Landover, [Maryland,] enterprising workers made sure that they had all the comforts of home. They created personal rec rooms with televisions, radios, chairs and couches. On the walls were photos, calendars and pinups. For entertainment, they had books, magazines and videos. If they got hungry, they could grab something from a refrigerator and pop it into a microwave.
>
> The crown jewel of their hideaway—which stored EPA office furnishings—was a 30-by-45-foot athletic center, cobbled together from "surplus" EPA gym equipment and decked out with a music system provided via "other agency inventory items," according to a recently released inspector general's report.[58]

But at least the EPA doesn't wrongfully disclose citizens' confidential information, like the IRS did, right?

Wrong:

> According to a letter from a group of Senators to Acting EPA Administrator Bob Perciasepe, the EPA "released farm information for 80,000 livestock facilities in 30 states as the

result of a Freedom of Information Act (FOIA) request from national environmental organizations. It is our understanding that the initial release of data contained personal information that was not required by the FOIA request for ten states including Arizona, Colorado, Georgia, Indiana, Illinois, Michigan, Montana, Nebraska, Ohio and Utah. This release included **names and personal addresses.**" (Emphasis in original)[59]

Pursing companies without evidence of wrongdoing, leaking personal information, hiding official emails, giving awards to fictitious people . . . this is exactly the wrong agency to obtain additional power, but as this book was being written the EPA was actively seeking the authority to garnish citizens' wages without a court order.[60]

Our federal bureaucracies are not self-regulating. They will not limit their own power. They constantly seek more. They are on a power trip and incapable of self-correcting.

Our federal bureaucracies are not self-regulating. They will not limit their own power. They constantly seek more.

And that's why we must resist. Our liberty is at stake, our economy is at stake, and even our own jobs can be at stake.

Don't believe me? Let's turn to the National Labor Relations Board, the NLRB, the agency that's trying to tell Americans where they can—and can't—work.

9

THE NLRB

Does Overreach Have Its Limits?

The South has gone through much-needed changes since I first moved to Atlanta as a teenager from New York in 1970. I went to college in Atlanta and law school in Macon, Georgia.

While the South's record of racial progress is well-known and much welcomed, its economic transformation has also been remarkable.

I can still remember the days when sleepy southern towns had few industries and depended almost entirely on agriculture, and their citizens had to look to cities outside the region for a shot at a decent income and financial security for their families. I can remember an Atlanta that most residents today would barely recognize, a city of modest size but big ambitions.

Nashville, Raleigh, Charlotte, Atlanta, Austin—all of these cities have transformed in recent years, and indeed the South has led the nation in internal migration (the movement of citizens between states).[1] In 2012, six of the top eight states in internal migration were in the South, gaining a total of 250,000 residents: Texas, Florida, North Carolina, Tennessee, South Carolina, and Georgia.[2]

The top losers? New York, Illinois, New Jersey, and California.
Why does the South do so well? Obviously the climate is
better than, say, New York's or New Jersey's. But it's not better
than California's, where some areas enjoy year-round sun and mild
temperatures.

Yes, the taxes can be much lower in the South. In Texas, Tennessee, and Florida there's no state income tax, and workers moving
to those states can see an immediate increase in their take-home
pay. But not every southern state has low taxes, and many of the
top-growing states have income taxes with rates comparable to
states in the West and Northeast.

So we have to look beyond taxes for a sufficient explanation.

But here's another: jobs. For almost two full generations, the
South has been consistently outpacing other American regions not
just in population growth but also in economic growth.[3]

Why?

The South is not union country. As a result, large-scale manufacturers have made their home there, bringing with them an enormous amount of economic opportunity.

Talk to many southerners from the new manufacturing regions,
like Georgetown, Kentucky; Smyrna, Tennessee; Chattanooga,
Tennessee; and others, and they all have a similar story to tell—of
struggling towns transformed by stable, high-paying jobs, of new
subdivisions, of new schools, and of new hope for a better life.

The automobile industry has become a dominant force in the
South, with foreign car companies moving into Kentucky, Tennessee, Alabama, Mississippi, South Carolina, Georgia, and Texas.[4]
Alabama, for example, went from producing not one single car
to becoming, by 2008, "the nation's fifth-largest auto-producing
state."[5]

And one can't measure the impact of any given car plant (or
other large manufacturer) merely by counting the total jobs at that
one facility:

"Every job in auto production supports five other jobs in the economy in steel, tires, rubber, programmers, and auto dealers," says Robert Scott, senior international economist at the Washington, D.C.–based Economic Policy Institute. Toyota's Kentucky operations support 28,000 jobs in the state. In 2007, according to the Association of International Automobile Manufacturers, foreign automakers employed 92,700 workers directly and 574,500 indirectly, accounting for 33 percent of U.S. auto production. By contrast, the Big Three (General Motors, Ford, and Chrysler) employ about 240,000 workers.[6]

There's no doubt that foreign manufacturers like Toyota have been attracted to the South's nonunion culture, and there's equally little doubt that major American unions have tried long and hard to unionize these new plants.

They have failed every time.

Not only has the United Automobile Workers (UAW) failed, but it's been shrinking—dramatically. According to the *Wall Street Journal*, "all of the employment growth in the U.S. auto industry since 1980 was in nonunion plants while the UAW's membership has shrunk to fewer than 400,000 from 1.5 million in 1979."[7]

To be sure, not all the shrinkage is the unions' fault. America emerged from World War II as the only great power whose industrial base had been untouched by war, so much of our earlier market dominance was an artifact of the ruined cities in Europe and Japan. When those countries' economies recovered, so did their market share, thereby shrinking the American market share and unionization.

To be fair, the union workers don't design or market cars, they just make them. It's hardly their fault that American automakers were caught flat-footed in the late 1990s by demand for more fuel-efficient vehicles. They did not design the Edsel (Ford's iconic failed model), nor did they bloat the upper management of General

Motors with its legendary, inflexible bureaucracy. All of these factors were out of the workers' control. So they can't be blamed for the UAW's declining membership.

Perhaps the single most frustrating challenge for America's left-wing labor unions is their persistent failure to unionize the new auto plants that have sprung up across the South. Again and again they've tried, and again and again they've been defeated, often by resounding margins.

Simply put, the nonunion southern plants pay a very good wage, provide excellent benefits, and treat their workers well. Why pay union dues to a national organization that likely does not share the workers' values or political views?

So why—in democratic elections—would workers in the South choose to align with the entity (big labor) that's lost many members over their status quo, over one that's given them financial security for decades?

But the will of the voters isn't the whole story. It's barely even the beginning of the story. When the bureaucracy is partisan it takes care of its key constituencies. And there are few constituencies more important to the Democratic Party and its partisan bureaucratic allies than big labor.

Just look at the dollars at stake.

From 1989 to 2014, 11 of the top 20 political givers were labor unions, with the vast majority of their dollars going to Democrats. Opensecrets.org tells the tale, with 10 of the 11 unions strongly tilting Democratic, with only one (the National Education Association) on the fence.[8]

If anything, a mere analysis of political donations understates the power of unions in Democratic politics. Here's the *Wall Street Journal*:

> Organized labor spends about four times as much on politics and lobbying as generally thought, according to a *Wall*

Street Journal analysis, a finding that shines a light on an aspect of labor's political activity that has often been overlooked.[9]

While unions spent a whopping $1.1 billion in direct contributions reported to the Federal Election Commission, they reported an additional $3.3 billion spent on other political activities to the Department of Labor.[10]

With this amount of money at stake, unions are simply too influential to fail. And thus the National Labor Relations Board, which oversees employee/union relations and has broad powers to adjudicate labor disputes, stepped in. It launched an effort early in the Obama administration that would have dramatically expanded federal power in the South, doomed much of the region's future manufacturing growth, and brought labor unions their biggest victory in years—unionizing of southern plants.

All because Boeing wanted to build a new airliner in the Palmetto State.

The Battle of South Carolina

On Friday, June 10, 2011, the state of South Carolina celebrated the latest chapter in the South's great economic renaissance, the opening of a Boeing 787 "Dreamliner" plant.

The Dreamliner is perhaps the world's most advanced airliner. Made out of composite materials, it promises longer and more fuel-efficient, more comfortable flights for passengers worldwide. It was easily one of the most anticipated new airplane designs in modern passenger aviation history. Representing a decisive response to Airbus, the European aircraft manufacturer, it meant that an American company employing American workers would continue to build the world's best aircraft.

But to the NLRB's general counsel, Lafe Solomon, the wrong Americans were building this airliner. To him, the right Americans to build the world's most advanced passenger jet belonged to a union and should work in the state of Washington, a union stronghold for Boeing workers. The wrong Americans were the nonunion Americans in South Carolina.

And so he filed a complaint with the NLRB to block production of the Dreamliner in South Carolina and send it to Boeing's Washington (union) facility. The core of his claim was that Boeing opened its plant in South Carolina primarily as a form of retaliation against union workers who kept striking in Washington State.[11]

Pro-union ideologues immediately understood the importance of this case. The *New York Times* was particularly enthusiastic, calling the complaint a "welcome effort to defend workers' rights to collective bargaining."[12] Yet even as it proclaimed its support for Solomon's suit, even the *Times* had to acknowledge that the law allowed Boeing to consider labor costs when it located a plant, and it could also consider "production stability" in its decision-making.[13]

In other words, there is absolutely no fair reading of the law that required Boeing to operate a union plant in a union-friendly state.

In fact, it was difficult to argue that Boeing was hostile to organized labor, having run union plants for years. The *Times* even noted that opening the plant in South Carolina would not cause a single layoff in its union operations in Washington.

Despite these facts, however, the NLRB's Solomon kept pursuing the case.

Typically the public is barely conscious of the NLRB's existence. The vast majority of Americans don't even know what "NLRB" stands for, much less understand what it does or comprehend the extent of its power. Its powerful legal staff works in near anonymity, even though its decisions have far-reaching consequences.

But all that changed with the Boeing complaint, and in that change lie the seeds of hope for reforming our bureaucracy.

Conservative political leaders understood the stakes.

Our federalist system creates a healthy economic competition among our states. Through this competition, states have strong incentives to improve their education systems and transportation infrastructures, and to keep taxes low, in essence, to make their state attractive to business and individuals alike. In many southern states, the desire to attract new business has been the prime catalyst for education reform and has led to dramatic gains.

Without this competition, it's entirely possible that many foreign companies wouldn't have located plants *anywhere* in the United States, leaving hundreds of thousands of jobs and billions of dollars in wages and investments overseas.

Aside from attracting foreign investment, competition between states can keep domestic corporations from pulling up stakes and taking all their manufacturing jobs overseas.

So, when the NLRB filed its complaint, GOP presidential candidates Tim Pawlenty and Mitt Romney immediately blasted it, with Pawlenty declaring that the Obama administration

is giving Big Labor veto power over where American companies can and cannot build their production facilities, and South Carolina doesn't make the cut for an investment that would provide new jobs and American products to be shipped around the world.[14]

Romney, for his part, noted that the NLRB action reflected a fundamental "distrust" of states in favor of nationalized labor policies. Newt Gingrich chimed in as well, claiming the suit "punished" right-to-work states—those states that prohibit unions from mandating employee membership.

It's difficult for me to recall a single NLRB action or case that triggered such extensive comment from presidential candidates, but the scrutiny didn't stop there. Conservatives didn't just understand the stakes; they took action.

The House of Representatives' Oversight Committee held a "rare" hearing in Charleston, South Carolina, on the matter, with the committee requiring Solomon himself to testify to justify his legal position.[15] The facts that emerged were illuminating. In essence, the unions were demanding that Boeing "return" to Washington. Boeing, however, had "already invested $1 billion in the new plant," and argued that "thousands of local jobs are at stake."[16] Boeing officials also noted that "frequent union strikes" had "cost the company billions of dollars."[17] The strikes were so disruptive that "several companies that do business with Boeing had threatened to cut off relations with [the] airline manufacturer."[18]

> There is also the fact that Boeing did not "move" any business out of Washington and into South Carolina, but rather opened an entirely new plant. Not a single union worker lost a job or benefit as result, in fact employment at the Washington plant has actually increased.[19]

The case just kept escalating. GOP candidates went from criticizing the NLRB in print to touring the plant and calling for a cutoff in NLRB funding. The House passed a bill to "strip the Board of its enforcement power" while a Senate committee "narrowly rejected" a conservative attempt to "deny funding for the NLRB to pursue any order threatening Boeing's South Carolina production."[20]

South Carolina politicians rightly went ballistic. The state's senior senator, Lindsey Graham, pledged "nasty, very, very nasty consequences" for the NLRB, promising to go after it with "full guns a blazing."[21] Senator Graham threatened to block President

Obama's nominee for commerce secretary, and South Carolina's then junior senator, Jim DeMint, filed an open-records request to determine if the NLRB colluded with the Obama administration.

Solomon professed to be taken by surprise by the backlash against his effort to essentially force unionization on South Carolina workers backed by the threat of a massive federal response, including a potential plant closing. He told *The Hill*, "I never could have imagined the fallout."[22]

It might seem astonishing that a government lawyer, a powerful bureaucrat, could truly be taken by surprise at a furious response to a case that threatened to yank billions of dollars in wages and investment from a state, but by now you are aware that bureaucrats are used to enjoying incredible power with near-total anonymity and minimal accountability.

Why should he face the backlash? After all, his agency and other federal agencies have been regulating America for years—without consequence.

But this time was different. Not only were the stakes so obvious—the public can easily understand the impact of a plant closing—but the conservative movement was rediscovering a Reagan-era political truth: It doesn't just matter who runs the government. In reality, government itself can be the problem. With size and power come inherent complexity and increased potential for partisan corruption.

In the end, Boeing won.[23] Solomon dropped the case after Boeing and union leaders in its Washington plants reached a deal on wages and production in Washington. Boeing kept its South Carolina plant and kept its South Carolina nonunion labor, where workers are today making premium wages producing the world's most sophisticated airliner.

The lesson was clear: when facing bureaucratic overreach and lawlessness, practice massive resistance.

The Battle of Tennessee and the Power of Defiance

Faced with a legacy of failure, the United Auto Workers put an enormous amount of hope in its most recent organizing drive—in the Chattanooga, Tennessee, Volkswagen plant.

And there was reason for the UAW's hope.

Volkswagen, a German company, is unionized in Germany and enjoys relative labor peace. Moreover, a key part of its management strategy involved setting up "works councils," collaborative efforts between blue-collar and white-collar employees designed to facilitate and improve production and efficiency.

Unfortunately, Volkswagen was concerned that America's convoluted labor laws—the very laws that grant the NLRB so much power with little oversight—rendered "works councils" unlawful as so-called company unions. So Volkswagen signed a "neutrality agreement" that meant it would not oppose the UAW's effort to unionize its Tennessee plant.

That was the UAW's golden opportunity. In effect, the union was running a campaign without true opposition. It would have unfettered, unopposed access to employees, and the company would not counter union messaging. In such circumstances, electoral victory is usually guaranteed.

But not everyone was happy about a union presence. Many Volkswagen workers looked at GM's and Chrysler's recent government bailouts and the overall job losses at union plants and didn't want to follow their model. Tennessee citizens and political leaders worried that unionization would lead to less investment in Tennessee and fewer jobs.

So they did what the Constitution allows them to do. They spoke out. Against the union.

And the UAW lost. The vote was extremely close (712–626), but it lost . . . an election that, thanks to the neutrality agreement, it was almost guaranteed to win.[24]

So naturally the UAW lashed out, claiming that "outside interference" (Tennesseeans' free speech) caused the loss, and specifically blamed Tennessee governor Bill Haslam and Tennessee senator Bob Corker for discussing the likely negative economic consequences of unionization.

Apparently, to the union, an election is "fair" only if the union is the *sole* advocate, and there is no meaningful opposition.

So the union tried to pull a Boeing. In the Boeing case, the NLRB's action began with a union complaint that soon became a complaint from the NLRB general counsel. In the Volkswagen case, the union started this same process, filing an unfair labor practice charge against third parties (Haslam and Corker) who merely used their freedom of speech to make an economic argument.

In the Boeing case, the union enlisted the federal government in an effort to control where companies could locate.

In the Volkswagen case, the union tried to enlist the federal government in an effort to control free speech during an election.

This time, however, conservatives were on their guard. This time they started resisting early.

In April 2014, Senator Corker declared that he would not comply with a UAW subpoena to testify before a regional NLRB hearing. Governor Haslam and his community development commissioner, Bill Hagerty, also said they would "likely refuse."[25] Corker's statement was clear:

> "Everyone understands that after a clear defeat, the UAW is trying to create a sideshow, so we have filed a motion to revoke these baseless subpoenas," Todd Womack, Corker's chief of staff, told the *Tennessean*. "Neither Sen. Corker nor his staff will attend the hearing on Monday."[26]

Faced with this resistance, the UAW caved. Three days after Senator Corker's defiance, the UAW dropped its complaint.[27]

Can the Tide Be Turned?

Legislative or public pressure isn't the only method for stopping bureaucratic overreach. Federal court—specifically the Supreme Court—can be crucial as well.

It is true that federal courts are often remarkably deferential to federal agencies, especially when those agencies are acting within the very broad scope of their statutory mandates, but it is also true that this deference often disappears when constitutional issues are at stake.

In other words, the Supreme Court isn't going to be more deferential to an unconstitutional executive action than it would be to an unconstitutional statute.

President Obama and the NLRB learned this the hard way in June 2014.

But first, some background.

In January 2012, President Obama—frustrated at his inability to receive Senate approval for his highly partisan nominees to the NLRB—unilaterally declared that the Senate was not in session (even though the Senate declared that it was) and made so-called recess appointments to the board.

While presidential nominees typically have to receive Senate consent before they can take office, the Constitution does permit temporary "recess" appointments when the Senate is not in session. Presidents have long utilized this power, but in so doing they always abided by Senate rules to determine when the Senate was, in fact, in session.

In this case, however, the president made his appointments while the Senate was in a "pro forma session"—a type of proceeding that typically involves a lesser amount of Senate action than during more "normal" proceedings.[28]

The president tried to override the legislators' own definitions and rules, defined the pro forma session as a sham, and appointed his favored appointees. Despite their highly irregular appointment, they took office immediately and began ruling on NLRB matters, issuing ultimately hundreds of decisions.

Soon after the appointments, Noel Canning, a soft-drink distributor, sued the NLRB, claiming that since the Obama administration exceeded its constitutional authority when it appointed three of the five NLRB members who ruled on Canning's case, the board lacked a quorum and its ruling should be set aside.

The case made it all the way to the Supreme Court. I represented the Speaker of the House before the Supreme Court in the case. We pointed out that "the Senate is part of a co-equal branch of government that is entitled to set its own rules, and the president simply can't step in and override them."[29]

In fact, the ACLJ got directly involved in the dispute, representing the Speaker of the House of Representatives, John Boehner, and filing an amicus brief on his behalf.[30]

On June 26, 2014, the Supreme Court issued its ruling. It unanimously rejected the Obama administration's arguments and invalidated the recess appointments, holding:

> In our view, however, the pro forma sessions count as sessions, not as periods of recess. We hold that, for purposes of the Recess Appointments Clause, the Senate is in session when it says it is, provided that, under its own rules, it retains the capacity to transact Senate business. The Senate met that standard here.[31]

This is an eminently sensible statement. Justice Stephen Breyer—a Clinton appointee—wrote the Court's opinion and explained that the constitutional standard allowed for limited exceptions and the Senate has the latitude to determine when and how to conduct its sessions.

Again, all this is quite sensible. The Senate defines its rules and sessions, not the president.

The result was a win for the Constitution's system of checks and balances and a crushing defeat for bureaucratic overreach.

The NLRB—in its astounding arrogance—kept conducting business as usual with its illegitimately appointed board members in spite of Noel Canning's pending lawsuit and in spite of a D.C. Circuit Court of Appeals opinion earlier in the proceedings striking down the appointments. The result? Hundreds of NLRB decisions were subject to legal challenge:

> The Democratic-controlled board of the NLRB, a federal agency that oversees private-sector union-organizing elections and referees management-employee disputes, decided 436 cases during the 18 months two of the three now-invalid appointees were seated, an NLRB spokesman said. The third appointee stepped down after several months on the job.
>
> The current board must decide whether to protectively redo those 436 rulings to try to shield them from new challenges, though labor lawyers said that in general, the vast majority of board decisions aren't controversial. Many of the NLRB orders have likely already been implemented, such as workers being rehired or collective-bargaining contracts being negotiated and implemented. It would be hard to undo such things and likely not worthwhile for parties to challenge, labor lawyers said.

The ruling impacted federal litigation across the nation:

> Still, more than 100 of the 436 decisions were challenged by companies in federal court and could be sent back by the courts to the board to be re-decided—if they haven't been otherwise resolved, labor lawyers said. . . .[32]

What a colossal, avoidable mess.

But a mess is preferable to living under a lawless regime, where illegitimately appointed bureaucrats rule with near impunity. With every case that has to be relitigated, the NLRB will be reminded of the costs of its own overreach, when it responded to litigation challenging its illegitimate appointees by proceeding with business as usual.

While I could easily continue for thousands more words providing one bureaucratic horror story after another, I won't. I trust you've gotten the point. The bureaucracy is out of control, it's lawless, and it's partisan. Moreover, the problem isn't confined to any one agency but instead stretches from the IRS to the DOJ to the VA to the NLRB to the EPA and beyond.

But to say that the bureaucracy is out of control is not the same thing as saying it is uncontrollable. In fact, you might be surprised at the ease with which—with a little bit of public awareness and a lot of action—any given regulatory action can be defeated.

You might be surprised at the ease with which—with a little bit of public awareness and a lot of action—any given regulatory action can be defeated.

You might also be surprised at the simplicity of the necessary legal reforms. While I believe we must ultimately abolish the IRS— the rot runs too deep—even the IRS can be improved short of abolition. So can the EPA. So can the VA. The public may not yet be ready for wholesale eliminations of executive agencies, but it is definitely ready for a better government, for a government that doesn't hurt its veterans, target its citizens, and damage its economy.

Better means smaller. But better also means accountable.

In the chapters that follow, I'll outline some of those reforms— providing a blueprint for legislators and citizen activists who wish to reintroduce sanity and fairness to our sprawling bureaucracy. In fact, many of these reforms will make sense at the state level as well. Sadly, bureaucracy abuse reaches all levels of government.

The public may not yet be ready for wholesale eliminations of executive agencies, but it is definitely ready for a better government, for a government that doesn't hurt its veterans, target its citizens, and damage its economy.

But in discussing the more modest, immediately attainable reforms, we shouldn't take our eyes off the much bigger prize— restoring a constitutional system of government, including constitutional checks and balances, and limitations on government's growth and reach.

Reform is necessary, but it will be merely temporary until there is a true restoration—a restoration of the liberty-protecting system of government that, when combined with a liberty-loving people, makes America truly exceptional.

I've presented the problem. I've told the horror stories. Now get ready for the hope.

10

THE BLUEPRINT
Resist, Reform, and Restore

One of the most fearsome villains of 1990s science fiction was a terrifying mechanical force called, simply and collectively, "the Borg." They were first introduced on the television show *Star Trek: The Next Generation* and then carried over into additional Star Trek shows and movies. The Borg were a seemingly unstoppable force—flying in massive cubical spaceships—that would invade, defeat their enemies, and then take over the enemies' bodies to turn them into hybrid robots. Their goal was to assimilate all living beings into one collective mind.

(Yes, I know it sounds strange, but remember this is science fiction.)

When the Borg attacked, they would always say the same thing, repeating it again and again—an ominous threat:

"Resistance is futile."

"You will be assimilated."

When facing the vast federal government, populated as it is with hundreds of thousands of public officials empowered by expansive federal laws, I'm reminded of this impersonal, seemingly unstoppable force from science fiction.

Is resistance truly futile?

Will the regulatory state always triumph?

In reality, resistance is *not* futile, and the regulatory state does not always win. In fact, the federal government can be surprisingly vulnerable in the face of determined resistance. A determined public backed by engaged and motivated members of Congress can rout the forces of bureaucracy and government intimidation.

In this book, I've discussed in great detail the ways the various federal agencies have violated the Constitution, but it's critical to remember that while they have violated the Constitution, they have not *repealed* the Constitution.

In other words, we still have a Bill of Rights. There still exist limits on government power. We just have to turn off the bureaucracy's power switch.

To be sure, the bureaucracy has exempted itself from accountability through its protective civil service rules, and it has stretched the reach and scope of the federal government further than any of our nation's Founders could imagine, but we still possess fundamental liberties.

These liberties not only allow us to resist government lawlessness; they also allow us to advocate for critical reforms, and they allow us to raise our voice to restore our republic—to educate our fellow citizens about the vision of the Founders, a vision that all too many of our friends and neighbors have never understood. This is what freedom of speech, religion, and the press are about.

Let's begin with "resist," the first step in stopping the government's most dangerous branch. And to resist, you have to know your rights.

Your Bureaucracy Bill of Rights

There can be few things more intimidating than your first encounter with a hostile bureaucrat. I can remember discussing the adoption audits I described in chapter 3 with a new adoptive family. They had stretched their family finances to the breaking point, were working to acclimate a beautiful little girl into their family, and were finally starting to feel just a little bit secure.

Then they got the audit letter from the IRS.

The fear and confusion were palpable. Had they done something wrong? Were the hundreds of hours of paperwork somehow not enough? How could they prove cash expenses when receipts were in foreign languages or sometimes not legible in any language? Would they be financially ruined?

Fortunately, they—like virtually every audited adoptive family—had done everything right, and so the IRS audit was a gigantic waste of time. No, it was worse than a waste of time. It was harassment, and harassment has costs.

That family, even as it was harassed, had rights—rights that each of us enjoys when the federal government knocks on the door. The IRS even has a taxpayer bill of rights.

The bureaucracy is incredibly complex, but you cannot and must not allow busy or aggressive bureaucrats to keep you from the information you need.

First, as a general rule, you have a right to *information*. This might sound remarkably basic, but in many ways it's the most important right that we'll discuss—the right to learn not just what the government wants, but what your rights are in each interaction. The bureaucracy is incredibly complex, but you cannot and must not allow busy or aggressive bureaucrats to keep you from the information you need and have a right to—information to determine how to answer their inquiries, or if you have to respond at all. You need to determine if you have rights to appeal or challenge the government's action against you.

Don't let bureaucrats bully you into compliance. When the government makes its demands, ask the following questions:

- What is the authority for your action?
- When must I respond?
- What is the consequence for not responding?
- How may I challenge your action?

Answers to these questions should be immediately forthcoming. If they are not—or if you have the slightest concerns regarding the government's good faith—seek legal counsel. While the government doesn't have to pay for your lawyer (unless you're indigent and facing criminal charges), it can't deny you access to legal counsel.

Second, you have a right to your *faith and viewpoint*. Religious speech and worship are constitutionally protected forms of expression. The government is all too willing to target and harass citizens merely because of their religious or political beliefs. This is not only unconstitutional, but can render unlawful an otherwise legitimate government action.

For example, the government can audit any given family. Audits are not, by themselves, illegal actions. But if the government chooses to audit me because I've opposed the Obama administration's policies, then that lawful audit becomes immediately illegal. One of the questions we posed during the adoption audits, for example, is whether these families were attacked because of their presumed religious and political viewpoints. If so, then a hurtful and immoral practice was also illegal.

Third, you have a right to *challenge* the government's actions. No, this does not mean you automatically have the right to sue. There are a variety of statutes and legal doctrines that can shield the federal government and federal employees from liability. But you always have a right to challenge. Challenges can take the form of lawsuits, administrative appeals, letters to your elected representatives, or sometimes a phone call to the local news.

You have a right to *challenge* the government's actions.

Critically, the government can't retaliate against you when you lawfully challenge its actions. In fact, even mere threats and bluster in response to you exercising your free speech rights or your rights to file administrative appeals or lawsuits are typically unlawful. Simply put, the government cannot make you keep your mouth shut.

Finally, the government cannot deprive you of your liberty or property (or life, for that matter) without granting you *due process*. What is due process? In many ways it's a combination of the rights I've already outlined. Put most simply, it's notice (information) combined with an opportunity to be heard (the challenge).

The government cannot deprive you of your liberty or property (or life, for that matter) without granting you *due process*.

But it's more than that: the notice and the opportunity to be heard must meet precise legal requirements. These requirements vary depending on the issue, but unless the government *fully* meets those obligations, its actions will not be legitimate. In other words, unless the government gives you all the information it's required to give, it won't satisfy its obligations merely by giving you *some* information. Unless it provides you with the exact kind of process (appeals, etc.) that it's required to give, it won't satisfy its obligations merely by giving you *some* process. What is required of you is reciprocally required of the government.

Taking the Offensive

Armed with these rights, it's time to take the offensive, to challenge the vast and growing bureaucracy head-on.

In the chapters that follow, I'll describe each of the three key steps to save our republic from its most dangerous branch.

Resist—you'll read stories of hope, when citizens refused to accept government abuse and rose up to challenge the most powerful bureaucracy on earth. In story after story, you'll learn the power of "no"—a power that resonates with the public and can change the dynamics of debate.

Reform—you'll read of legislation that is both modest and ambitious. There are attainable, small changes that will incrementally protect your liberty, and there are ambitious, sweeping changes that will decisively roll back federal authority.

Restore—this is the most difficult challenge. We can win individual cases, and we can even win legislative battles, but we cannot truly "keep our republic" unless we win the hearts of the people.

We live in an era where millions upon millions of Americans are taught that the solution to all challenges—public and even private—lies with the federal government. They're taught that applying the right federal program to our problems will ease economic insecurity and ensure our personal safety and our children's futures.

Ridiculous.

We have to be able to show our friends and neighbors that there's a better way, a constitutional way, to govern our society, and that liberty is of far greater value than regulation, intrusion, and all-encompassing government by even the most well-meaning bureaucrat.

That's not to say that government and regulation doesn't have its proper scope and place. Of course we need to have a well-functioning government, and—yes—that will include some degree of bureaucracy, but a government that focuses on securing the liberties of its people is very different from a government focused on managing all aspects of our lives.

Restoration means education.

And education starts with resistance.

II

RESIST

The Government Can Be Beaten

Did you know that a fourteen-year-old girl can defeat the full might of the federal government?

If her name is Emily Echols, she can.[1]

In 2002, Congress passed—and President George W. Bush signed—the "Bipartisan Campaign Reform Act." (Indeed, both political parties are fully capable of violating citizens' constitutional rights.) The Campaign Reform Act was an immensely complicated piece of legislation, limiting campaign contributions, regulating election expenditures, and doing much, much more. But one part offended Emily more than any other.

It banned political contributions to candidates or political parties by anyone seventeen or younger. In other words, it prohibited kids from using their own money to express their own political views.

Yet the Supreme Court has long held that children enjoy First Amendment rights, and it's so much a part of American public life that we take it for granted.

If you see kids gathered around a school flagpole, praying for their school, that's free speech.

If you see kids meeting in empty classrooms, debating politics or studying scripture, that's free speech.

If you see kids outside a city hall, waving signs and asking that the mayor save their charter school, that's free speech.

The examples are endless, and so are the cases that explain again and again that the circumstances where the state can restrict that speech are limited indeed.

But in the Campaign Reform Act, Congress and the president told Emily that she couldn't give her own money to the candidate of her choice because they didn't trust her honesty, or her parents' honesty. They were afraid that parents would funnel money to their kids, and that kids would essentially be a conduit for parents who wanted to break the law.

Never mind that setting up sham donations was already illegal; the federal government—in its infinite wisdom—decided that the price for stopping what it deemed "bad speech" was shutting down every child's speech. In other words, to stop the wrongdoing of the few, the federal government shut down the political speech of the many.

Emily Echols decided to resist. She gave a Republican Senate candidate some money she had saved and then exercised her right to challenge the Campaign Reform Act in court. Her case made it through every layer of the federal court system until it landed in the Supreme Court of the United States, where I had the honor of representing Emily.

Emily prevailed, and we won 9–0 at the Supreme Court. The Court declared that there was "scant evidence" to support the federal government's contention that it had to suppress the rights of all children to prevent the wrongdoing of a few.[2]

If one person can make a difference—if one person can resist—can more than sixty-seven thousand?

Let's ask the U.S. Forest Service.

Preserving a War Memorial

The war in Italy is often referred to as a forgotten part of World War II. In late 1944 and 1945, while the world watched, transfixed, as American and British forces landed at Normandy and then marched mile by bloody mile through Western Europe, hundreds of thousands of Allied troops were fighting their own battles against entrenched Germans, battling up the length of the Italian peninsula.

As the fight moved into the Alps, weary American soldiers on occasion came across statues of Jesus in the mountains, put there by churches long ago. For many of these soldiers, the statues were deeply moving, reminding them of peace and grace amid the savagery of war.

Years later, many of these veterans placed a statue of Jesus on Big Mountain in Montana to honor the service and sacrifice of fellow veterans and to remind themselves of the very real solace they felt in the mountains of Italy.

The statue was placed on land leased from the federal government, in the Whitefish Mountain Resort, and there it stood, without controversy or complaint, as the decades rolled by.

But then, in 2011, the Freedom from Religion Foundation attacked. The FFRF, a group of angry atheists who are trying to cleanse the public square of any form of religious expression, claimed that the lease represented a violation of the Establishment Clause of the U.S. Constitution and called the war memorial a "ruse and a sham."[3]

A ruse? A sham?

After the FFRF complaint, the Forest Service decided not to renew the lease, an action that meant the statue would come down.

One veteran said the decision was "a slap in the face of the men and women who served their country and built this community."[4]

But the bureaucracy had spoken. What could you do?

Resist.

At the ACLJ we launched a petition drive, asking Americans to sign on to our letter demanding that the Forest Service reconsider.[5] But we don't just make demands; we make arguments. We explained in detail how the war memorial was constitutional and how the FFRF's complaint had no legal merit.

Americans responded, by the tens of thousands. Within days, we had accumulated more than sixty-seven thousand signatures, and we sent our letter to the Forest Service, to let them know that there was another side to this story, and that Americans weren't simply going to accept yet another attack on our nation's heritage or on the sacrifice of our nation's veterans.[6]

And we won. The bureaucracy reversed course and decided to renew the lease. The Jesus statue remained on Big Mountain.[7]

Furious, the angry atheists filed a federal lawsuit, but as of late fall 2014, they were "shocked" to lose in federal court just as decisively as they lost in the court of public opinion.[8]

The case continues on appeal, but it continues only because Americans stood up. Because Americans resisted.

Is this resistance unusual? Are these stories merely exceptions to a rule that says that the federal government almost always wins?

Not at all.

Just ask the Federal Communications Commission.

Saying No to Newsroom Monitors

The FCC is yet another of those federal agencies that most Americans rarely consider but whose power is vast. As it states on its website, the FCC "regulates interstate and international communications by radio, television, wire, satellite and cable in all 50 states, the District of Columbia and U.S. territories." This means that every television show you watch, every radio show you listen to, and indeed most Internet sites you visit are subject to some form of FCC influence.[9]

While this fact is troubling enough, the FCC's own complicated history with free speech should cause greater concern.

For decades the FCC imposed the "Fairness Doctrine" on American broadcasters, a regulation that essentially prevented stations from advancing a single point of view, requiring that they offer "multiple perspectives" on any given issue.[10] The practical effect was that radio shows like Sean Hannity's—or my own show, for that matter—were not viable as long as the Fairness Doctrine was in place. The requirement to offer equal time would essentially swallow the show and its host's perspective.

While most people react favorably to words like *fairness* or even—in theory—like to hear "balanced perspectives," in reality this doctrine helped entrench the mainstream media's power, closed down the marketplace of ideas, and stifled the conservative movement. And when the Fairness Doctrine was finally repealed in 1987, conservative media flourished.

But as conservative media has flourished, the Left has been looking for ways to either restore the Fairness Doctrine or otherwise utilize the FCC's broad regulatory powers to monitor or suppress conservative speech.[11]

Which brings us to the FCC's "Multi-Market Study of Critical Information Needs." Rarely has a more dangerous initiative been wrapped in a more dull package. At its core, the study was designed to examine whether radio and television stations were meeting the public's perceived information "needs."[12]

To accomplish this purpose, the FCC would send monitors to newsrooms across the country to ask a series of questions about the station's philosophy. Rather than simply ask questions of owners and managers, the "study" encouraged FCC employees to gain access to confidential employee data and interview employees about their relationships with their bosses.

Here were the questions for station owners, managers, or human resources personnel:

- What is the news philosophy of the station?
- Who is your target audience?
- How do you define critical information that the community needs?
- How do you ensure the community gets this critical information?
- How much does community input influence news coverage decisions?
- What are the demographics of the news management staff (HR)?
- What are the demographics of the on-air staff (HR)?
- What are the demographics of the news production staff (HR)? [13]

And here were the questions for on-air staff:

- What is the news philosophy of the station?
- How much news does your station air every day?
- Who decides which stories are covered?
- How much influence do you have in deciding which stories to cover?
- Have you ever suggested coverage of what you consider a story with critical information for your customers (viewers, listeners, readers) that was rejected by management?
- If so, can you give an example?
- What was the reason given for the decision?
- Why do you disagree? [14]

The problems are obvious. It is no concern of the government whether reporters and editors disagree about stories. Moreover, the philosophy of the station is the station's business, not the government's.

But the study was worse than that. Written in dense bureaucratic language, it effectively attempted to monitor newspapers (which are outside the FCC's jurisdiction) to distinguish between news that people wanted to hear versus the news the FCC believed they needed to hear, and actively sought to cultivate government informants.

The very idea that the federal government should play any role in determining the content and editorial direction of the news is antithetical to any conception of free speech.

Imagine the chilling effect of a government monitor watching a radio host broadcast his program, and studiously taking notes. Imagine the chilling effect of knowing the government was contacting your coworkers, trying to find out information about *you*. This is behavior one would expect out of Castro's Cuba, not the American government.

And yet, the FCC was pressing forward, preparing to send its monitors across the country.

We decided to resist.

On February 10, 2014, one of the FCC's own commissioners, Ajit Pai, broke ranks and sounded the alarm in the *Wall Street Journal*:

Last May the FCC proposed an initiative to thrust the federal government into newsrooms across the country. With its "Multi-Market Study of Critical Information Needs," or CIN, the agency plans to send researchers to grill reporters, editors and station owners about how they decide which stories to run. A field test in Columbia, S.C., is scheduled to begin this spring.

The purpose of the CIN, according to the FCC, is to ferret out information from television and radio broadcasters about "the process by which stories are selected" and how often stations cover "critical information needs," along with "perceived station bias" and "perceived responsiveness to underserved populations."[15]

As soon as I read his story, I knew we had to fight. While Pai's op-ed was necessary to begin the battle, it was not—by itself—sufficient for victory. So we mobilized the full resources of the ACLJ.

First, we launched a petition drive, asking our ACLJ members to sign a simple petition declaring:

The federal government has no place putting monitors in America's newsrooms. Stop this unconstitutional assault on free speech and freedom of the press.[16]

We launched the petition online, through social media, and over the airwaves—reaching more than two million Americans in less than twenty-four hours. Immediately, the petition became one of our fastest-growing ever, with tens of thousands of signatures rolling in during the first hours of the campaign.

At the same time, we reached out directly to friendly media contacts and sympathetic members of Congress. Within the day, the story went from largely dormant to dominating Fox News and much of conservative media.

We began our full assault on February 19, 2014—nine days after Pai's op-ed. My own op-ed about the study appeared on FoxNews .com on February 20, and other ACLJ attorneys posted similar stories across the Web.[17]

By the afternoon of February 21, just two days after we launched our campaign, the FCC surrendered, issuing a statement retracting the study:

However, in the course of FCC review and public comment, concerns were raised that some of the questions may not have been appropriate. Chairman [Tom] Wheeler agreed that survey questions in the study directed toward media outlet managers, news directors, and reporters overstepped the bounds of what is required. Last week, Chairman Wheeler informed lawmakers that that Commission has no intention of regulating political or other speech of journalists or broadcasters and would be modifying the draft study. Yesterday, the Chairman directed that those questions be removed entirely.

To be clear, media owners and journalists will no longer be asked to participate in the Columbia, S.C. pilot study. The pilot will not be undertaken until a new study design is final. Any subsequent market studies conducted by the FCC, if determined necessary, will not seek participation from or include questions for media owners, news directors or reporters.[18]

The lesson here is the same one learned in the victories against the NLRB: resistance works. The federal government simply cannot justify in public the abuses it hopes to accomplish in private, outside the public eye.

In other words, when advancing its ideological agenda, the bureaucratic branch of government often depends on public ignorance or apathy.

In other words, when advancing its ideological agenda, the bureaucratic branch of government often depends on public ignorance or apathy.

The FCC's proposed "study" required public ignorance. If Americans actually knew that the FCC wanted to send monitors to newsrooms, they'd be outraged. And, in fact, they were outraged—so outraged that when the FCC looked for allies on Capitol Hill, there were few to be found.

So it surrendered. Quickly.

Sometimes, however, bureaucracies can't depend on ignorance—their misconduct is in plain view—so they depend instead on apathy, or maybe even public sympathy.

Using National Parks as a Partisan Weapon

In October 2013, disagreements over funding ObamaCare and the imposition of its individual mandate (which of course had been saved from oblivion by the lawless IRS, as outlined in chapter 3) led to a protracted government "shutdown."

It was never really a shutdown. It was more like a government slowdown. Unable to reach agreement on a budget, the government was unable to spend the vast majority of "discretionary" funds—those funds that require annual appropriations and whose expenditures are not mandated by federal law "Entitlement" spending—spending, like Social Security, that is mandated by law—was largely untouched.

This meant that Social Security recipients still received their checks, but other "nonessential" branches of government faced severe cutbacks.

The shutdown infuriated the Democrats, who argued that it was nothing but an attempt to strong-arm changes to the "settled law of the land," ObamaCare. And if an action enrages the party of government, it will always enrage the government itself.

No agency punished America with more zeal than the National Park Service.

And so the bureaucracy acted—to punish the American people into submission, to cause maximum pain to demonstrate to America how much we *needed* our bureaucracy, how we couldn't live without them.

No agency punished America with more zeal than the National Park Service.

Americans understandably love our national parks. The Park Service in many ways can represent government at its finest, preserving national landmarks and our nation's incredible natural beauty for future generations. We want the Statue of Liberty to stand as a beacon of freedom. We want Independence Hall to preserve our constitutional and revolutionary legacy. We want to visit war memorials and honor those who gave their "last full measure of devotion" to preserve our liberty.

If you've visited our parks recently, you know the Park Service typically does an admirable job. You can walk through Great Smoky Mountains National Park and enjoy unspoiled natural beauty as far as the eye can see. You can walk the fields at Gettysburg, stand atop Cemetery Ridge, and look across the field where Pickett launched his charge into Union lines.

But in the midst of the shutdown, the Park Service abandoned its duty to the public and instead led the charge for the Democratic Party. How?

By maliciously shutting off access to our nation's most hallowed grounds, our open-air war memorials.

Hours after the shutdown began, the Park Service, rather than wind down operations, immediately *expended money* to blockade the World War II Memorial and other memorials on the National Mall in Washington, D.C. It put up steel barricades and employed security to stop people from breaching them. These were areas open twenty-four hours per day, seven days per week. The bureaucrats actually spent taxpayer dollars to put up barricades to keep people out of open areas.

When can the Park Service expend money to enforce a shutdown? When it's trying to punish the American people.

Now, keep in mind that the National Mall typically offers free and open access twenty-four hours per day, seven days per week.

There are no gates to walk through to see the Washington Monument, the Marine Corps Memorial, the Vietnam War Memorial, the Lincoln Memorial, or any of our other national treasures in the open air of our nation's capital. The National Park Service had to build a fence.

The goal? In the words of one Park Service employee: "To make life as difficult for people as we can."[19]

When this malicious act impacted "honor flights," flights of World War II veterans who are escorted to the World War II Memorial to see it before they pass away, millions of Americans were fed up.

So they resisted. And so did the ACLJ.

Because of our constitutional training, we immediately recognized that the Park Service's action was blatantly illegal. Open-air monuments and parks must remain open for First Amendment activities. In fact, under Supreme Court case law, public parks are essentially "held in trust" for public use, and that use can be regulated only through "reasonable" time, place, and manner restrictions. Closing parks—and spending money to do so—was hardly reasonable. I have been arguing these types of cases at the Supreme Court for three decades.

On October 4, 2013, we sent a demand letter to the National Park Service, stating that it had to open the World War II Memorial to honor flights but also to the general public, to those who also wanted to exercise their First Amendment rights to honor veterans and to educate themselves about America's fight for its very existence.[20]

But we didn't just send a letter. We mobilized our radio listeners and our millions-strong Internet and social media audience. My son, Jordan, went to the memorials during live radio and politely confronted Park Service personnel, demanding to know why the Park Service was deliberately and maliciously violating the First Amendment.

Members of Congress soon joined the fray, as they escorted honor flights to the World War II Memorial and dared the Park Service to stop them. Peaceful civil disobedience spread, as citizens moved the barricades on their own, walked into the memorials, and exercised their rights as American citizens to learn about their nation's blood-bought heritage of constitutional liberty.

On October 8, 2013, the Park Service went too far, displaying its partisan bias for all to see. Days after spending money to block access to the National Mall, it opened the park—to a leftist Democrat pro-immigration rally.

Once again, the government showed favoritism to the party of government.

By October 9, the Park Service's legal position was utterly hopeless. It surrendered, opening the memorials to "First Amendment activities" and allowing unimpeded access.

While the Park Service continued to close other parks, often depriving Americans of their long-planned vacations, in the highly visible center of the nation's capital, it failed. Resistance was *not* futile.

In my years of fighting for liberty, I've learned that millions of Americans *want* to fight back; they often just don't know how. The ACLJ is working to make the "how" easy, to facilitate and empower resistance to government abuse.

First, we know that you have to go around the mainstream media to raise public awareness. Through radio, our own television show, conservative TV, email, and now—critically—social media (where we reach millions), we can go directly to the American people, to the most politically engaged members of the public.

Second, we know that public anger needs to be focused on achievable objectives. That's why we always have a "call to action"— such as joining a legal brief, signing a petition, or engaging directly with members of Congress. With awareness must come action.

Third, we know that resistance requires persistence. Simply

put, we don't quit after one day or two days or two weeks of effort. We will pursue the same issue, relentlessly, for years if we must. Bureaucratic abuse can often (but not always, obviously) survive short-term expressions of outrage, but it typically can't survive long-term campaigns that include congressional and judicial responses.

Fourth, we're not afraid to file a lawsuit. In the more than twenty-five years of the ACLJ, we've prevailed in countless lawsuits against the federal government. And each one of them depended on a brave citizen or brave citizens to stand up, be counted, and as a plaintiff challenge the bureaucracy. A plaintiff is at the tip of the spear, and we are honored to stand behind them.

Awareness, focus, persistence, and litigation—that's the formula for resistance. It's a formula that works so well that we typically don't have to progress all the way to litigation to achieve results. Sometimes we don't even have to go public. The threat of massive resistance alone is enough to get even the most fearsome of public agencies to back down. Just ask a certain small business that faced an unjust IRS audit.

"Tell Them No"

As I described in the third chapter, the IRS has a disturbing habit of auditing conservatives, especially conservatives who have the audacity to use their rights to free speech to challenge leftist policies.

At the ACLJ we saw this dynamic firsthand when the IRS sent one of our clients—who was then suing the Obama administration for a violation of his religious liberty rights—a notice that his business was being audited.

The IRS can trigger audits randomly or because there was something amiss in a tax return. Just because the IRS has abused its auditing power does not mean that *every* audit or even most audits are illegitimate.

So we didn't raise the alarm. Instead, the client cooperated and quickly received a clean bill of health. There was nothing wrong with his business's tax return, and he moved on.

But he did not dismiss his lawsuit. Instead, he not only pursued the suit, but gained a key—and very public—injunction against the Obama administration, one that provided yet another round of embarrassing news coverage for a scandal-plagued, lawless administration.

And so he received a second audit notice.

At this point, we'd had enough. One audit notice could be legitimate. But a second notice in mere months?

Absolutely not.

My response was simple, a statement of pure defiance.

"Just tell them no."

No, we would not cooperate. No, this audit was not legitimate. No, we would not put up with a cycle of abuse and intimidation.

No.

And the IRS caved. They did so without a press release, without a public campaign, without a petition, and without litigation. They just backed down.

And that leads me to the final lesson of resistance: victory begets victory.

Victory begets victory.

In other words, once you establish a pattern of public resistance, you are no longer a soft target, and a bureaucracy that is used to bullying citizens into compliance will often move on when it encounters a real adversary, and look for easier prey.

But, sadly, resistance does not always work. If it did, there would be no need for structural reform. While our partisan agencies will often back down from individual fights, they do not back down from their larger goals. If one conservative resists the IRS, the agency will audit another conservative. If the IRS grudgingly approves a Tea Party group, it will enthusiastically leak another's confidential information. If the agency timidly withdraws questions about the content of prayers, it will ask another what church they attend. And the EPA? It may slow down regulatory activity for political reasons, but it will pursue its agenda as soon as it believes the time is right. And the NLRB will continue to invent ways to reward unions and punish corporations and nonunion workers.

A bureaucracy that is used to bullying citizens into compliance will often move on when it encounters a real adversary, and look for easier prey.

Reform Is Necessary

Thus, we have to reform the system—not only to alter incentives so thoroughly that even the most partisan of bureaucrats thinks twice before violating your rights, but also to strip them of their power to pass tens of thousands of regulations without meaningful democratic oversight.

Many of these agencies are incapable of self-correcting or self-policing. The problem inside these agencies is systemic. However, the election of a new president does not cure them. These problems are much deeper than an election cycle. True reform begins with accountability, not just accountability for individual misconduct but also accountability for departmental actions and agendas. The bureaucracy has to become subject to Congress and the Constitution. A bureaucracy that is more enduring and powerful than even the people's elected representatives represents a grotesque subversion of our constitutional structure.

In many ways, reform is more difficult than resistance. After all, the Left has no incentive to reform a system it has so painstakingly constructed for generations. The bureaucracy is its instrument of one-party rule.

At the same time, however, the bureaucracy has become its own worst enemy. Not everyone in the United States is a leftist, and even partisans can't justify or rationalize the abuses and incompetence in the VA, for example.

The time is right for reform, but what form should it take? How can we mobilize the American people?

Let's take a look at the plan.

12

ACCOUNTABILITY AND DEMOCRACY
The Mandatory Elements of Reform

There are few political sentences better calculated to put an audience to sleep than the declaration, "As your congressman, I will support comprehensive regulatory reform!"

No amount of volume or emphasis can make that sentence more interesting or meaningful. After all, every president and every congressman supports regulatory reform of some kind. No one likes the system just as it is.

In the Clinton administration, Vice President Al Gore was put in charge of "reinventing government," an effort that was successful only if one can imagine that today's bureaucracy could actually be worse.[1]

The George W. Bush administration's reforms were of little consequence, consisting of such game changers (I'm being sarcastic) as the use of so-called prompt letters to *speed up* the regulatory process and the implementation of Information Quality Act guidelines that proved to have minimal real-world impact.[2]

Yes, the Obama administration has jumped into the regulatory reform game as well, issuing, for example, Executive Order 13563, called "Improving Regulation and Regulatory Review."[3] As with all regulatory reform efforts, the goals seem laudable, but the means, well, are laughable. In fact, the order itself is nearly as incomprehensible as the bureaucracy it purports to reform.

The bottom line? The last three presidents have attempted or offered regulatory "reform" efforts that have had little to no impact on the actual regulatory process—or at least little to no discernible impact. The fundamental power of the bureaucracy is unchanged, with regulatory reform merely nibbling at the edges. We are left with a fourth branch of government, made up of increasingly powerful, largely untouchable bureaucrats, an unelected branch that writes far more laws than Congress and impacts almost every area of our lives.

And this powerful fourth branch is not mentioned or authorized by a Constitution that set up a careful system of checks and balances among *three* branches, legislative, executive, and judicial. There is no provision for a bureaucratic branch. Nor should there be. If we return to a constitutional framework, reform will be much easier than you might think.

Even when outside groups offer "bold" suggestions, these suggestions don't alter the fundamentals of bureaucratic power. Take, for example, a proposal for a "New Civil Service Framework" from the Partnership for Public Service,[4] a proposal that government unions immediately opposed.[5]

While the report was long and contained multiple proposals (such as shrinking the number of pay classifications in the federal system), it still didn't address employee discipline in a meaningful way.

It still granted public sector employees much greater job protections than the vast majority of private sector employees.

Think for a moment of the sectors of American life where job protection is at its greatest: the union private sector, the union public sector, and nonunion federal employment.

Are our public schools—staffed with virtually unfireable teachers supported by powerful unions—models of efficiency and productivity? Of course not. While some public schools are good and some public school teachers are outstanding, our inner-city schools are a national disgrace, and the most powerful nation in the world lags on almost every measure of academic achievement.

Are our union industries thriving? Hardly. Union industries have competed so poorly in the marketplace that private sector unions have declined dramatically, with virtually all the growth in union employment occurring in the public sector, where there's no real competition.

And what about federal employment? As we've discussed throughout this book, there is a greater chance in many agencies for a worker to die on the job than get fired. Is the VA functioning well? The EPA? The IRS?

However, our nation's military is an interesting case study in the effectiveness of incentives. When bureaucracy reigns, the best and brightest leave. But when the military performs its core function—engage and destroy our nation's enemies on the field of battle—it is unsurpassed. In that arena, the incentives are clear, and success or failure is not defined by boards of bureaucrats but instead by life and by death.

To reform our bureaucracy and introduce accountability, we must introduce the concept of life and death to our federal workforce—not actual life and death of course, but career life and death.

The Civil Service Accountability Act

To reform the bureaucracy, let's supplement accountability with fundamental fairness. Our public servants should not enjoy greater job security than the public they serve. We live our lives (in general) as at-will employees, and so should they.

Here's what I would like to propose:

First principle: Federal public employee unions must either be abolished or their rights to collectively bargain matters involving job security completely removed.

Public employee unions enjoy vast leverage over the public— leverage that private sector unions do not enjoy—through their absolute monopoly over the services they provide.

If GM employees strike, Americans aren't cut off from the supply of automobiles. They can buy a Ford or Toyota or Honda. And while GM may suffer from a strike and be forced to provide concessions, the larger public is untouched.

But what happens if public employees strike? Citizens can lose access to critical, irreplaceable services. Who steps in during the strike? Who replaces police departments? Who replaces fire departments? Who replaces teachers?

Ronald Reagan understood this danger and established his leadership style early in his presidency when he fired more than 11,000 striking air traffic controllers.[6] Air traffic control is an irreplaceable public service, and the strike punished the public—the passengers and the airlines—whom the traffic controllers purportedly served, *not* the federal government employer. By smashing the strike, President Reagan protected the public interest.

Public servants serve us. We do not serve them.

Public servants serve us. We do not serve them.

Second principle: Make federal workers at-will employees, like most of us. That means they can be fired for any reason or no reason at all, so long as the reason does not violate antidiscrimination statutes.

While this provision seems harsh, it's the default position for nonfederal workers. It simply means that private sector employees don't have a right to a job, but they do have a right to nondiscrimination on the basis of race, gender, or religion

To prevent partisan housecleaning during election cycles, I'd also include one, and one only, special protection for nonpolitically appointed federal workers: the right not to suffer discrimination on the basis of their actual or perceived political viewpoint.

In fact, such a protection already exists. The First Amendment to the Constitution already protects citizens (including government employees) from retaliation or other punitive actions based on their constitutionally protected expression. It would be important, however, to take this further and establish required punishments for violating any citizens' constitutional rights (including public employee citizens).

And that brings us to the next principle.

Third principle: Violation of citizens' constitutional rights shall result in mandatory termination and payment of personal damages. Any public employee who is found by a court of competent jurisdiction (and after all appeals are exhausted) to have violated the constitutional rights of any person (including government workers) shall be immediately terminated; they may not be rehired under any circumstances, and they shall not be reimbursed by the government for any damages they're required to pay.

Currently, it is extraordinarily difficult to hold a federal employee individually liable for unconstitutional actions. A series of statutory defenses combined with sovereign immunity means that individual citizens can find it difficult to obtain compensation when the government violates their rights. Civil service reform must mean that government employees face risks similar to those faced by employees of private corporations, who are always vulnerable to lawsuit when they violate your rights.

In other words, bureaucrats will have to bear the full costs of their unconstitutional actions.

Fourth principle: Terminated employees have to leave work immediately, without pay, and their right of "appeal" will be the same as most citizens'—the right to file a lawsuit.

Civil service reform must mean that government employees face risks similar to those faced by employees of private corporations, who are always vulnerable to lawsuit when they violate your rights.

If I could pinpoint a prime failing of the current system, it's that the termination process often means an extended paid vacation as the government works through the process. The public is left suffering the worst of all worlds: it is paying the worst workers to do nothing, while managers are deterred from pursuing the discipline process because of its sheer, daunting complexity.

Lawsuits, on the other hand, can deter frivolous appeals (lawyers, contrary to public belief, do not generally take meritless cases on a mass scale) while increasing the consequences for wrongful termination. What's a better deterrent to manager misconduct: an adverse ruling from an internal review that has no real consequence for the manager's job, or an adverse court ruling that (under principle three) could result in the manager's immediate termination?

Think of the application of these principles to the VA, to the IRS, or to the Department of Justice. Rather than see prosecutors promoted who've thrown innocent Americans in jail for invented crimes, we'd see them terminated and disbarred.

I think that would certainly deter prosecutorial misconduct.

Rather than watch, helplessly, as VA employees systematically lie and cover up failures with no terminations and few suspensions (with pay), a housecleaning would have the same effect as it would in the private sector.

And would the IRS launch a national targeting scheme if its employees knew that the inspector general's findings would likely lead to their terminations and require them to pay damages out of their own pockets?

Now, I fully recognize that this solution isn't perfect. I fully recognize that some managers and partisans would do their best to abuse the system to stock the bureaucracy (even more) with like-minded partisans, but at least an accountability-based system contains built-in checks and balances that we know work in the private sector.

The bureaucracy is too entrenched. It's essentially immune from public accountability. It's time for the pendulum to swing back from absolute job security to enhanced *insecurity*. Our public servants should fear failure.

Our public servants should fear failure.

The Democracy Restoration Act

At the beginning of this chapter, I noted that regulatory reform must be guided by two principles: accountability and democracy.

Civil service reform can introduce accountability, but the problem of our bureaucracy isn't merely bureaucrats failing to do their job; it's bureaucrats who do their jobs all too well. They're the ones who write thousands of pages of regulations that govern virtually every aspect of our lives, all without any real congressional oversight.

Congress has recognized this problem before and has taken steps to rein in agencies that overstep the bounds of their enabling statute. A now-defunct method of reintroducing democratic accountability was the "legislative veto."

Under the legislative veto, one or both houses of the legisla-

ture can invalidate an agency regulation. For example, under Section 244(c)(2) of the Immigration and Nationality Act, one house of
Congress could vote to override the decision to allow a deportable
alien in the United States—"vetoing" an action by the executive
branch.

In the 1983 case of *INS v. Chadha*, the Supreme Court struck
down that section of the Immigration and Nationality Act, and
with it the legislative veto itself on separation-of-powers grounds,
declaring that the legislative veto violated provisions of the Constitution that require acts of Congress to be passed by both houses and
presented to the president for his signature. One house of Congress
could not act alone.[7]

The lesson was clear. Congress could not bypass the constitutional processes to act with the force of law. Both houses had to
act, it had to be presented to the president of the United States, the
president had to have the opportunity to veto, and Congress had to
have the opportunity to override the veto.

If that seemed cumbersome, well, that's too bad. It's what the
Constitution required:

But in our modern regulatory process, Congress and the president have created an out-of-control monster that creates law while
bypassing bicameralism, presentment, vetoes, and veto overrides
every single day, thousands of times per year.

It's time to reintroduce the constitutional process to our federal
agencies.

Under my proposed reform, federal agencies would be stripped
of their authority to unilaterally issue significant regulation. A significant regulation or regulations would be defined as a regulation
with an impact on the constitutional rights of citizens; or an economic or budgetary monetary impact exceeding $10 million.

Instead, agencies could propose only regulation that would then
be legislatively ratified through a bill passed through the conventional, bicameral process and presented to the president.

The deterrent effect on runaway regulation would be profound. Agencies would propose only those significant regulations they felt confident could get through Congress. Our elected representatives would suddenly have to take ownership of our regulatory state and would be deprived of their current privilege of decrying bureaucracy while taking no real responsibility for its actions. In other words, they would have to engage and could no longer hide behind layers and layers of bureaucracy.

The concept of legislative ratification is not new. In fact, Florida passed a similar statute in 2010 (over the governor's veto).[8] And the bill had a number of commonsense exceptions—particularly when the public health and safety were at stake—that would prevent dangerous regulatory paralysis.

But the bottom line was and should be clear: no significant regulations without approval from the people's elected representatives. There's another word for this concept:

Democracy.

But the bottom line was and should be clear: no significant regulations without approval from the people's elected representatives.

Transform—Then Abolish—the IRS

Finally, no discussion of reform would be complete without sending the strongest message possible. There are circumstances where a federal agency spirals so far out of control that it is incapable of reforming itself and is virtually immune to meaningful external reform.

The IRS is one such agency.

The IRS has unilaterally reshaped immigration policy.

The IRS has unilaterally reshaped welfare policy.

The IRS has unilaterally reshaped our health-care system.

I said it earlier and I'll repeat it here: the IRS must be abolished.

While I understand where we must go, I'm also a political realist. I don't think the IRS can be abolished immediately. The process of agreeing upon alternative revenue collection models will be long and arduous. But in the meantime—in addition to the reforms outlined above—there is an IRS-specific rule that would dramatically impact the IRS's ability to persecute Americans.

Change the burden of proof.

At present, the IRS enjoys a power that virtually no federal agency enjoys: when it suspects wrongdoing and audits American taxpayers, *the taxpayer* bears the burden of proving that their taxes are correct. This is exactly backward from the norm. When other agencies suspect Americans are violating the law, they, the agencies, have to prove it. This burden-of-proof requirement prevents untold amounts of government abuse.

By contrast, the IRS is positively empowered and encouraged to go after Americans. Think about the adoption audits I outlined in chapter 3—when the IRS launched an assault on adoptive families, auditing up to 70 percent of families that used the adoption tax credit in two tax years. Under the current system, thousands of middle-class families were forced to dig through receipts and voluminous adoption files—often translating documents from obscure languages—just to prove they had, in fact, adopted and they had, in fact, incurred substantial expenses.

The IRS had the luxury of sending out audit notice after audit notice while the taxpayers bore the burden of doing all the work.

By changing the burden of proof, Congress could dramatically limit the IRS's ability to audit. The effects would be immediate, with audit decisions made on the basis of—essentially—probable cause rather than random chance or targeting. The IRS simply wouldn't have the resources to issue mass-scale audits, and without reason for the audit, the taxpayer could simply sit back and force the IRS to prove its case.

The taxpayer could simply sit back and force the IRS to prove its case.

But merely changing the burden of proof is not enough. The IRS must be made to pay when it's wrong. Current law typically requires taxpayers to pay the IRS, then sue for a refund if it believes tax assessments are wrongful. This gives the IRS enormous leverage when dealing with cash-strapped individuals or businesses, leading them often to settle with the IRS rather than fight for their rights.

If taxpayers contest tax assessments, the law should prevent the IRS from collecting tax until the case is concluded. If taxpayers prevail, they should be entitled not just to attorneys' fees but also to documented, compensatory damages (if any) caused by the IRS's wrongful tax assessment.

Current law rests on the untenable assumption that you are simply a caretaker for the government's money, until you can prove ownership. In reality, your wages and compensation are *yours*, until the government can prove its right to tax.

Some will argue that this proposal will enable a greater level of tax fraud because the IRS will have to actually prove its cases. This is nonsense. Once simplified, the tax code will allow for less fraud, not because of loopholes but because of its simplicity. Our constitutional republic can survive a simplified tax code, but it cannot survive having its most powerful civilian agency turned into a weapon of vengeance and retribution against political dissent.

These three reforms are simple and can be profoundly effective.

- It's simply fair that bureaucrats face the same level of accountability and risk that private sector Americans face in their own jobs.

- It's simply prudent to make sure that our nation's elected representatives are responsible for significant rules that impact our economy and our rights.
- It's simply necessary that an abusive agency face consequences for its misconduct because evading responsibility only emboldens wrongdoing.

But simple reforms are still difficult to pass, especially when they are consequential. The government and the party of government will object, loudly, using nothing short of apocalyptic language. Reform advocates should be prepared for incremental improvement. In the meantime, we cannot neglect the critical task of public education.

My vision is to restore America not just to its constitutional roots but to its understanding of itself. American exceptionalism, how this nation was the "hope of the earth," was, in fact, the hope of my own family when my grandfather escaped the horror of religious persecution in Russia.

And you can help. Write your legislators. Attend town halls. Write letters to editors of local papers. Comment on social media like Facebook and Twitter. Do the little things necessary to put the big issues squarely in the public eye. When candidates run for office, they must state their position on these reforms, and voters must hold them accountable. They are either for these reforms, or they are not.

Together, we must restore the vision of our Founding Fathers—a vision so important that unless we can pass it from generation to generation, this government "of the people, by the people, and for the people" will indeed perish from this earth.

13

RESTORE OR PERISH

When my grandfather's family fled Russia, they didn't just change continents; they changed from one governing philosophy to another. I'm not just talking about the transformation from oppression to liberty. That part is obvious. I'm talking about changing the very concept of the purpose of government itself.

For centuries in Europe, the government existed primarily to nurture and protect itself, as embodied by the ruling class. First, the royal ruling classes exercised power, and then—much later—permanent bureaucracies sprang up in the aftermath of world war

The goal—the aim—of government by philosophy and practice was first to sustain itself and then, second, to sustain and protect the people. In czarist and then communist Russia, sustaining the people was never a priority. The people were merely cannon fodder for the dreams of the rulers. In other European nations, rulers were more benign, but despite their sometimes benevolent nature, they still exercised power for a purpose far different from the American constitutional model.

The American model, by contrast, is that government exists not to sustain itself but rather to protect and defend the liberty of its people. A government that cannot protect and defend liberty is not a government worth sustaining.

America's greatest mistakes have always centered on the failure to safeguard liberty, but its greatest triumphs have been when America has corrected those mistakes.

Our nation was born with hundreds of thousands of our brothers and sisters toiling in the bondage of slavery.

But our nation at its best liberated the slaves, peacefully defeated Jim Crow, and now leads the fight against slavery and human trafficking worldwide.

This didn't "just happen." Thomas Jefferson—a slave owner himself—wrote the immortal words that "all men are created equal, that they are endowed by their Creator with certain unalienable rights, that among these are Life, Liberty, and the Pursuit of Happiness." But those words, once written, could not be contained, and their inexorable moral force ultimately doomed the institution of slavery.

But while the Declaration of Independence expressed our nation's highest ideals, it did not have the force of law. One does not govern through aspirations. Instead, we needed a constitution, a document that would provide our nation with the legal structures that help make those ideals a reality.

Put another way, if Thomas Jefferson's legendary words in the Declaration of Independence represent the ends, then the Constitution represents the means.

That's why so many of our public servants take an oath of office, promising first to defend the Constitution. In fact, that should be at the top of the job description of every single federal employee: defend the Constitution and safeguard the constitutional rights of the people you're hired to serve.

That's the exceptional ideal of American government and American public service.

And that's precisely the ideal we're losing.

As you've learned by reading horror story after horror story, our bureaucratic government is transitioning—indeed, has transitioned—from one that focuses on defending constitutional liberty to one that focuses on implementing its own agenda. The bureaucratic government lives for itself, protects itself, and serves itself and the ideological allies who sustain it.

Was the IRS defending constitutional liberty and upholding the Constitution when it audited tens of thousands of adoptive families, throwing their lives into chaos?

Was the EPA defending constitutional liberty and upholding the Constitution when it hid public communications behind fictitious email addresses and conspired to influence the outcome of the 2012 presidential elections?

Was the Justice Department defending constitutional liberty and upholding the Constitution when it prosecuted an innocent Republican senator, thus decisively tipping the balance of power in the United States Senate?

Was the NLRB defending constitutional liberty and upholding the Constitution when it attempted to dictate which American workers in which American state enjoyed the right to high-paying jobs?

Was the VA defending constitutional liberty and upholding the Constitution when it turned its back on the very warriors it was created to serve, killing them with its incompetence and corruption?

Was the FCC defending constitutional liberty and upholding the Constitution when it plotted to place monitors in newsrooms across the country?

The result of these failures is a government that is seen as an instrument of ideological warfare, not a servant of the people and a guardian of their freedom. The result isn't just the oppression described in these pages but also a division that threatens the very fabric of our nation.

When constitutional liberty is properly protected, no elected government and no bureaucrat can do anything so drastic as restrict your fundamental freedoms, take away your right to earn a livelihood, or—at its worst—take away your very liberty through wrongful prosecutions. But when constitutional liberty is discarded, government is weaponized, and here is perhaps the most destructive side effect of all: the American people are turned against each other.

How?

When government is weaponized, you no longer have to persuade citizens of the rightness of your cause. You no longer have to build coalitions. You simply use raw power.

Over the last decade or so there's been much discussion that our politics seem less civil, that Americans seem more divided. And while some of that discussion has been dismissed as alarmist, the numbers tell a different tale.

We are not just more divided politically than we have been in generations; we're more divided emotionally.

In other words, we Americans don't tend to like each other that much anymore.

On June 12, 2014, the Pew Research Center for the People and the Press released the results of a comprehensive survey showing the extent of our partisan political divide. Its conclusions were startling:

> Republicans and Democrats are more divided along ideological lines—and partisan antipathy is deeper and more extensive—than at any point in the last two decades. These trends manifest themselves in myriad ways, both in politics and in everyday life. And a new survey of 10,000 adults nationwide finds that these divisions are greatest among those who are the most engaged and active in the political process.[1]

This is hardly surprising. After all, it's the knowledgeable and engaged Americans who've followed Washington's scandals and are likely to have either been targeted by the government themselves or know people who have. By the same token, many of the most engaged people on the Left are actively cheering on the government and the party of government as it works cooperatively to defeat those they loathe and whose views they despise.

Think of the response to the *Citizens United* decision that I raised early in the book. Rather than accept a Supreme Court declaration that actually protected liberty--specifically the right to free speech enshrined in the First Amendment—activists in the government worked to undermine it at every turn, specifically through punishing Americans who chose to exercise the very rights the Supreme Court rightfully recognized.

In 2014, the Pew Research Center released a comprehensive report showing a dramatically increasing partisan divide between Republicans and Democrats, with the median Republican and the median Democrat farther apart on the ideological spectrum than at any time in the last twenty years.[2]

Obviously, there are many reasons for this vast and growing disparity. There is, for example, a degree of self-sorting as Americans move to neighborhoods where neighbors agree with their values. Additionally, with the growth in cable and Internet and social media communications channels, we can increasingly get our news mainly from like-minded sources. And these trends become increasingly self-reinforcing as time goes by.

It is interesting, however, that well before the avalanche of government abuse outlined in this book, we Americans were much closer together. As we separated, our bureaucratic government enabled and empowered that separation—by decisively taking sides in the critical moral, cultural, economic, environmental, and political issues of our day.

And when the government takes sides, employing all the power of the state on behalf of one side against the other, the result is not just division but divisiveness—real anger and antipathy. The Pew Research Center's numbers are startling, showing both Democrats and Republicans as more than twice as likely to view the opposing party as a "threat to the nation's well-being" as they were twenty years ago.[3]

Lest you think this study is an aberration and just one organization's view of American realities, the *Washington Post* published similar information, from Emory University's Alan Abramowitz, showing dramatic decreases in regard for the opposing party, with only 7 percent of Americans having positive feelings for both parties, down from 35 percent from 1978 to 1980.[4]

Again, I want to be clear: I am not arguing that our bureaucratic government is the sole cause of this phenomenon, but I am arguing that it is exacerbating our divisions. It is understandable for individuals who see their government as decisively siding with their ideological opponents to become angry and embittered, especially when that government *breaks the law* to achieve its preferred ideological outcomes.

I communicate with millions of Americans every day through radio and TV broadcasts, as well as social media that reach millions.

Our audience consists of many of the most engaged members of their communities, including pastors, church leaders, pro-life leaders and activists, longtime members of the conservative establishment, and Americans who've given their time and money to protect religious liberty at home and abroad. These folks are the "salt of the earth," the backbone of our democracy.

And they are angry.

They are angry that their government is turning against them. They're angry that misconduct is not just overlooked but positively encouraged. They're angry that leftist members of Congress serve as cheerleaders and enablers of blatantly unlawful activity. And they're angry that too many of their fellow citizens look at IRS abuse, DOJ bias, and NLRB overreach and say, "Those conservatives get what they deserve."

And while that anger motivates, it can also be dangerous—leading Americans to believe that they must fight fire with fire, to defeat the other side in the same way, using the same tools.

That is a recipe only for further division, for further animosity, and—ultimately—for increased government abuse.

There's Another Way: Restoration

It's past time for the most engaged Americans to take a step back from the ideological battle of the moment and think of a larger goal: restoring in the American people the notion that government doesn't exist to help you win a fight but instead as an instrument for ensuring that, indeed, all men are created equal—that, indeed, we all enjoy the rights to Life, Liberty, and the Pursuit of Happiness.

At the ACLJ we're increasingly using our vast platform not merely to fight specific legal cases and specific government abuses—as vital as that work is—but also to remind Americans of our constitutional roots, to teach them about our constitutional heritage.

We've disseminated thousands upon thousands of copies of *Foundations of Freedom*, a booklet that includes the Constitution, the Declaration of Independence, and the Gettysburg Address.

On social media we've been sharing far and wide the great quotes and thoughts of our Founding Fathers, with some of the images reaching millions.

We've created videos that tie the words of great Americans past and present into a seamless web of liberty, showing that even men and women with greatly divergent worldviews can agree on freedom for all Americans, even for their political and ideological opponents.

These are small gestures, to be sure, but important nonetheless. And we're certainly not alone in these efforts. In fact, the lead plaintiff in our ACLJ lawsuit on behalf of forty-one conservative and pro-life groups in twenty-two states was engaged in just such an effort to educate young Americans about our founding principles when it found itself in the IRS's crosshairs.

Linchpins of Liberty is a small, Tennessee-based group that intended to teach small groups of kids about our nation's history and constitution. The IRS found this so offensive that not only did it delay the organization's nonprofit application, it also asked unconstitutionally intrusive questions, such as demanding to know the names of the children Linchpins taught.

Restoration, obviously, will not be easy.

We have to overcome not only those—particularly in the mainstream media and the academy—who deny American exceptionalism and indeed the very existence of virtue in our founding or national story; we also must overcome a bureaucratic government that is fully invested in the status quo, and has been for a long time. Earlier I discussed the number of regulations passed year by year in recent years, but the regulatory state has been very busy for a very long time. Look at these numbers:[5]

Table I. Total Number of Final Rules Published in Recent Years, 1997–2012

Calendar Year	Number of Final Rules
1997	3,930
1998	4,388
1999	4,336
2000	4,079
2001	3,423
2002	3,559
2003	3,744
2004	3,661
2005	3,301
2006	3,065
2007	2,947
2008	3,085
2009	3,471
2010	3,261
2011	3,835
2012	2,482

Source: Government Accountability Office's Federal Rules Database; data retrieved on February 22, 2013. Data provided are the numbers of rules published each year in the Federal Register and submitted to GAO under Section 801 of the Congressional Review Act, which requires that agencies submit their rules to GAO and to both houses of Congress.

There is a word that comes to mind when I see those tens of thousands of rules and regulations.

That word is *power*.

Hidden behind those numbers is enormous legal power exercised by hundreds of thousands of federal bureaucrats—bureaucrats who are disproportionately connected with one political party.

But this raw power does not mean the fight is hopeless, just that it is challenging. Critically, I am not the only person who recognizes the threat of an out-of-control federal government or the need to restore our constitutional republic.

In fact, that word is in the subtitle of my friend Mark Levin's outstanding bestseller *The Liberty Amendments: Restoring the American Republic*, where he advocates using Article V of the Constitution to pass specific constitutional amendments that would severely limit federal power.

Article V contains a provision that enables constitutional amendments without any congressional involvement at all, a method for circumventing the federal government entirely. Article V states (in relevant part):

> The Congress, whenever two thirds of both Houses shall deem it necessary, shall propose Amendments to this Constitution, *or, on the Application of the Legislatures of two thirds of the several States, shall call a Convention for proposing Amendments*, which, in either Case, shall be valid to all Intents and Purposes, as Part of this Constitution, when ratified by the Legislatures of three fourths of the several States, or by Conventions in three fourths thereof as the other Mode of Ratification may be proposed by the Congress. . . .
> (Emphasis added)

In other words, two-thirds of the states can call a constitutional convention. Levin is not the only person to call for such a remedy.

George Will, widely considered to be the dean of conservative pundits, in 2014 endorsed using Article V to pass a balanced budget amendment, an amendment that would immediately and dramatically limit government power.[6]

Organizations like Citizens for Self-Governance have also joined the call for an Article V Convention, with the aim of limiting federal power over the states. In response to this growing call for more radical change, on March 6, 2014, Georgia became the first state to pass a convention of states resolution.[7]

But the Article V remedy is not the only method for limiting our bureaucratic government. Indeed, the more modest reforms I proposed in the previous chapter would fundamentally transform the regulatory landscape and restrict not just federal power but also the very potential for abuse—all by statute.

I do not pretend those reforms would be a cure-all, but I do know they would be an improvement.

In reality, however, it is less important in this moment to endorse any specific remedy than it is to fight against despair, the one thing—the only thing—that can truly destroy our constitutional republic.

In reality, however, it is less important in this moment to endorse any specific remedy than it is to fight against despair, the one thing—the only thing—that can truly destroy our constitutional republic.

In fact, even as I hear the anger of many of our friends and supporters, I sometimes also hear despair, a feeling that nothing we can do matters and that all proposed solutions—no matter how interesting or creative—are ultimately futile. The forces of big government have won, and all we can do is defend our shrinking liberties as long as we can.

I understand the temptation of despair. It's hard to read the stories in this book and not see the situation as grave, and the voice of one man or woman among 300 million can feel small. We feel like we have little impact.

But we shouldn't think so much about our impact. Instead, let's think about responsibilities—to ourselves, to our families, to our children, and to our children's children. That gives us real motivation and great hope.

I love to study American history. The lessons I draw from the past are deep and meaningful, and when we forget the past we forget who we are. There's a reason, for example, why angry atheists constantly try to change our perceptions of the past by attacking war memorial crosses or displays of the Ten Commandments, or—most egregiously in recent memory—even the display of historically significant symbols like the legendary Ground Zero cross in the National September 11 Memorial & Museum.[8]

When you change perceptions of the past, you can alter the present and transform the future.

Sometimes, when times are bleak and I begin to lose hope, I go back to the past—to crises so great that they dwarf what we face today.

I think of the Civil War, and not just of triumphs like Gettysburg, where the Union was saved amid displays of indescribable heroism, but instead of the darkness before the dawn, when the Union army failed again and again to breach Confederate lines, and our nation teetered on the brink of extinction.

Did the Union soldiers at Fredericksburg, at Chancellorsville, at the Battles of Bull Run—did they feel like world-bearers, like they were making all the difference?

No, but they knew their duty, and they did their duty. Ultimately, they were victorious.

Similarly, I think of World War II, and not of the triumphs like Midway or D-Day, when every soldier present knew they were part of history, but instead of the dark days on Wake Island, or Bataan, or Corregidor, when victory seemed far away and the odds were overwhelming. Or what of the Marines at Chosin Reservoir in the Korean War, with a vast Chinese army surrounding them, attacking from every side?

Did these men feel like they were striking a key blow for liberty, or were they hanging on by their fingernails? Fighting for the person next to them, fighting for the chance just to stay alive?

Those men knew their duty, and they did their duty.

That is American greatness. That is why we have hope.

And it's not just the history of courage in war that gives me hope. There was a time in this country—not too long ago—when our brothers and sisters lived as second-class citizens in their own country. They couldn't eat at the same lunch counters. They couldn't drink from the same water fountains. They couldn't sit in the same seats on the same bus.

There are names that echo in history from the civil rights movement. Rosa Parks. John L. Lewis. Martin Luther King Jr. But in addition to these great leaders, there were countless others who sat where they had a right to sit, who peacefully faced attack dogs and fire hoses, all to confront a system that defied our constitutional promises, but a system so entrenched that no one alive could remember a different way. Did those people do what they did believing that their own effort would make all the difference?

No, these men and women knew what was right, and they acted, with love and courage.

That is American greatness.

As I write this book, I've been touched by the story of a young American doctor who went to Liberia—a desperately poor country in Africa—to provide medical care in the most difficult of circumstances. As I write, this doctor has faced death from the worst of diseases, the Ebola virus, not because he believes he can change an entire nation or provide health care to all its people, but because he believes that it is his duty, his obligation, to do what he can—whatever that may be.

That is American greatness.

That is the spirit of this country. That is the spirit that gives me hope. The answer to our challenge lies not in any specific idea—as important as ideas are—but instead in our own resolve. We are heirs to a great nation, and we are caretakers of that nation's Constitution and liberty, its blood-bought liberty.

Impatient presidents don't get to change the law. The same goes for unelected bureaucrats. It is time to turn the power switch off and reclaim our republic.

With that understanding, and with that sacred trust, and with the knowledge that America has confronted much longer odds in much darker times, I have confidence—I have hope—that we can, in fact, answer Benjamin Franklin's challenge and keep our constitutional republic.

AFTERWORD

The fight against regulatory agencies run amok never ends. In order to protect our freedoms from the encroachment of our power-hungry federal government ruled by unaccountable bureaucrats, we must continue fighting in our communities, in courts, and on Capitol Hill.

In fact, if I've learned anything in my work at the ACLJ, and as I travel the nation discussing the problems and solutions laid out in this book, it's that the bureaucracy will do anything to defend itself against those who threaten its power and influence.

Since the first edition of this book was released, I've continued to fight for justice in courts across this great nation for those everyday Americans unconstitutionally targeted by the Obama administration's IRS. I've also returned to Capitol Hill to testify at hearings about the bureaucracy's broad collusion with other corrupt agencies to stop grassroots conservative activists.

We at the American Center for Law and Justice have certainly achieved key victories. Unfortunately, the fight is far from over.

Though our requests for answers and information from the IRS and the Obama administration are slow in coming, we continue to fight for justice in Congress and the federal courts.

Congress

On July 29, 2015, I testified before a key Senate Judiciary Committee subcommittee on behalf of the American Center for Law and Justice, our clients, and 185,000 of our members to address the IRS-targeting scandal denying tax-exempt status to conservative organizations. The fact that this follow-up hearing even took place is a victory in and of itself because it demonstrates that Congress is still listening, still seeking the truth, and doing its constitutional duty to hold the Obama IRS accountable. It is critically important to speak up for the American people when U.S. senators are asking questions that demand answers.[1] These investigations are some of Congress's most important work.

I testified on the Hill not just on behalf of our thirty-eight clients from twenty-two different states from coast to coast, but also on behalf of the American people as a whole. Make no mistake—it's the everyday American people working to provide for their families and love their neighbors who suffer when an unelected bureaucracy reigns unchecked. The IRS must be held accountable for its actions. My clients were subjected to unconstitutional intimidation, delays, and questioning simply because they were conservative organizations applying for tax-exempt status.

At this crucial hearing last summer, former Federal Election Commission (FEC) official Lawrence Noble also testified. He was not there to protest the IRS's selective targeting of conservative groups. Instead, he complained that the IRS (as well as the FEC) was not doing *enough* to enforce the tax code. According to Noble, the IRS is failing in its responsibility to enforce the requirements for organizations claiming to be exempt from taxation under section 501(c)(4) of the IRC.[2]

In other words, Noble argued that the IRS wasn't doing enough to target Americans and unconstitutionally infringe on their fundamental freedoms. Like President Obama and Lois Lerner, he wanted to wield the bureaucracy as a partisan weapon.

Ironically, Noble complained about outside pressure on the IRS "to let the past abuses of 501(c)(4) status flourish."[3] That is ironic because Noble himself has been implicated in doing the very same thing: pressuring the IRS—to go after 501(c)(4)'s for their "political" activity. Noble was Lois Lerner's boss at the FEC before she began her career at the IRS, where she infamously and unconstitutionally targeted conservative Americans.

In one of the numerous emails uncovered through the litany of investigations, Lerner wrote to top IRS staff:

As I mentioned yesterday, there are several groups of folks from the FEC world that are pushing tax fraud prosecution for (c)(4)s who report that they are not conducting political activity when they are (or these folks think they are). One is my ex-boss Larry Noble, former General Counsel at the FEC, who is now President at Americans for Campaign Reform. This is their latest push to shut down these groups.[4]

She continues:

One IRS prosecution would make an impact, and they would not feel so comfortable doing this stuff. So do not be fooled about how this is being articulated. It is all about 501(c)(4)s orgs and political activity.[5]

Let's recap what exactly is being said here. Lois Lerner is writing to encourage a multiagency crackdown on nonprofit groups engaged in political activity—activity they are legally allowed to conduct and which happens to be constitutionally protected.

Imagine my surprise when seated just a few chairs from me in the hearing was Larry Noble himself. The same Larry Noble who, according to Lerner's own emails, was among the FEC "folks" pressuring the IRS "to shut down these groups" with criminal prosecution.

Yet that day he sat at the witness table with me, and testified to Congress that outside "pressure" on the IRS was hampering its work; he warned of the "dangers this presents to our democracy."

So let's get that straight: he was complaining about outside pressure keeping the IRS from doing its job and called the distraction dangerous to democracy at the very same time he was putting *outside pressure* on the IRS to limit freedoms to certain Americans. Naturally, I drew attention to this irony and had Lerner's email incorporated into the record.

You want to talk about dangers to our democracy? Okay, let's talk about dangers to our democracy. Let's talk about the danger of unrestrained power. Let's talk about the damage done by the leftist elite's horde of bureaucratic drones.

Our clients have been subjected to intentional targeting, delay, intimidation, and a fully unnecessary and unconstitutional investigation by the IRS. And while some of them finally received their tax-exempt status after years of delays, we still have numerous clients waiting. In fact, one client has been waiting six years for a determination by the IRS—and is still waiting today.

Meanwhile, the IRS continues to swirl in either outright deception or, at best, hopeless self-denial. For example, consider the congressional testimony of IRS commissioner John Koskinen. At the Senate hearing, Koskinen brazenly insisted there was no evidence of any outside influence on the IRS concerning its targeting of conservative groups. But remember Lerner's March 27, 2013, email describing pressure applied by Noble "and others" in the FEC labyrinth? In Lerner's own words: "This is their latest push to shut down these groups," and "do not be fooled," it is "all about . . . political activity."

If that is not outside influence, I do not know what is. Still, Koskinen and the IRS would have us believe there was no outside influence. The left complains that outside "pressure" from Congress and oppositional groups is a "danger" to democracy—even though it pressured the IRS to criminally target those holding differing political views.

But the outside influence doesn't stop with the FEC. Another one of Lerner's uncovered emails, sent on May 8, 2013, goes even further.

According to Lerner, yet another Obama administration executive agency—the very agency supposedly responsible for investigating the IRS—was part of the targeting scandal from the beginning. The Department of Justice is supposed to be the epitome of independent, unbiased, and evenhanded law enforcement, defending our nation's laws and Constitution. Yet in her email, Lerner outlined how a senior DOJ official expressed to her that "DOJ wants to talk to the right folks at IRS" to coordinate and "piece together" criminal prosecution of certain unnamed (c)(4) organizations.[6]

This doesn't exactly sound independent, unbiased, or evenhanded to me.

It would be laughable if the consequences weren't so severe.

Fortunately, the shadowy antics of the IRS, the FEC, and the DOJ came to light before they got as far as launching criminal prosecutions. Imagine the nightmare we would be witnessing if our clients, and other targeted groups, hadn't spoken up when they did. Only left-leaning progressive groups would have their tax-exempt status and their constitutional freedoms to engage in the public square while conservative groups would be diminished and sidelined.

Even still, the steps taken by the IRS before the corruption was revealed have had an immeasurably chilling effect on free speech and associational rights for conservative organizations. Large donors withheld checks that could have grown and sustained these groups. Without contributions, some of them were forced to close down. Others had to cut activities and operations, limiting their contributions to the good of our country and a thriving political discourse. But while we cannot undo the intimidation and abuse our clients have endured at the hands of the IRS, we are making progress in ensuring their rights are protected and that nothing like this ever happens again.

The Courts

The IRS also repeatedly fails to cooperate in federal courts. At the ACLJ, we are actively demanding accountability in two federal lawsuits. In both, the IRS is attempting to thwart the legal process at every turn.

As I mentioned, after we filed our case, the IRS granted tax-exempt status to most of our clients as the litigation wound through the courts. In a sense, this was not surprising. By granting the exemptions, the IRS and DOJ were trying to moot the case out. So when one federal judge predictably dismissed some of our case, we immediately appealed. We needed to remain in the fight for our clients who were still waiting, and to ensure this never happens again.

As we appealed, a separate case making its way through the United States Court of Appeals for the District of Columbia Circuit, *Z Street v. Koskinen*, helped immensely. Z Street is a pro-Israel group suing the IRS because the IRS purposefully delayed their application for tax-exempt status solely because they promote pro-Israel viewpoints.

Sound familiar?

The federal bureaucracy picks winners and losers, with traditional conservative speech and viewpoints unconstitutionally targeted, limiting their fundamental First Amendment freedoms of speech, association, and more.

Z Street also contended that the IRS had created a "special unit in Washington, D.C." to determine whether the group's activities and connection to Israel "contradict[ed] the Administration's public policies."[7] The facts we have uncovered in our own case certainly support this assertion. While we do not represent Z Street, we have followed it closely for the good of our clients and all concerned Americans.

Here's the fundamental constitutional argument: Can the IRS lawfully delay processing tax-exempt applications merely because the viewpoint of the applying group may be different from the current administration? A recent ruling by the D.C. Circuit in *Z Street* answers resoundingly in the negative. The court's ruling has allowed the pro-Israel organization to continue with its claims and in so doing, bolsters our own case before this same court.

In addition to this ruling, IRS officials are finally starting to be held accountable, forced to answer under oath for their discriminatory conduct. Thus far, for years, the IRS has been able to avoid answering for their actions. But our fights in the courts are paying off, shedding light on their actions, which are catching up with them.

The importance of the ruling in *Z Street* cannot be overstated. It makes perfect sense because it is common sense. If our nation was founded on any principle, it's that people have the fundamental right to speak out against the policies and practices of those in power. If this isn't allowed to happen anymore, we cease to live in the same United States of America that has been a beacon of freedom for more than two centuries.

The court's message in *Z Street* is crystal clear: "in administering the tax code, the IRS may not discriminate on the basis of viewpoint."[8]

It is precisely this type of conduct—the abuse of unfettered discretion by the IRS to discriminate in the administration of the tax code and its resulting harms—that our clients are challenging in their federal lawsuit against the IRS.

Like Z Street, our clients are all nonprofit organizations seeking tax-exempt status that have been victimized by a discriminatory policy—a "targeting scheme"—by which the IRS "intentionally and systematically targeted for additional and unconstitutional scrutiny conservative organizations applying for tax-exemption," because their conservative viewpoint is at odds with that of the current administration.[9]

The resounding message of the recent *Z Street* order is that the IRS will no longer be permitted to discriminate on the basis of viewpoint in administering the tax code. They can no longer cower behind broad, obscure, or obsolete statutory interpretations, allowing American taxpayers to suffer blatant violations of their First Amendment rights.

This is exactly what the ACLJ lawsuits are about. After all, the IRS admitted it intentionally and systematically targeted *for additional unconstitutional scrutiny* those organizations applying for tax-exempt status that discussed certain topics and held certain viewpoints.

An organization seeking tax-exempt status is not required to wait 270 days—or until the IRS actually denies its exemption—to challenge the agency's blatant constitutional violations.[10] However, the Obama administration claims this time period is reasonable because of an existing statute—one that doesn't even apply to egregious violations like what the IRS had done with conservative groups. But the D.C. Circuit concluded that for the IRS "to process exemption applications pursuant to different standards and at different rates depending upon the viewpoint of the applicants" would constitute "a blatant violation of the First Amendment."[11]

We were encouraged that the judges hearing the Z *Street* case were as outraged by the IRS's targeting scheme as we were. Our clients are encouraged, and you should be, too. Expressing his frustrations during oral argument, Chief Judge Merrick B. Garland made the following remarks to the IRS attorneys:

> I think if I were you I would go back and ask your superiors whether they want us to represent that the government's position in this case is that the government is free to unconstitutionally discriminate against its citizens for 270 days.
>
> I would be stunned if the current Attorney General agreed with that. Or the last Attorney General. Or the one before that, or the one before that. Or anyone. That can't be the position. Now, do you want to think about it again, whether you really want that to be your position.[12]

Shockingly, the attorney for the IRS responded that this was precisely the government's position.[13]

It's remarkable. But it's the natural position for this bumbling agency that has faced no accountability for far too long. This contempt for the rule of law by a government attorney representing the Obama administration only further reveals the IRS's brazen disregard for the constitutional rights of the citizens of this nation.

While the IRS attorney's honesty is laudable, the arrogance is maddening.

Imagine the audacity it takes to stand before a federal judge and admit your belief that you have the right to violate the fundamental constitutional rights of taxpaying, law-abiding citizens—just because they hold an opposing view. This is America's unelected bureaucracy at its finest. And this is why we fight. Unelected, unchecked power consumes freedom like a cancer.

At the hearing on Capitol Hill, we were able to inform key Senate committee members of these recent developments in federal courts and further underscore the gross injustices perpetrated by the IRS. The IRS and the DOJ have proven they are completely compromised on this investigation. That is why I demanded that the Department of Justice appoint a special counsel. And it is why I demanded that Congress begin the process of truly reforming the IRS.

The targeting of Americans based upon their personal beliefs is repugnant to the Constitution. An IRS that can do it once can do it again. Americans have been outraged for quite some time, and it is time for a thorough investigation.

We need to know what happened. We need finality and closure. We need accountability. Those responsible for this scandal must be brought to justice. Individual organizations are winning important victories in court. But more must be done to ensure the government never does this again. We are not alone. Earlier in 2015, calls for Commissioner Koskinen's impeachment began circulating. As of October 2015, the House of Representatives stated his impeachment is "inevitable."[14] This is the kind of response we need: holding those in power accountable for their actions and firing them when they abuse their position.

We must seize the momentum and press forward until justice is met and freedom for all citizens, not just some, is restored. The various proceedings, congressional committee hearings, and our ongoing litigation have all led us to discover vital evidence that otherwise would have remained swept under the rug by the Obama administration. But we must keep digging until the scales of justice have been balanced.

The Fight Against IRS Bureaucracy Continues

While we have seen positive developments and even victories, rest assured, many battles remain. This administration and its horde of bureaucratic ideologues won't take their sights off "dissident" nonprofits without a fight. We must demand accountability under the law, and we must be consistently heard.

The IRS is in desperate need of reform. Even the Government Accountability Office (GAO) agrees. In July 2015, an official from the GAO testified before the Subcommittee on Oversight in the House Ways and Means Committee.[15] In its congressional testimony, the GAO described continuing deficiencies increasing the risk that the IRS could continue to select organizations for examination in an unfair manner.[16]

Even Commissioner Koskinen admitted the IRS improperly identified organizations. He just asserts that the problems have been corrected and we can all go about business as usual.[17] Unsurprisingly, the Obama administration's DOJ agrees with this conclusion. Last October, after two years of a supposed investigation that we advised our clients not to participate in once we realized it was partisan, the DOJ closed the case without recommending any criminal charges against any of the IRS officials. While they admitted to finding "substantial evidence of mismanagement, poor judgment and institutional inertia leading to the belief" that the IRS targeted groups for their political views, the DOJ concluded that "poor management is not a crime."[18]

However outrageous and appalling the result, this is the predictable outcome of one branch of the bureaucracy attempting to save another. President Obama declared there was "not even a smidgeon of corruption"[19] while the investigation—conducted by a top Obama donor[20]—was still ongoing.

Though the IRS and other agencies continue to flout the law and the Constitution, we will continue fighting for the truth. Justice will be served.

We must not grow weary in our efforts to make meaningful and lasting reform a reality.

As long as an unelected IRS bureaucracy holds the reins of power, we must assume the worst. They continue to rewrite ObamaCare in order to save the law from itself.[21] Christian schools and ministries tell us they are bracing for what they see as inevitable: scrutiny of their tax-exempt status—especially in light of recent Supreme Court rulings on social issues.

But friends, here's the good news: We won't back down. We will stand in the gap. We will not go down without a fight. The American Center for Law and Justice will continue to stand for freedom in this arena just as we have in so many others.

The fight continues in court, where our litigation matters. We will continue to pursue our IRS-targeting lawsuit, *Lynchpins of Liberty v. United States*, until justice is served. We recently appealed on behalf of our clients when the district court dismissed their claims based on the erroneous notion that the targeting scheme was no longer in place. On September 23, 2015, the Court of Appeals entered an order calling for a briefing and oral arguments, noting that "[t]he merits of the parties' positions are not so clear as to warrant summary action."[22] We remain hopeful, especially in light of the Court of Appeals decision in *Z Street*, that we will be allowed to return to the district court and vindicate our clients' rights.

We will also continue to pursue our FOIA case, *Citizens for a Strong New Hampshire, Inc. v. Internal Revenue Service*, based on the IRS's failure to comply with its obligations under the Freedom of Information Act to disclose communications between Lois Lerner and Democrats in Congress from New Hampshire leading up to the vital 2014 elections.

In August 2015, the United States District Court for the District of New Hampshire ordered the IRS to turn over key, potentially incriminating documents it withheld so the court could undertake its own independent review. This ruling forced the IRS to turn over materials that could potentially reveal collusion between liberal legislators and the IRS in targeting conservative groups. This is, first, so a federal judge—not a bureaucrat— can determine if those documents are responsive to our client's FOIA request, and second, to ensure their safekeeping as this case continues. We were confident the IRS had not meaningfully searched for the documents, and the court agreed, rejecting the IRS's ridiculous assertions that it did not collude with other agencies to target conservative groups.

In another welcome development, the court denied the IRS's motion for summary judgment.[23] And so the fight for justice continues.

Consider this success in context: Less than one percent of FOIA cases actually go to trial. Most get resolved without a trial, and without the plaintiff ever learning any details about the government's search for responsive documents. Because the court has ordered this discovery, the IRS will have to turn over key documents containing information previously unrevealed. The bureaucracy's stonewalling is beginning to crumble. A favorable outcome in this case will shed tremendous light on the IRS's secretive conduct.

We are working diligently in numerous federal courts to bring to light the IRS's flagrant abuses of power and to ensure it answers for its corruption. But experience teaches us that it will likely be quite some time before these cases are resolved. Therefore, it is even more important that we persevere and show resilience in the face of the bureaucratic attempts to conceal the truth. We must never stop the fight to keep our government transparent and responsive to the needs of the citizenry.

We continue to resist the notion that our government exists to serve the people—we continue to fight against statism and progressivism that says people only have as much freedom as the supposedly all-knowing government allows them. That's not why our Founding Fathers risked everything to establish our great nation. That's not why civil rights activists fought for freedom in the 1960s. That's not why the men and women of our military put their lives on the line every day to safeguard our security at home.

We continue the important work to reform the broken system. This requires long-term strategy and diligence, building coalitions and establishing and strengthening institutions that impact our culture. So elections can succeed in giving us representatives and leaders who fear the people instead of instilling fear in the people.

Finally, we continue to restore our republic—the America that has made us that "shining city on a hill" where people from all over the world risk everything to come here for a chance to succeed.

These fights are important. The federal bureaucracy wants us to think that one American can't change the course of history. They want us to be apathetic and they want us to feel defeated.

But we are achieving real victories—in courts, on Capitol Hill, and in communities from coast to coast.

Join us in ensuring that we will always be a government of the people, by the people, for the people and that government will not perish from the earth.

NOTES

INTRODUCTION: THE BUREAUCRATIC BLOCKBUSTER

1 http://www.washingtonpost.com/politics/clintons-raised-nearly-2
-billion-for-foundation-since-2001/2015/02/18/b8425d88-a7cd-11e4
-a7c2-03d37af98440_story.html.

2 Ibid.

3 http://www.dailymail.co.uk/news/article-3201367/Hillary-s-email
-firm-run-loft-apartment-servers-BATHROOM-raising-new
-questions-security-sensitive-messages-held.html.

4 http://www.usnews.com/news/articles/2015/06/23/opm-tries-to
-calm-hacking-cybersecurity-fears.

5 http://www.wired.com/2015/07/senator-sasse-washington-still-isnt
-taking-opm-breach-seriously/.

6 Ibid.

7 Ibid.

8 Ibid.

9 http://www.usatoday.com/story/money/columnist/2015/06/13
/hacking-opm-weisman/28697915/.

10 http://www.usatoday.com/story/money/columnist/2015/06/13
/hacking-opm-weisman/28697915/.

11 http://www.wsj.com/articles/hillary-clinton-vs-foia-1443136818.

12 http://www.nytimes.com/2015/03/04/us/politics/using-private
-email-hillary-clinton-thwarted-record-requests.html?_r=0.

13 For example, Clinton and her lawyers could simply claim that the
emails remaining on the server are private and not subject to FOIA
requests or claim that any emails there aren't subject to FOIA
requests, requiring a court or DOJ to subpoena the email server.

14 http://www.nytimes.com/2015/09/23/us/politics/investigators-find
-emails-hillary-clinton-said-were-erased.html.

15 https://www.washingtonpost.com/blogs/fact-checker
/wp/2015/08/27/clintons-claims-about-receiving-or-sending
-classified-material-on-her-private-email-system/.

16 http://www.politico.com/story/2015/03/colin-powell-personal
-email-secretary-of-state-115707.

17 http://www.wsj.com/articles/hillary-clintons-personal-email-use
-came-before-recent-rule-changes-1425415233.

18 http://time.com/3739541/transcript-hillary-clinton-email-press
-conference/.

19 http://www.wsj.com/articles/investigation-sought-into-hillary
-clintons-emails-1437714369.

20 https://www.archives.gov/isoo/faqs/identifying-handling-classified
-records.html.

21 Ibid.

22 http://www.wsj.com/articles/hillary-clintons-personal-email-use
-came-before-recent-rule-changes-1425415233.

23 Ibid.

24 Ibid.

25 https://www.fbi.gov/about-us/faqs.

26 http://www.wsj.com/articles/hillary-clinton-to-turn-over-private
-email-server-to-federal-authorities-1439344172.

27 Ibid.

28 http://www.nytimes.com/2015/09/08/us/politics/second-review
-says-classified-information-was-in-hillary-clintons-email.html.

29 http://news.yahoo.com/ap-exclusive-top-secret-clinton-emails
-drone-talk-071308584--election.html.

30 http://www.nytimes.com/2015/09/26/us/politics/string-of-emails
-raises-questions-about-when-hillary-clinton-began-using
-personal-account.html?_r=0.

31 http://freebeacon.com/politics/clinton-aide-shared-classified
-information-with-foundation-email-shows/.

32 http://www.politico.com/story/2015/09/hillary-clinton-email-state
-department-release-214246#ixzz3nFtfn81y.

33 Ibid.

34 http://www.foxnews.com/politics/2015/10/07/fbi-probe-hillary
-clinton-emails-expands-to-second-tech-company/?intcmp=hpbt2.

35 http://freebeacon.com/politics/fbi-seizes-four-state-department
-servers-in-clinton-email-probe/.

36 http://bigstory.ap.org/article/5ad0f6bb57eb487f84e98fe9a74a08b1
/clinton-subject-hack-attempts-china-korea-germany.

37 https://www.law.cornell.edu/uscode/text/44/3101.

38 http://www.nationalreview.com/corner/414777/yes-hillary-clinton
-broke-law-ian-tuttle.

39 http://www.ecfr.gov/cgi-bin/text-idx?SID=86eb52e506c845f12d3c12
cd60e8b207&node=se36.3.1236_122&rgn=div8.

40 https://www.law.cornell.edu/uscode/text/18/793.

41 https://www.law.cornell.edu/cfr/text/18/3a.11.

42 http://www.thedailybeast.com/articles/2015/08/12/the-spy-satellite
    -secrets-in-hillary-s-emails.html.

43 https://www.law.cornell.edu/uscode/text/18/1924.

44 http://nypost.com/2015/09/27/yes-hillary-clinton-broke-the-law/.

45 https://www.law.cornell.edu/uscode/text/18/2071.

46 Ibid.

47 http://www.nationalreview.com/article/414835/did-hillary-commit
    -felony-shannen-coffin.

CHAPTER ONE: ONE DAY IN MAY

 1 See Second Amended Complaint, *Linchpins of Liberty v. United
    States*, Case 1:13-cv-00777, located at http://media.aclj.org/pdf
    /second-amended-complaint-filed-redacted.pdf (hereafter "Second
    Amended Complaint").

 2 Editors, "The I.R.S. Does Its Job," *New York Times*, March 7, 2012,
    http://www.nytimes.com/2012/03/08/opinion/the-irs-does-its-job
    .html?src=tp&_r=2&.

 3 Lucy Madison, "Justice Dept. to Investigate IRS Targeting," CBS
    News, May 14, 2013, http://www.cbsnews.com/news/justice-dept
    -to-investigate-irs-targeting/.

 4 Katie Pavlich, "Breaking: New Emails Show Lois Lerner Was
    in Contact with DOJ About Prosecuting Tax Exempt Groups,"
    Townhall.com, April 16, 2014, http://townhall.com/tipsheet
    /katiepavlich/2014/04/16/breaking-new-emails-show
    -lois-lerner-contacted-doj-about-prosecuting-tax-exempt
    -groups-n1825292.

 5 See generally Second Amended Complaint.

 6 Rick Hasen, "Transcript of Lois Lerner's Remarks at Tax Meeting
    Sparking IRS Controversy," Election Law Blog, May 11, 2013,
    http://electionlawblog.org/?p=50160.

 7 Stan Veuger, "Yes IRS Harassment Blunted the Tea Party Ground
    Game," American Enterprise Institute, June 20, 2013, located at
    http://www.aei.org/article/economics/yes-irs-harassment-blunted
    -the-tea-party-ground-game/.

 8 Ibid.

 9 Ibid.

10 Dave Boyer, "Obama Blames Founding Fathers 'Structural' Design
    of Congress for Gridlock," *Washington Times*, May 23, 2014, http://

www.washingtontimes.com/news/2014/may/23/obama-blames
-structural-design-congress-gridlock/.

11 Benjamin Goad, "Government report finds Regulations have spiked
under Obama," *Hill*, May 15, 2013, http://thehill.com/regulation
/administration/299617-government-report-shows-spike-in
-regulations-under-obama.

12 Ibid.

13 "Abortifacients," Life Issues Institutes Inc., http://www.lifeissues
.org/abortifacients/.

14 James Hohmann, "Pelosi: People Won't Appreciate Reform Until It
Passes," *Politico*, March 9, 2010, http://www.politico.com/livepulse
/0310/Pelosi_People_wont_appreciate_reform_until_it_passes
.html.

15 Katherine Q. Seelye, "Health Care's Share of U.S. Economy
Rose at Record Rate," *New York Times*, February 4, 2010, http://
prescriptions.blogs.nytimes.com/2010/02/04/us-health-care
-spending-rose-at-record-rate-in-2009/.

16 Review & Outlook, "The 60th ObamaCare Vote," *Wall Street
Journal*, March 6, 2012, http://online.wsj.com/articles/SB100014240
52970203753704577255570396264602.

17 Dennis Cauchon, "Some Federal Workers More Likely to Die
than Lose Jobs," *USA Today*, July 19, 2011, http://usatoday30
.usatoday.com/news/washington/2011-07-18-fderal-job-security_n
.htm.

18 On May 30, 2014, the VA secretary, Eric Shinseki, resigned
under pressure. See Greg Jaffe and Ed O'Keefe, "Obama Accepts
Resignation of VA Secretary Shinseki," *Washington Post*, May 30,
2014, http://www.washingtonpost.com/politics/shinseki-apologizes
-for-va-health-care-scandal/2014/05/30/e605885a-e7f0-11e3
-8f90-73e071f3d637_story.html. The author is unaware of any
termination of a civil-service-protected VA employee in connection
with the VA wait list scandal.

19 Tony Lee, "Obama Admin Will Allow Amnesty Rally on National
Mall During Gov't Shutdown," Breitbart.com, October 7, 2013,
http://www.breitbart.com/Big-Government/2013/10/07/Obama
-Admin-Will-Allow-Amnesty-Rally-on-National-Mall-During
-Govt-Shutdown.

20 Kevin D. Williamson, "The Emerging Junta," *National Review
Online*, May 16, 2014, http://www.nationalreview.com/article
/378115/emerging-junta-kevin-d-williamson.

21 Cass R. Sunstein, "The Law of Group Polarization," John M. Olin Law & Economics Working Paper No. 91, 2d Series, December 7, 1999, http://www.law.uchicago.edu/files/files/91.CRS_.Polarization.pdf.

CHAPTER TWO: AMERICA, STILL EXCEPTIONAL?

1 "News Conference by President Obama," White House press release, April 4, 2009, http://www.whitehouse.gov/the-press-office /news-conference-president-obama-4042009.
2 See http://www.merriam-webster.com/dictionary/republic.
3 See http://www.lyricsmania.com/im_just_a_bill_lyrics _schoolhouse_rock.html.
4 See https://www.youtube.com/watch?v=JUDSeb2zHQ0.
5 See "Dodd-Frank Progress Report," Davis Polk, periodic reports, http://www.davispolk.com/Dodd-Frank-Rulemaking-Progress-Report/.
6 Ibid.
7 Ibid.
8 "Avocados Grown in South Florida and Imported Avocados; Clarification of the Avocado Grade Requirements," Federal Register, June 23, 2014, https://www.federalregister.gov /articles/2014/06/23/2014-14405/avocados-grown-in-south-florida -and-imported-avocados-clarification-of-the-avocado-grade.
9 John Fund and Hans Von Spakovsky, *Obama's Enforcer: Eric Holder's Justice Department* (New York: Broadside Books, 2014).
10 Daniel Foster, "Firing Lois Lerner," *National Review Online*, May 23, 2014, http://www.nationalreview.com/article/349115/firing -lois-lerner-daniel-foster.
11 Ibid.
12 Andrew Stiles, "A Partisan Union at the IRS," *National Review Online*, May 20, 2013, http://www.nationalreview.com/article /348811/partisan-union-irs.
13 Ibid.
14 Andrew Stiles, "IRS Employees Disproportionately Donate to Obama," *National Review Online*, May 15, 2013, http://www .nationalreview.com/article/348417/irs-employees -disproportionately-donate-obama.
15 Michael Beckel, "IRS Employees Back Obama, Democrats," Center for Public Integrity, May 14, 2013, http://www.publicintegrity .org/2013/05/14/12661/irs-employees-back-obama-democrats.
16 Rob Nikolewski, "Gov't Workers Voted for Obama with Their Dollars," Watchdog.org, June 17, 2013, http://watchdog

.org/90798/govt-lawyers-overwhelmingly-gave-to-obama-over
-romney-in-2012/.

17 Frank Newport, "Majority of Union Members Favor Obama; a
Third Back Romney," Gallup, June 11, 2012, http://www.gallup
.com/poll/155138/majority-union-members-favor-obama-third
-back-romney.aspx.

18 See http://uselectionatlas.org/RESULTS/national.php?year=2012.

19 Betsi Fores, "Report: US States Less Free than Canadian Provinces,"
Daily Caller, November 28, 2012, http://dailycaller.com/2012/11/28
/report-us-states-less-free-than-canadian-provinces/.

20 For a description of the Canadian constitutional structure, see
http://www.justice.gc.ca/eng/csj-sjc/just/05.html.

CHAPTER THREE: THE IRS: AT WAR WITH CONSERVATIVES

1 *Citizens United v. Federal Election Commission*, 558 U.S. 310 (2010).

2 "Statement from the President on Today's Supreme Court Decision,"
White House, January 21, 2010, http://www.whitehouse.gov/the-
press-office/statement-president-todays-supreme-court-decision-0.

3 "Remarks by the President in State of the Union Address," White
House, January 27, 2010, http://www.whitehouse.gov/the-press
-office/remarks-president-state-union-address.

4 Louis Jacobsen, "Why Alito Shook His Head: Obama Exaggerates
the Impact of Supreme Court Ruling on Foreign Companies,"
Politifact.com, January 27, 2010, http://www.politifact.com/truth
-o-meter/statements/2010/jan/27/barack-obama/obama-says
-supreme-court-ruling-allows-foreign-com/.

5 Mark Hemingway, "IRS's Lerner Had History of Harassment,
Inappropriate Religious Inquiries at FEC," *Weekly Standard*, May 20,
2013, http://www.weeklystandard.com/blogs/irss-lerner-had
-history-harassment-inappropriate-religious-inquiries-fec_725004
.html?page=1; testimony also at http://
www.campaignlegalcenter.org/attachments/LEGISLATION/941.pdf.

6 Ibid.

7 Ibid.

8 See http://waysandmeans.house.gov/uploadedfiles/lerner_email_a
.pdf.

9 Ibid.

10 Ibid.

11 "Weekly Address: President Obama Challenges Politicians
Benefiting from Citizens United Ruling to Defend Corporate

Influence on Our Elections," White House, August 21, 2010, http://
www.whitehouse.gov/the-press-office/2010/08/21/weekly-address
-president-obama-challenges-politicians-benefiting-citizen.

12 Paul Roderick Gregory, "The Timeline of IRS Targeting of
Conservative Groups," *Forbes*, June 25, 2013, http://www.forbes
.com/sites/paulroderickgregory/2013/06/25/the-timeline-of-irs
-targeting-of-conservative-groups/.

13 Ibid.

14 Sam Stein, "Obama, Dems Try to Make Shadowy Conservative
Groups a Problem for Conservatives," *Huffington Post*, September 21,
2010, http://www.huffingtonpost.com/2010/09/21/obama-dems-try
-to-make-sh_n_733133.html.

15 Tamara Keith, "Report: IRS Scrutiny Worse for Conservatives,"
NPR.org, July 30, 2013, http://www.npr.org/blogs/itsallpolitics
/2013/07/30/207080580/report-irs-scrutiny-worse-for
-conservatives.

16 David French, "A Broad-Based IRS Assault on the Tea Party?"
National Review Online, March 2, 2012, http://www.nationalreview
.com/corner/292475/broad-based-irs-assault-tea-party-david-french.

17 *National Association for the Advancement of Colored People v. Patterson*,
357 U.S. 449 (June 30, 1958).

18 Ibid.

19 See French, "A Broad-Based IRS Assault on the Tea Party?"

20 "IRS Chief: Agency Not Targeting Tea Party Groups," Fox News,
March 22, 2012, http://www.foxnews.com/politics/2012/03/22/irs
-chief-agency-not-targeting-tea-party-groups/.

21 See Second Amended Complaint.

22 Ibid.

23 Mackenzie Weinger, "IRS Pays $50k to Anti-Gay Marriage Group,"
Politico, June 24, 2014, http://www.politico.com/story/2014/06/irs
-nom-lawsuit-108266.html.

24 Ibid.

25 Kim Barker and Justin Elliott, "IRS Office That Targeted Tea Party
Also Disclosed Confidential Docs from Conservative Groups,"
ProPublica, May 13, 2013, http://www.propublica.org/article/irs
-office-that-targeted-tea-party-also-disclosed-confidential-docs.

26 Stephen Dinan, "House Republicans Find 10% of Tea Party
Donors Audited by IRS," *Washington Times*, May 7, 2014, http://
www.washingtontimes.com/news/2014/may/7/house-republicans
-find-10-of-tea-party-donors-audi/?page=all.

27 Joe Otto, "Tea Party Donors 1000% More Likely to be Audited,"
   Conservative Daily, http://www.conservative-daily.com/2014/05/10
   /tea-party-donors-1000-more-likely-to-be-audited/.
28 Matthew Mosk, "IRS Suspicion Widens: GOP Donors Question
   Audits," ABC News, May 15, 2013, http://abcnews.go.com/Blotter
   /irs-suspicion-widens-gop-donors-question-audits/story?id
   =19184358.
29 Ibid.
30 Congressman Dave Camp, "Camp Opening Statement:
   H.R. 3865, 'Stop Targeting of Political Beliefs by the IRS
   Act of 2014,'" Committee on Ways and Means, February 11,
   2014, http://waysandmeans.house.gov/news/documentsingle
   .aspx?DocumentID=369556.
31 Rachel Bade, "Lois Lerner Sought Audit of Group Invite to GOP
   Senator," *Politico*, June 25, 2014, http://www.politico.com/story
   /2014/06/lois-lerner-irs-chuck-grassley-108322.html.
32 Susan Ferrechio, "Here's the Backstory Behind Chuck
   Grassley and Lois Lerner," *Washington Examiner*, June 27,
   2014, http://washingtonexaminer.com/heres-the-backstory
   -behind-chuck-grassley-and-lois-lerner/article/2550252?utm
   _campaign=FoxNews&utm_source=foxnews.com&utm
   _medium=feed.
33 "Republicans Slam IRS Scrutiny of Pro-Life Groups," Associated
   Press, May 22, 2013, http://www.foxnews.com/politics/2013/05/22
   /republicans-slam-irs-scrutiny-pro-life-groups/.
34 Penny Starr, "IRS Urged Pro-Life Group Seeking Tax-Exempt
   Status Not to Protest at Planned Parenthood Clinics," CNSNews
   .com, June 4, 2013, http://www.cnsnews.com/news/article/irs
   -urged-pro-life-group-seeking-tax-exempt-status-not-protest
   -planned-parenthood.
35 Ibid.
36 See http://www.irs.gov/pub/irs-tege/rp_1986-43.pdf.
37 Kimberly Winston, "IRS Agrees to Monitor Churches for
   Electioneering," *Washington Post*, July 21, 2014, http://www
   .washingtonpost.com/national/religion/irs-agrees-to-monitor
   -churches-for-electioneering/2014/07/21/99815d32-1118-11e4-ac56
   -773e54a65906_story.html.
38 See http://www.judicialwatch.org/document-archive/jw1559-00105/.
39 Ibid.
40 Ibid.

41 Eliana Johnson, "Report: IRS Sent Database Containing Confidential Taxpayer Information to FBI," *National Review Online*, June 9, 2014, http://www.nationalreview.com/corner/379897 /report-irs-sent-database-containing-confidential-taxpayer -information-fbi-eliana.

42 "IRS Claims to Have Lost Over 2 Years of Lerner Emails," House Committee on Ways and Means, press release, June 13, 2014, http://waysandmeans.house.gov/news/documentsingle.aspx ?DocumentID=384506.

43 Ibid.

44 Eliana Johnson, "IRS Has Lost More E-mails . . ." *National Review Online*, June 17, 2014, http://www.nationalreview.com/corner /380576/irs-has-lost-more-e-mails-eliana-johnson.

45 Matthew Clark, "Obama Thinks You Won't Notice," American Center for Law and Justice, http://aclj.org/irs-lost-more-emails -obama-administration-thinks-you-wont-notice.

46 See http://www.irs.gov/PUP/newsroom/IRS%20Letter%20to%20 Senate%20Finance%20Committee.pdf.

47 Francesca Chambers, "Lois Lerner Emails Show She Was Concerned About Congress Being Able to Subpoena IRS Employees' Online Chats," *Daily Mail*, July 9, 2014, http://www.dailymail.co.uk /news/article-2686856/Lois-Lerner-emails-concerned-Congress -able-subpoena-IRS-employees-online-chats.html.

48 Ibid.

49 Ibid.

50 Patrick Howley, "IRS 'Lost' Emails From Official That Met With Top Obama Assistant," *Daily Caller*, June 19, 2014, http://dailycaller .com/2014/06/19/irs-lost-emails-from-official-that-met-with top -obama-assistant/.

51 See http://watergate.info/impeachment/articles-of-impeachment.

52 Josh Hick, "Obama Donor Leading Justice Department's IRS Investigation," *Washington Post*, January 9, 2014, http://www .washingtonpost.com/politics/federal_government/obama-donor -leading-justice-departments-irs-investigation/2014/01/09 /980c010a-796a-11e3-8963-b4b654bcc9b2_story.html.

CHAPTER FOUR: THE IRS: AUDITING ADOPTION, BREAKING THE LAW

1 David French, "IRS Morality: Defend Planned Parenthood, Deluge Adoptive Families with Audits," *National Review Online*, May 22, 2013, http://www.nationalreview.com/corner/349077/irs-morality

-defend-planned-parenthood-deluge-adoptive-families-audits-david
-french.

2 Peggy Bogadi, "The IRS's Compliance Strategy for the Expanded
Adoption Tax Credit Has Significantly and Unnecessarily Harmed
Vulnerable Taxpayers, Has Increased Costs for the IRS, and Does
Not Bode Well for Future Credit Administration," Taxpayer
Advocate Service 2012 Annual Report to Congress, http://www
.taxpayeradvocate.irs.gov/userfiles/file/Full-Report/Most-Serious
-Problems-Adoption-Credit-Delays.pdf.

3 Ibid.

4 See http://kateswish.blogspot.com/2011/06/irs-audit-of-adoption
-tax-credit.html.

5 Ibid.

6 Taxpayer Advocate Service 2012 Annual Report.

7 See http://www.gao.gov/assets/590/586423.html.

8 Ibid.

9 David French, "Is the Left Launching an Attack on Evangelical
Adoption?" National Review Online, April 25, 2013, http://
www.nationalreview.com/corner/346643/left-launching-attack
-evangelical-adoption.

10 Laura Barcella, "How the Christian Right Perverts Adoption,"
Salon.com, May 4, 2013, http://www.salon.com/2013/05/04/how
_the_christian_right_perverts_adoption/.

11 First Person Plural, "Adoption History," PBS.org, 2000, http://
www.pbs.org/pov/firstpersonplural/history.php.

12 See http://elections.nytimes.com/2012/results/president/exit-polls.

13 Ibid.

14 Ibid.

15 Ibid.

16 Julian Hattem, "IRS Overpaid Up to $13.6B in Low-Income Tax
Credits, Report Find," Hill, April 22, 2013, http://thehill.com
/regulation/administration/295353-irs-overpaid-up-to-136b-in-low
-income-tax-credits-report-finds.

17 Ibid.

18 Kyle Pomerleau, "Summary of Latest Federal Income Tax Data,"
Tax Foundation, December 18, 2013, http://taxfoundation.org
/article/summary-latest-federal-income-tax-data.

19 Michael F. Cannon, "ObamaCare Architect Jonathan Gruber: 'If
You're a State And You Don't Set Up an Exchange, That Means
Your Citizens Don't Get Their Credits,'" Forbes, July 25, 2014,

http://www.forbes.com/sites/michaelcannon/2014/07/25/obamacare
-architect-jonathan-gruber-if-youre-a state and-you-dont-set-up
-an-exchange-that-means-your-citizens-dont-get-their-tax-credits/.

20 Sam Baker, "How the Supreme Court Can Kill ObamaCare
Without Overturning It," *National Journal*, November 17, 2014,
http://www.nationaljournal.com/health-care/how-the-supreme
-court-can-kill-obamacare-without-overturning-it-20141117.

21 Kimberly Strassel, "The ObamaCare-IRS Nexus," *Wall Street
Journal*, July 24, 2014, http://www.wsj.com/articles/kim-strassel
-the-obamacare-irs-nexus-1406244677.

22 Ibid.

23 See http://www.foxnews.com/politics/interactive/2014/07/22
/federal-appeals-court-decision-on-obamacare-subsidies/.

24 Stephen Dinan, "Bungling Bureaucrats Dole Out Billions in Tax
Credits to Illegal Immigrants," *Washington Times*, October 14, 2013,
http://www.washingtontimes.com/news/2013/oct/14/tax-credits-to
-illegals-likely-from-midlevel-repor/?page=all.

25 Ibid.

26 Terence P. Jeffrey, "IG: IRS Made 'Policy Decision' to 'Legalize
Illegal Aliens'; Ended Up Paying Illegals $4.2B in Refundable
Credits in 1 Year," CNSNews.com, July 12, 2013, http://cnsnews
.com/news/article/ig-irs-made-policy-decision-legalize-illegal
-aliens-ended-paying-illegals-42b.

27 Ibid.

28 See http://www.treasury.gov/tigta/auditreports/reports/094505fr.pdf.

29 Ibid.

30 Ed O'Keefe, "IRS Training Videos Spoof 'Star Trek,' 'Gilligan's
Island' and 'Cupid Shuffle,'" *Washington Post*, June 1, 2013, http://
www.washingtonpost.com/blogs/post-politics/wp/2013/06/01/irs
-training-videos-spoof-star-trek-gilligans-island-and-cupid-shuffle/.

31 Ed O'Keefe, "IRS Faces New Scrutiny for Excessive Spending
on Conferences," *Washington Post*, June 1, 2013, http://www
.washingtonpost.com/politics/irs-faces-new-scrutiny-for-excessive
-spending-on-conferences/2013/06/01/e1469324-cab2-11e2-9245
-773c0123c027_story.html.

CHAPTER FIVE: THE VA: WHEN INCOMPETENCE KILLS

1 See http://www.va.gov/opa/publications/celebrate/vamotto.pdf.

2 Louis Jacobson, "Katrina vanden Heuvel Says Congress Has
'Slashed Funding for Veterans' Benefits in Recent Years," Politifact

.com, May 21, 2014, http://www.politifact.com/punditfact
/statements/2014/may/21/katrina-vanden-heuvel/katrina-vanden
-heuvel-says-congress-has-slashed-fu/.

3   "Timeline: The Road to VA Wait-time Scandal," *Arizona Republic*,
    November 24, 2014, http://www.azcentral.com/story/news/arizona
    /politics/2014/05/10/timeline-road-va-wait-time-scandal/8932493/.
4   Ibid.
5   Ibid.
6   Ibid.
7   Ibid.
8   Ibid.
9   Ibid.
10 Ibid.
11 Ibid.
12 Ray Sanchez, "Audit That Led to Shinseki's Resignation Paints
    Scandal in Starkest Terms," CNN.com, May 30, 2014, http://www
    .cnn.com/2014/05/30/us/va-hospitals-audit/.
13 Ibid.
14 Ibid.
15 Ibid.
16 Ibid.
17 Katie Zezima, "Everything You Need to Know About the VA—
    And the Scandals Engulfing It," *Washington Post*, May 30, 2014,
    http://www.washingtonpost.com/blogs/the-fix/wp/2014/05/21/a
    -guide-to-the-va-and-the-scandals-engulfing-it/.
18 Ibid.
19 Ibid.
20 Ibid.
21 Ibid.
22 "The Waiting Wounded," *Economist*, March 23, 2014, http://www
    .economist.com/news/united-states/21573984-government-failing
    -keep-faith-ex-soldiers-waiting-wounded.
23 "Top 10 Outrageous VA Employee Behaviors," *Stars and Stripes*,
    June 24, 2014, http://www.stripes.com/news/veterans/top-10
    -outrageous-va-employee-behaviors-1.290426.
24 Ibid.
25 Ibid.
26 Ibid.
27 Ibid.
28 Ibid.

29 Mark Flatten, "Veterans Affairs Spies, Stonewalls on People Investigating It," *Washington Examiner,* July 15, 2014, http://washingtonexaminer.com/article/2550854#.U8VhMkl_fNc.twitter.

30 Ibid.

31 David Wood, "Scandal-Plagued VA Is Overpaying Workers by Millions of Dollars, Internal Audits Find," *Huffington Post,* July 10, 2014, http://www.huffingtonpost.com/2014/07/10/va-overpaid-workers_n_5564766.html.

32 Andrew Johnson, "Acting VA Secretary: Firing VA Employees Is a 'Bunch of Crap,'" *National Review Online,* June 16, 2014, http://www.nationalreview.com/corner/380476/acting-va-secretary-firing-va-employees-bunch-crap-andrew-johnson.

33 Ezra Klein, "Does the Government Run Health Care Better?" *Washington Post,* June 3, 2009, http://voices.washingtonpost.com/ezra-klein/2009/06/does_the_government_run_health.html.

34 Ibid.

35 Nicholas Kristof, "Health Care That Works," *New York Times,* September 2, 2009, http://www.nytimes.com/2009/09/03/opinion/03kristof.html.

36 Ibid.

37 Ibid.

38 Paul Krugman, "Vouchers for Veterans," *New York Times,* November 13, 2011, http://www.nytimes.com/2011/11/14/opinion/krugman-vouchers-for-veterans-and-other-bad-ideas.html?_r=0.

39 Daniel Halper, "Obamacare Now Estimated to Cost $2.6 Trillion in First Decade," *Weekly Standard,* July 11, 2012, http://www.weeklystandard.com/blogs/obamacare-now-estimated-cost-26-trillion-first-decade_648413.html.

40 Tim Kane, "Why Our Best Officers Are Leaving," *Atlantic,* January 4, 2011, http://www.theatlantic.com/magazine/archive/2011/01/why-our-best-officers-are-leaving/308346/.

41 J. R. Dunn, "Bureaucratic Failure," *American Thinker,* May 2, 2007, http://www.americanthinker.com/articles/2007/05/bureaucratic_failure.html.

42 Ibid

43 James Q. Wilson, "The Bureaucracy Problem," *National Affairs,* Spring 2012, http://www.nationalaffairs.com/publications/detail/the-bureaucracy-problem.

44 Roger Cheng, "Farewell Nokia: The Rise and Fall of a Mobile Pioneer," CNET, April 25, 2014, http://www.cnet.com/news /farewell-nokia-the-rise-and-fall-of-a-mobile-pioneer/.

CHAPTER SIX: THE DEPARTMENT OF JUSTICE—MAKING IT UP AS THEY GO ALONG

1 Charlie Savage, "Prosecutors Face Penalty in '08 Trial of Senator," *New York Times*, May 24, 2012, http://www.nytimes .com/2012/05/25/us/politics/2-prosecutors-in-case-of-senator-ted -stevens-are-suspended.html?_r=1.

2 Del Quentin Wilber, "Judge Orders Probe of Attorneys in Stevens Case," *Washington Post*, April 8, 2009, http://www.washingtonpost .com/wp-dyn/content/article/2009/04/07/AR2009040700338 .html.

3 Amanda Becker, "In Wake of Stevens Trial, Push to Reform Rules," *Roll Call*, March 17, 2012, http://www.rollcall.com/news/In-Wake -of-Stevens-Trial-Push-to-Reform-Rules-213184-1.html?pos =hftxt.

4 Ibid.

5 Ibid.

6 Savage, "Prosecutors Face Penalty in '08 Trial of a Senator."

7 Sidney Powell, "All the President's Muses: Obama and Prosecutorial Misconduct," *New York Observer*, June 13, 2014, http://observer .com/2014/06/all-the-presidents-muses-obama-and-prosecutorial -misconduct/. For further discussion of the Enron cases and Ms. Powell's extensive documentation of the case and alleged prosecutorial misconduct, see Sidney Powell, *Licensed to Lie: Exposing Corruption in the Department of Justice* (Dallas: Brown Books Publishing, 2014).

8 Editorial Board, "Rampant Prosecutorial Misconduct," *New York Times*, January 4, 2014, http://www.nytimes.com/2014/01/05 /opinion/sunday/rampant-prosecutorial-misconduct.html.

9 Brad Heath and Kevin McCoy, "Prosecutors' Conduct Can Tip Justice Scales," *USA Today*, September 23, 2010, http://usatoday30 .usatoday.com/news/washington/judicial/2010-09-22-federal -prosecutors-reform_N.htm.

10 See Powell, "All the President's Muses."

11 Fred Lucas, "Obama Has Touted al Qaeda's Demise 32 Times Since Benghazi Attack," CNSNews.com, November 1, 2012, http:// cnsnews.com/news/article/obama-touts-al-qaeda-s-demise-32-times -benghazi-attack-0.

12 Elias Groll, "5 Highlights from Susan Rice's Diplomatic Career," *Foreign Policy*, June 5, 2013, http://foreignpolicy.com/2013/06/05/5 -highlights-from-susan-rices-diplomatic-career/.

13 Powell, "All the President's Muses."

14 Ibid.

15 Ibid.

16 Ibid. The Fifth Circuit opinion Ms. Powell refers to is *United States of America v. James A. Brown, et al.* (Fifth Circuit Court of Appeal, 2006) and can be read at: http://www.ca5.uscourts.gov/opinions%5 Cpub%5C05/05-20319-CR0.wpd.pdf.

17 Ibid.

18 Sidney Powell, "War on Wall Street: Obama Appoints Anti-Business Activist Head of DOJ Division," *New York Observer*, June 25, 2014, http://observer.com/2014/06/war-on-wall-street -obama-appoints-anti-business-activist-head-of-doj-division/.

19 Ibid.

20 Craig Havighurst, "Why Gibson Guitar Was Raided by the Justice Department," NPR, August 31, 2011, http://www.npr.org/blogs /therecord/2011/08/31/140090116/why-gibson-guitar-was-raided -by-the-justice-department.

21 Ibid.

22 Bill Frezza, "Lumber Union Protectionists Incited SWAT Raid on My Factory, Says Gibson Guitar CEO," *Forbes*, May 26, 2014, http://www.forbes.com/sites/billfrezza/2014/05/26/lumber-union -protectionists-incited-swat-raid-on-my-factory-says-gibson-guitar -ceo/.

23 "Gibson Guitar Corp. Agrees to Resolve Investigation into Lacey Act Violations," Department of Justice Office of Public Affairs, press release, August 6, 2012, http://www.justice.gov/opa/pr/gibson -guitar-corp-agrees-resolve-investigation-lacey-act-violations.

24 See http://www2.gibson.com/Products/Electric-Guitars/Les-Paul /Gibson-USA/Government-Series-II-Les-Paul.aspx.

25 Nina Totenberg, "The Supreme Court Takes Up the Case of the Missing Fish," NPR, November 5, 2014.

26 Dahlia Lithwick, "Scales of Justice," *Slate*, November 5, 2014, http://www.slate.com/articles/news_and_politics/supreme_court _dispatches/2014/11/supreme_court_fish_destruction_of_evidence _case_jokes_outrage_and_hating.html.

27 Totenberg, "The Supreme Court Takes Up the Case of the Missing Fish."

28 Lithwick, "Scales of Justice."

29 Harvey Silverglate, *Three Felonies a Day: How the Feds Target the Innocent* (New York: Encounter Books, 2011).

30 L. Gordon Crovitz, "You Commit Three Felonies a Day," *Wall Street Journal*, September 27, 2009, http://www.wsj.com/articles/SB1 0001424052748704471504574438900830760842.

31 Ibid.

32 Jonah Bennett, "Operation Choke Point Hearing Reveals DOJ Threats and Strong-Arming," *Daily Caller*, July 18, 2014, http://dailycaller.com/2014/07/18/operation-choke-point-hearing-reveals-doj-threats-and-strong-arming/.

33 Ibid.

CHAPTER SEVEN: THE DEPARTMENT OF JUSTICE—PERMANENTLY RIGGING THE GAME

1 https://www.uschamber.com/sites/default/files/documents/files /SUEANDSETTLEREPORT-Final.pdf.

2 Larry Bell, "EPA's Secret and Costly 'Sue and Settle' Collusion with Environmental Organizations," *Forbes*, February 17, 2013, http:// www.forbes.com/sites/larrybell/2013/02/17/epas-secret-and-costly -sue-and-settle-collusion-with-environmental-organizations/.

3 https://www.uschamber.com/sites/default/files/documents/files /SUEANDSETTLEREPORT-Final.pdf.

4 Ibid.

5 Ibid.

6 Sharon LaFraniere, "U.S. Opens Spigot After Farmers Claim Discrimination," *New York Times*, April 25, 2013, http://www .nytimes.com/2013/04/26/us/farm-loan-bias-claims-often -unsupported-cost-us-millions.html?pagewanted=all&_r=0.

7 Ibid.

8 Ibid.

9 Ibid.

10 Ibid.

11 Ibid.

12 http://www.justice.gov/agencies/list.

13 "A Review of the Operations of the Voting Section of the Civil Rights Division," Office of the Inspector General Oversight and Review Division, March 2013, http://www.justice.gov/oig/reports /2013/s1303.pdf.

14 Ibid.

15 Ibid.

16 Ibid.

17 Ibid.

18 Ibid.

19 Ibid.

CHAPTER EIGHT: THE EPA: THE WORLD'S LEAST DEMOCRATIC AGENCY

1 https://www.uschamber.com/sites/default/files/documents/files
/SUEANDSETTLEREPORT-Final.pdf.

2 Andrew Simms, "Apocalypse? No. But Unless We Change Tack,
the Planet Is Running Out of Time," *Guardian*, March 1, 2013,
http://www.theguardian.com/environment/2013/mar/01/100
-months-apocalypse-warnings.

3 Kevin D. Williamson, "The Problem with Science," *National Review
Online*, July 7, 2014, http://www.nationalreview.com/article
/382067/problem-science-kevin-d-williamson.

4 Mark J. Perry, "18 Spectacularly Wrong Apocalyptic Predictions
Made Around the Time of the First Earth Day in 1970, Expect
More This Year," American Enterprise Institute, April 21,
2014, http://www.aei ideas.org/2014/04/18-spectacularly-wrong
-apocalyptic-predictions-made-around-the-time-of-the-first-earth
-day-in-1970-expect-more-this-year/.

5 Ibid.

6 Ibid.

7 Ruth Alexander, "Does a Child Die of Hunger Every 10 Seconds,"
BBC News Magazine, June 17, 2013, http://www.bbc.com/news
/magazine-22935692.

8 Perry, "18 Spectacularly Wrong Apocalyptic Predictions."

9 Ibid.

10 Ibid.

11 Ibid.

12 http://www.indexmundi.com/energy.aspx?product=oil&graph
=production.

13 Grant Smith, "U.S. Seen as Biggest Oil Producer After Overtaking
Saudi Arabia," Bloomberg, July 4, 2014, http://www.bloomberg
.com/news/2014-07-04/u-s-seen-as-biggest-oil-producer-after
-overtaking-saudi.html.

14 Perry, "18 Spectacularly Wrong Apocalyptic Predictions."

15 David Rose, "Global Warming Stopped 16 Years Ago, Reveals Met
Office Report Quietly Released . . . And Here Is the Chart to Prove
It," *Daily Mail*, October 16, 2012, http://www.dailymail.co.uk

/sciencetech/article-2217286/Global-warming-stopped-16-years
-ago-reveals-Met-Office-report-quietly-released—chart-prove-it
.html?ito=feeds-newsxml.

16 Michael Bastasch, "Top 5 Failed 'Snow Free' and 'Ice Free'
Predictions," *Daily Caller*, March 4, 2014, http://dailycaller
.com/2014/03/04/top-5-failed-snow-free-and-ice-free-predictions/.

17 Robert Zubrin, "The Truth About DDT and Silent Spring," *New
Atlantis*, September 27, 2012, http://www.thenewatlantis.com
/publications/the-truth-about-ddt-and-silent-spring. Zubrin's article
is an outstanding resource for anyone interested in a brief history of
DDT. I rely on it heavily here.

18 Ibid.

19 Ibid.

20 Ibid.

21 Ibid.

22 Ibid.

23 Ibid.

24 Ibid.

25 Ibid.

26 Ibid.

27 Ibid.

28 Ibid.

29 42 U.S.C. Section 7602(g).

30 Robert B. Semple Jr., "Remember Kyoto? Most Nations Don't,"
New York Times, December 3, 2011, http://www.nytimes.com/2011
/12/04/opinion/sunday/remember-kyoto-most-nations-dont.html.

31 *Massachusetts v. Environmental Protection Agency*, 549 U.S. 497
(2007).

32 http://www.epa.gov/climatechange/endangerment/.

33 http://www.epa.gov/climatechange/EPAactivities/regulatory
-initiatives.html.

34 Ibid.

35 Ibid.

36 "Obama Administration Finalizes Historic 54.5 MPG Fuel
Efficiency Standards," White House press release, August 28, 2012,
http://www.whitehouse.gov/the-press-office/2012/08/28/obama
-administration-finalizes-historic-545-mpg-fuel-efficiency
-standard.

37 "CAFÉ Standards Sacrifice Lives for Oil," Heartland Ideas, March
8, 2013, http://heartland.org/ideas/cafe-standards-sacrifice-lives-oil.

38 Juliet Eilperin, "Autos Must Average 54.5 MPG by 2025, New
EPA Standards Say," *Washington Post*, August 28, 2012, http://
www.washingtonpost.com/national/health-science/autos-must
-average-545-mpg-by-2025-new-epa-standards-are-expected-to
-say/2012/08/28/2c47924a-f117-11e1-892d-bc92fee603a7_story.html.

39 Ramesh Ponnuru, "Trampling Democracy to Fight Climate
Change," Bloomberg, June 9, 2014, http://www.bloombergview.com
/articles/2014-06-09/trampling-democracy-to-fight-climate-change.

40 Benjamin Goad, "House Republicans Take Aim at EPA Climate
Rules," *Hill*, July 15, 2014, http://thehill.com/regulation/212308
-panel-advances-spending-bill-that-would-block-epa-regs.

41 Christopher Helman, "EPA Official Not Only Touted 'Crucifying'
Oil Companies, He Tried It," *Forbes*, April 26, 2012, http://www
.forbes.com/sites/christopherhelman/2012/04/26/epa-official-not
-only-touted-crucifying-oil-companies-he-tried-it/.

42 Becket Adams, "EPA Official on Non-Compliant Companies:
'Hit Them as Hard as You Can' & 'Make Examples Out of Them,'
Cites Crucifixion," *Blaze*, April 25, 2012, http://www.theblaze.com
/stories/2012/04/25/epa-official-on-non-compliant-companies-hit
-them-as-hard-as-you-can%E2%80%99-make-examples-out-of
-them/.

43 Helman, "EPA Official Not Only Touted 'Crucifying' Oil
Companies, He Tried It."

44 Ibid.

45 "Top EPA Official Resigns After 'Crucify' Comment," Fox News,
April 30, 2012, http://www.foxnews.com/politics/2012/04/30/top
-epa-official-resigns-after-crucify-comment/.

46 Mark Hendrickson, "The EPA: The Worst of Many Rogue Federal
Agencies," *Forbes*, March 14, 2013, http://www.forbes.com/sites
/markhendrickson/2013/03/14/the-epa-the-worst-of-many-rogue
-federal-agencies/.

47 Ibid.

48 Ibid.

49 Ibid.

50 Benjamin Goad, "'Secret Science' Must End, Republicans Declare,"
Hill, February 6, 2014, http://thehill.com/regulation/energy
-environment/197701-gop-bill-would-outlaw-epas-secret-science.

51 Seth Shulman, "Smoke and Mirrors: Who's Really Fueling Those
Bogus EPA Attacks?" LiveScience, May 5, 2014, http://www
.livescience.com/45362-attacks-on-epa-bogus.html.

52 "Secret Science Reform Act: Another Attack on Science,"
   Observation Deck, May 6, 2014, http://observationdeck.io9.com
   /secret-science-reform-act-another-attack-on-science-1572468495.

53 John Fund, "E-mail Scandal at the EPA," *National Review Online*,
   January 5, 2013, http://www.nationalreview.com/articles/336995/e
   -mail-scandal-epa-john-fund.

54 Ibid.

55 Darren Samuelsohn and Jonathan Allen, "President Obama's
   Administration Slow-Walks New Rules," *Politico*, July 12, 2012,
   http://www.politico.com/news/stories/0712/78419.html.

56 http://www.landmarklegal.org/uploads/MemorandumInSupportof
   SanctionsFINALJULY24.pdf.

57 Stephen Dinan, "Newly Released Emails Show EPA Director's
   Extensive Use of Fictional Alter Ego," *Washington Times*, June 2,
   2013, http://www.washingtontimes.com/news/2013/jun/2/newly
   -released-emails-show-epa-directors-extensive/?utm_source=feedly.

58 Lenny Bernstein, "Workers Turned EPA Warehouse in Landover
   into Personal Rec Rooms, Audit Finds," *Washington Post*, June 5,
   2013, http://www.washingtonpost.com/national/health-science
   /workers-turned-epa-warehouse-in-landover-into-personal-rec
   -rooms-audit-finds/2013/06/05/ed5514fc-ce17-11e2-8845-d970ccb
   04497_story.html.

59 Katie Pavlich, "Senators Call Out the EPA for Leaking Private
   Info of Farmers to Radical Environmental Groups," Townhall.com,
   June 7, 2013, http://townhall.com/tipsheet/katiepavlich/2013/06/07
   /why-is-the-epa-leaking-private-farm-info-to-radical
   -environemental-groups-n1615456.

60 "EPA Claims It Has the Power to Garnish Wages Without Court
   Approval," Fox News, July 9, 2014, http://www.foxnews.com
   /politics/2014/07/09/epa-claims-it-has-power-to-garnish-wages
   -without-court-approval/.

CHAPTER NINE: THE NLRB: DOES OVERREACH HAVE ITS LIMITS?

1 Joel Kotkin, "How the South Will Rise to Power Again,"
   Forbes, January 31, 2013, http://www.forbes.com/sites/joel
   kotkin/2013/01/31/how-the-south-will-rise-to-power-again/.

2 Wendell Cox, "Moving to North Dakota: The New Census
   Estimates," New Geography, December 26, 2012, http://www
   .newgeography.com/content/003359-moving-north-dakota-the
   -new-census-estimates.

3 http://www.ops.fhwa.dot.gov/freight/freight_analysis/nat_freight
_stats/docs/11factsfigures/table1_2.htm.

4 Daniel Gross, "Big Three, Meet the 'Little Eight,'" *Slate*, December
13, 2008, http://www.slate.com/articles/business
/moneybox/2008/12/big_three_meet_the_little_eight.html.

5 Ibid.

6 Ibid.

7 John Schnapp, "The Long History of the UAW's Failed Southern
Strategy," *Wall Street Journal*, February 21, 2014, http://www.wsj
.com/news/articles/SB1000142405270230467550457939116333485
396.

8 "Heavy Hitters: Top All-Time Donors, 1989-2014," OpenSecrets
.org, 2014, https://www.opensecrets.org/orgs/list.php

9 Tom McGinty and Brody Mullins, "Political Spending by Unions
Far Exceeds Direct Donations," *Wall Street Journal*, July 10, 2012,
http://www.wsj.com/news/articles/SB10001424052702304782404577
488584031850026.

10 Ibid.

11 http://www.nlrb.gov/sites/default/files/attachments/basic-page/node
-3310/cpt_19-ca-032431_boeing__4-20-2011_complaint_and_not
_hrg.pdf.

12 Editorial, "Boeing and the NLRB," *New York Times*, April 25, 2011,
http://www.nytimes.com/2011/04/26/opinion/26tue2.html.

13 Ibid.

14 Tim Pawlenty, "The Federal Government vs. Job Creation,"
National Review Online, April 28, 2011, http://www.nationalreview
.com/corner/265917/federal-government-vs-job-creation-tim
-pawlenty.

15 Andrew Stiles, "GOP vs. NLRB," *National Review Online*, June 17,
2011, http://www.nationalreview.com/corner/269947/gop-vs-nlrb
-andrew-stiles.

16 Ibid.

17 Ibid.

18 Ibid.

19 Ibid.

20 Kendra Marr, "South Carolina Boeing Factory Turns Sour for
Obama," *Politico*, September 23, 2011, http://www.politico.com
/news/stories/0911/64199.html.

21 Kyung M. Song, "NLRB's Top Lawyer Still Feels Fallout from
Boeing, Union Case," *Seattle Times*, February 12, 2012, http://

seattletimes.com/html/businesstechnology/2017551565_solomon20.html.

22 Ibid.

23 Steven Green, "Labor Board Drops Case Against Boeing After Union Reaches Accord," *New York Times*, December 9, 2011, http://www.nytimes.com/2011/12/10/business/labor-board-drops-case -against-boeing.html?_r=0.

24 Neal E. Boudette, "Union Suffers Big Loss at Tennessee VW Plant," *Wall Street Journal*, February 15, 2014, http://online.wsj .com/news/articles/SB1000142405270230443410457938254122630 73 68?mg=reno64-wsj.

25 Sean Higgins, "Bob Corker, Other Tennessee Republicans Refuse Subpoenas from Big Labor," *Washington Examiner*, April 18, 2014, http://washingtonexaminer.com/bob-corker-other-tennessee -republicans-refuse-subpoenas-from-big-labor/article/2547438.

26 Ibid.

27 Steven Greenhouse, "UAW Drops Appeal of VW Vote in Tennessee," *New York Times*, April 21, 2014, http://www.nytimes .com/2014/04/22/business/auto-workers-union-drops-appeal-in -vw-vote.html.

28 Jay Sekulow, "Obama Cannot Set Senate Rules," American Center for Law and Justice, http://aclj.org/us-constitution/jay-sekulow -obama-cannot-set-senate-rules.

29 Ibid.

30 http://media.aclj.org/pdf/Noel%20Canning%20S%20%20Ct%20 %20amicus%20-%20final.pdf

31 NLRB v. Noel Canning, Docket No. 12-1281, 2014, http://www .law.cornell.edu/supremecourt/text/12-1281.

32 Melanie Trottman, "Supreme Court Ruling Forces NLRB to Scramble to Revisit Cases," *Wall Street Journal*, June 26, 2014, http://www.wsj.com/articles/supreme-court-ruling-forces-nlrb-to -scramble-to-redecide-cases-1403818711.

CHAPTER ELEVEN: RESIST: THE GOVERNMENT CAN BE BEATEN

1 Editorial, "Emily's Rights," *New York Sun*, May 20, 2003, http://www.nysun.com/editorials/emilys-rights/78005/.

2 *McConnell v. Federal Election Commission*, 540 U.S. 93 (2003), http://www.law.cornell.edu/supct/html/02-1674.ZS.html.

3 "FFRF Complaint to Move Jesus Statue from Montana Mountain," Freedom from Religion Foundation, October 20, 2011, http://ffrf

.org/news/news-releases/item/2824-ffrf-complaint-to-move-jesus -statue-from-montana-mountain.

4 Jeff Schapiro, "Congressman Wants Forest Service to Let Jesus Statue Stay," *Christian Post*, October 19, 2011, http://www .christianpost.com/news/congressman-wants-forest-service-to-let -jesus-statue-stay-58718/.

5 See http://aclj.org/american-heritage/defending-montana-jesus-statue.

6 See http://c0391070.cdn2.cloudfiles.rackspacecloud.com/pdf/letter -forest-service-support-montana-jesus-statue-war-memorial.pdf.

7 Billy Hallowell, " 'A Significant Victory': Atheists Lose Battle over Jesus Statue atop Montana Mountain," *Blaze*, January 31, 2012, http://www.theblaze.com/stories/2012/01/31/a-significant-victory -atheists-lose-battle-over-jesus-statue-atop-montana-mountain/.

8 Vince Devlin, "Atheists 'Shocked' by Judge's Decision Allowing Big Mountain Jesus," *Missoulian*, June 26, 2013, http://missoulian.com /news/local/atheists-shocked-by-judge-s-decision-allowing-big -mountain-jesus/article_a658be68-dda4-11e2-98a2-001a4bcf887a .html.

9 http://www.fcc.gov/what-we-do.

10 Dan Fletcher, "The Fairness Doctrine," *Time*, February 20, 2009, http://content.time.com/time/nation/article/0,8599,1880786,00 .html.

11 Ibid.

12 http://transition.fcc.gov/bureaus/ocbo/FCC_Final_Research _Design_6_markets.pdf.

13 Ibid.

14 Ibid.

15 Ajit Pai, "The FCC Wades into the Newsroom," *Wall Street Journal*, February 10, 2014, http://online.wsj.com/news/articles/SB10001424 052702304680904579366903828260732.

16 http://aclj.org/free-speech-2/no-government-monitors-in-newsrooms.

17 Jay Sekulow, "Is Obama Trying to Kill a Free Press?" Fox News, February 20, 2014, http.//www.foxnews.com/opinion/2014/02/20 /is-obama-trying-to-kill-free-press/.

18 http://www.berrybest.com/relay14.asp?df=022114&pf=DOC-325722 A1.pdf.

19 Wesley Pruden, "Pruden: The Cheap Tricks of the Game," *Washington Times*, October 3, 2013, http://www.washingtontimes .com/news/2013/oct/3/pruden-the-cheap-tricks-of-the-game/.

20 http://media.aclj.org/pdf/letter-to-national-park-service.pdf.

CHAPTER TWELVE: ACCOUNTABILITY AND DEMOCRACY: THE MANDATORY ELEMENTS OF REFORM

1 Charles Clark, "Reinventing Government—Two Decades Later," *Government Executive*, April 26, 2013, http://www.govexec.com /management/2013/04/what-reinvention-wrought/62836/.

2 Stuart Shapiro, "The Fate of Bush's Regulatory Reforms," CATO Institute, http://object.cato.org/sites/cato.org/files/serials/files /regulation/2009/2/v32n1-3.pdf.

3 "Executive Order 13563—Improving Regulation and Regulatory Overview," http://www.whitehouse.gov/the-press-office/2011/01/18 /improving-regulation-and-regulatory-review-executive-order.

4 https://ourpublicservice.org/issues/modernize-management/civil -service-reform.php.

5 Joe Davidson, "Partnership for Public Service Urges Civil Service Reform; Unions Object," *Washington Post*, April 1, 2014, http://www .washingtonpost.com/blogs/federal-eye/wp/2014/04/01/partnership -for-public-service-urges-civil-service-reform-unions-object/.

6 Andrew Glass, "Reagan Fires 11,000 Striking Air Traffic Controllers Aug. 5, 1981," *Politico*, August 5, 2008, http://www .politico.com/news/stories/0808/12292.html.

7 *INS v. Chadha*, 462 U.S. 919 (1983).

8 Larry Sellers, "The 2010 Amendments to the APA: Legislature Overrides Veto of Law to Require Legislative Ratification of 'Million Dollar Rules,'" *Florida Bar Journal*, May 2011, http:// www.floridabar.org/DIVCOM/JN/JNJournal01.nsf/c0d731e 03de9828d852574580042ae7a/f0d37b157bd38e3e8525788100696dbb! OpenDocument&Highlight=0,lawrence,sellers*.

CHAPTER THIRTEEN: RESTORE OR PERISH

1 "Political Polarization in the American Public," Pew Research Center for the People and the Press, June 12, 2014, http://www .people-press.org/2014/06/12/political-polarization-in-the -american-public/.

2 Ibid.

3 Ibid.

4 Chart reproduced in Chris Cillizza, "America Really Is Two Different Political Countries These Days," *Washington Post*, July 28, 2014, http://www.washingtonpost.com/blogs/the-fix/wp/2014/07 /28/america-really-is-two-different-political-countries-these-days/.

5 Maeve P. Carey, "Counting Regulations: An Overview of Rulemaking, Types of Federal Regulations, and Pages in the

Federal Register," Congressional Research Service, November 26, 2014, http://fas.org/sgp/crs/misc/R43056.pdf.

6 George Will, "Amend the Constitution to Control Federal Spending," *Washington Post*, April 9, 2014, http://www.washington post.com/opinions/george-will-amend-the-constitution-to -control-federal-spending/2014/04/09/00fa7df6-bf3c-11e3-bcec -b71ee10e9bc3_story.html.

7 Buzz Brockway, "Georgia Becomes First State to Pass Convention of States Resolution," *RedState*, March 6, 2014, http://www.redstate .com/diary/buzzbrockway/2014/03/06/georgia-become-first-state -pass-convention-states-resolution/.

8 See http://media.aclj.org/pdf/Am-Atheists decision-July-28.pdf.

AFTERWORD

1 http://www.judiciary.senate.gov/meetings/revisiting-irs-targeting -progress-of-agency-reforms-and-congressional-options.

2 *Revisiting IRS Targeting: Progress of Agency Reforms and Congressional Options, U.S. Senate Committee on the Judiciary, Subcommittee on Oversight, Agency Action, Federal Rights and Federal Courts*, 114th Cong. (2015) (statement of Lawrence M. Noble, Senior Counsel, Campaign Legal Center), http://www.judiciary.senate.gov/imo /media/doc/07-29-15%20Noble%20Testimony.pdf adfafg.

3 http://www.judiciary.senate.gov/imo/media/doc/07-29-15%20 Noble%20Testimony.pdf.

4 http://www.judicialwatch.org/press-room/press-releases/jw-obtains -irs-documents-showing-lerner-contact-doj-potential-prosecution -tax-exempt-groups/.

5 Ibid.

6 http://www.judicialwatch.org/wp-content/uploads/2014/04 /JW1559-0001051.pdf.

7 *Z Street v. Koskinen*, 44 F. Supp. 3d 48, 52 (D.D.C. 2014) (quoting Complaint ¶¶ 24–25).

8 *Ibid.* at *12, *15, **17–18.

9 *Ibid.* at *5 ("Z Street alleges that the IRS has an 'Israel Special Policy,' which mandates that applications from organizations holding views about Israel inconsistent with those espoused by the Obama administration be scrutinized differently and at greater length.")

10 Ibid. at **12, 17.

11 *Ibid.* at ^^16–17.

12 *Honesty: A Refreshing, But Legally Lethal, Policy for IRS*, American Center for Law and Justice, May 2015, http://aclj.org/free-speech /honesty-a-refreshing-but-legally-lethal-policy-for-irs.

13 Ibid.

14 http://www.breitbart.com/big-government/2015/10/06/rep-jim -jordan-says-house-will-impeach-head-irs/.

15 IRS Examination Selection, IRS Should Strengthen Internal Controls for Exempt Organization Selection: Testimony Before the Subcommittee on Oversight, Committee on Ways & Means, House of Representatives, 114th Cong. (2015) (statement of Jay McTigue, Director, Strategic Issues, U.S. GAO).

16 Ibid.

17 http://www.washingtontimes.com/news/2015/mar/31/john -koskinen-not-the-irs-of-years-past/.

18 http://www.cnn.com/2015/10/23/politics/lois-lerner-no-charges -doj-tea-party/index.html.

19 http://www.foxnews.com/politics/2014/02/03/not-even-smidgen- corruption-obama-downplays-irs-other-scandals/.

20 https://www.washingtonpost.com/politics/federal_government /obama-donor-leading-justice-departments-irs-investigation/2014 /01/09/980c010a-796a-11e3-8963-b4b654bcc9b2_story.html.

21 https://www.washingtonpost.com/news/volokh-conspiracy/wp/2015 /06/25/in-king-v-burwell-chief-justice-roberts-rewrites-the-ppaca -in-order-to-save-it-again/.

22 This simply means that the court finds legitimate areas of dispute and inquiry that cannot be disregarded by dismissing the case or declaring a summary judgment for one side or the other. Therefore, the legal issues must be briefed and argued before the court.

23 In a civil lawsuit, either party can submit a motion for summary judgment, which argues that based on the facts pled by both sides, there are actually no legitimate legal questions to be answered by the court and therefore a judgment can be issued for that side without any further discovery, briefing, or hearings.

ACKNOWLEDGMENTS

The thesis of this book—that bureaucrats have created an unconstitutional fourth branch of government—is something that we have litigated for almost three decades. My wife, Pam, has been my biggest supporter since I was eighteen years old. She still is, forty-one years later. Without her, none of my work would be possible, and her late-night critiques made this a better book. I also say *we* because these cases and issues move forward because of a team effort. This book, like so much of our work, represents the collective efforts of our team. My colleague, Major David French, is one of the best writers and thinkers that I have worked with. His ability to take complex concepts, issues, and ideas and put them into a coherent text is legendary. Thank you, David, for sharing your gifts. Our editor, Becky Nesbitt, kept us moving on pace and provided invaluable insight. Jonathan Merkh, our publisher, is in our hall of fame for his enthusiasm for this project. In fact, the entire team at Simon & Schuster, Howard Books, is deserving of our collective thanks. Curtis Wallace brought vision, energy, and drive to this project. His wise counsel made a key difference for this book. I also want to thank Carolyn Davis for reviewing this book, as only a librarian can. To Carolyn's husband and my friend, Joe Davis, whose advice I cherish, thank you.

INDEX

ABC News: IRS audit of
   conservatives story by, 74–75
abortion, 32–33, 60, 80. *See also*
   pro-life movement; *specific
   organization*
Abortion Must End Now (AMEN), 79
Abramowitz, Alan, 248
accountability
   and blueprint for change, 208,
      233–37, 241
   of civil service, 237
   of Clinton (Hillary), 7
   of federal bureaucracy, 10, 19,
      29–30, 33, 40, 56, 58, 111, 121,
      199, 229, 233–37, 256
   of federal prosecutors, 137, 147
   and freedom of information, 5
   of government, 5
   importance of, 29–30, 40, 264, 265
   job security and, 34–35, 233–37
   and Koskinen impeachment, 265
   laws about, 14
   and lawsuits, 261
   and partisanship, 56
   and prosecutorial misconduct, 137
   reform and, 40, 165, 205, 229,
      231–32, 233–37
   resistance and, 208
   as systemic problem, 163
   three R's and, 40
   truth about government, 34–36
   *See also specific federal department or
      agency*

"additional child tax credits"
   (ACTC), 107–9
"administrative leaves," 35
adoptions
   complexity of, 91, 93
   cost of, 91
   and evangelical adoption
      movement, 97–98
   foreign, 90, 91, 93
   IRS audits and, 91–98, 209, 210,
      240, 245
   socio-economic background and,
      94–95
   of special needs children, 95, 96
   tax credits for, 91–98, 240
   transracial, 97–98
advocacy issues
   and blueprint for change, 208
   NAACP v. Patterson case and,
      69–70
   nonprofit corporations and, 66
age: and political contributions,
   214
agencies, U.S.
   creation of, 48
   limiting of rulemaking authority
      of, 40
   partisanship in, 54–58
   power of, 48, 49
   "rulemaking process" and, 49–51
   as threat to democracy, 23
   *See also shadow government; specific
      person or agency*

Agriculture Department, U.S.:
    Pigford case and, 155–58
air pollution, 169, 176–81, 185
air traffic controllers: Reagan's
    firing of, 234
Alito, Samuel, 61
Allen, Bill, 134, 135
American Center for Law and
    Justice (ACLJ)
    adoption cases and, 90, 94, 95
    and FCC newsroom monitors
      controversy, 221–22
    FFRE case and, 217
    fight against Obama
      administration by, 256–57
    and FOIA requests, 187, 267
    founding of, 45–46
    and how to resist, 226–27
    IRS lawsuits filed by, 67, 71–72, 80,
      150–51, 152, 227, 249, 256–57,
      261–63, 264, 267
    and IRS "loss" of evidence, 86
    and IRS war on Tea Party, 71–72
    military veterans at, 113–14
    and National Park Service
      blockade of National Mall,
      225–27
    and Obama's recess appointments
      to NLRB, 203
    offices of, 21, 22, 47
    purpose of, 263, 264
    restoration efforts at, 249
    Sekulow at, 256
    victories of, 256
    See also specific litigation
American Civil Liberties Union
    (ACLU), 24, 25, 66
American Enterprise Institute
    (AEI), 26–27, 168
American exceptionalism
    and blueprint for change, 242, 250
    as goal of restoration, 206
    and how bills become laws, 43–44,
      57
    immigration and, 41–42, 43, 57, 58
    and improving the republic, 44–45
    IRS activities and, 28

liberals and, 42–43
partisanship in federal bureaucracy
    and, 57–58
questions about, 40
Sekulow's family background and,
    41–42, 43, 57, 58
three R's and, 40
what is, 43–44
American greatness, 254–55
American Revolution, 60
American Thinker magazine, 127, 157
Americans for Campaign Reform,
    258
Americans with Disabilities Act,
    159–60
amnesty rallies, 37–38, 226
anger, public, 248
anthrax attack (2001), 22
apathy: and advancement of
    ideology, 222, 223
appeals: by federal employees, 236
Arab Spring: Clinton emails about,
    12
Arizona Republic: VA wait-time
    story in, 114, 115
Armendariz, Al, 182–83, 184
Army, U.S.: and DDT, 171–73
Arthur Andersen LLP case, 139
Arthur, Chester A., 53
Article V (Constitution), 251–52
Association of International
    Automobile Manufacturers, 193
at-will employees, 165, 233, 234–35
atheists, 79–80, 216–17, 253
audits
    and knowing your rights, 210
    legal and illegal, 210
    of VA facilities, 115, 116
    See also audits, IRS
audits, IRS
    "additional child tax credits" and,
      107–9
    adoptions and, 91–98, 209, 240,
      245
    automotive industry and cost of
      cars, 180
    and burden of proof, 240–41

congressional limitations on, 240–41
of conservatives, 74–76, 227–28
and Earned Income Tax Credits, 98–101
fuel standards and, 179, 180, 193
of Grassley, 76–78
jobs in, 192–95
legitimate, 227–28
and power of IRS, 240
unions and, 193–95, 200–201
Avocado rule: language concerning, 50
awareness: and how to resist, 225–26, 227

bailouts, 59
balanced budget amendment, 252
banks
Dodd-Frank bill and, 48–49
DOJ targeting of, 146
Bedford VA Medical Center (Massachusetts): scandals involving, 119
Begich, Mark, 34, 133
Bell, Larry, 153
Benghazi, Libya: attack on, 137
Biden, Joe, 182
Big Mountain (Montana): Jesus statue on, 216–17
Bill of Rights, 44–45, 208
bills
and how bills become laws, 46–51, 57
See also specific bill
Billy Graham Evangelistic Association, 75
bin Laden, Osama: and SEAL's disability claim, 118
blueprint for change
and accountability, 208, 233–37, 241
and American exceptionalism, 242, 250
and American greatness, 254–55
challenges and, 210–11, 212–13

Constitution and, 232, 238–42, 244–55
despair and, 252–54
divisiveness and, 246–48
and education, 213, 242, 249–50
and knowing your rights, 208, 209–11
and power, 246
reform and, 205–6, 212, 229–30, 231–37, 239–42
resistance and, 208, 212, 213, 214–29
restoration and, 208, 212, 213, 237–39, 242, 249–55
and rights, 208, 209–11, 235–36, 242, 245–46
Boehner, John, 203
Boeing Corp.: unions-NLRB and, 195–99, 201
Bopp, James, 62–64
Borg (fictional character), 207
Bottini, Joseph, 135
Breyer, Stephen, 203
Browner, Carol, 185–86
burden of proof, 240–41
bureaucracy, federal
accountability of, 10, 19, 29–30, 33, 40, 56, 58, 111, 121, 199, 229, 233–37, 256
as activist government, 38–39
anonymity in, 199
as blocking justice and rule of law, 1
"by any means necessary" system of, 40
classification of information by, 11–12
as Clinton (Hillary) protector, 1, 5, 7, 9, 11, 12, 13, 19
complexity of, 121, 209
Congress compared with, 29
congressional oversight of, 229, 237–39, 242
Constitution and, 10, 30, 244–45, 251–52, 259
corruption in, 1, 3, 10, 29, 30, 33–34, 37, 57, 58, 89, 149, 256

bureaucracy, federal (*cont.*)
  and "creative destruction" concept,
    128–29
  evasion of questions by, 4
  as extension of Democratic Party,
    38, 55, 56
  fixing problems of, 128–29
  funding for, 129
  and gaps in laws, 31–33
  and government "shutdown," 223
  growth of, 36–37, 46
  and how bills become laws, 46–51,
    57
  and how bureaucracies fail, 125–29
  human nature in, 127
  importance of, 223
  incompetency of, 1, 3, 29, 33–34,
    37, 57, 58
  language of, 50
  liberals and, 128
  military as, 126–27
  overreach of, 237
  partisanship in, 29, 30, 37–40,
    54–58, 65, 109, 149, 181, 205, 251,
    256, 258
  power of, 19, 29, 57, 58, 65, 111,
    128, 190, 199, 229, 232, 251–52,
    256, 264
  presidential appointments to,
    148–49
  reform of, 39–40, 197, 205–6, 212,
    229–30, 231–37, 239–42, 256,
    266–68
  resistance to, 195–99, 229
  and restoration of constitutional
    democracy, 238–42, 249–55
  rewards for, 129
  "rulemaking process" and, 48–51
  self-correction of, 229
  as shadow government, 29, 46
  stonewalling by, 267
  targeting by, 261
  as threat to democracy, 37, 46, 89,
    259
  three R's and, 39–40
  transitioning of, 245
  See also employees, federal; job

  security; *specific department,
    agency, or issue*
Bush, George W., 22, 59, 132, 154,
    163, 214, 231
"by any means necessary" system,
    40

Caldwell, Leslie, 139
"call to action": resistance and,
    225–26, 227
Camp, Dave, 75–76, 85
Campaign Reform Act, 214, 215
Canada: freedom in, 57–58
Canning, Noel, 203, 204
carbon dioxide: as air pollutant,
    177–78, 179
cars. *See* automotive industry
Carson, Rachel, 174
Carter, Jimmy, 45
CATO Institute, 53
Center for Immigration Studies, 107
Center for Responsive Politics, 56
challenges
  and blueprint for change, 210–11,
    212–13
  forms of, 211
  and knowing your rights, 210–11
  and taking the offensive, 212–13
Chamber of Commerce, U.S.: and
    "sue and settle" cases, 152, 154,
    166–67
Chattanooga, Tennessee: and
    Volkswagen-UAW-NLRB
    controversy, 200–201
checks and balances, system of, 45,
    46, 204, 206, 232, 237
children
  and "additional child tax credits,"
    107
  adoption of, 90–98
  education of, 249–50
  foreign, 90, 91, 93
  Linchpins of Liberty and, 249–50
  political contributions of, 214–15
  special needs, 95, 96
China: as origin of cyberattacks, 13

Christian Broadcasting Network, 63
Christian Coalition, 62–64, 78
Chrysler Corporation, 193, 200
churches
 IRS monitoring of free speech in,
  79–81
 See also religion
CIA (Central Intelligence Agency)
 and Clinton emails, 11
 and Petraeus case, 17
Cigna Health, 61
Circuit Court of Appeals
 D.C., 105–6, 204, 262, 263,
  266–67
 Fifth, 138
 Fourth, 105
 Ninth, 136
*Citizens for a Strong New Hampshire,
 Inc. v. Internal Revenue Service,*
 267
Citizens for Self-Governance, 252
Citizens United v. FEC case (2010),
 59–61, 247
civil disobedience: peaceful, 225–27
Civil Rights Act, 159
Civil Rights Division (Justice
 Department), 149–65
civil rights movement, 60, 254
civil service
 accountability and, 237
 "administrative leave" rules of, 115
 and blueprint for change, 208,
  233–37
 and career life and death, 233
 and individual liability, 235
 and penalties for violation of
  constitutional rights, 235–36
 private sector compared with,
  233–37
 reform of, 40, 164–65, 233–37
 See also employees, federal; job
  security
Civil War, 171, 253
Clean Air Act, 153, 154, 176
Clean Water Act, 153
"climate change"
 democracy and, 176–81

EPA and, 168, 176–81
and growth of federal bureaucracy,
 36
Supreme Court decision about,
 178
Clinton administration: and "sue
 and settle" cases, 154
Clinton, Bill, 1, 2, 124, 138–39
Clinton, Hillary
 accountability of, 7
 aides to, 6
 bureaucracy as protector of, 1, 5, 7,
  9, 11, 12, 13
 civil cases against, 15
 criminal investigation/liability of,
  8–9, 10, 11, 15, 19
 cyberattacks on, 13
 donors for, 2
 elections of 2016 and, 13, 18
 email of, 2, 3, 4–9, 10–19
 investigations/reviews of, 7, 8–9,
  10, 11, 12–14
 laws pertaining to, 14–19
 legal case against, 13–14
 power of, 1–2
 as source for Hollywood ideas, 1
 violation of laws by, 2, 7, 15,
  17–18
Clinton Foundation, 2, 11
Club of Rome, 173
CNN: and VA wait-time scandal,
 116
CNS News: immigration story by,
 108
Coalition for Life, 77
Coalition for Life of Iowa, 77–79
Coburn, Tom, 118–20
Coffin, Shannen, 18
Colmery-O'Neil VA Medical Center
 (Kansas): sexual abuse at, 118
competition: among states, 197
conferences, IRS, 110–11
confidential information
 DOJ sharing of, 163, 164, 165
 EPA sharing of, 189–90
 IRS disclosure of conservatives',
  72–74, 229

Congress, U.S.
  and ACLJ fight for freedom and
    justice, 257, 264, 265
  adoption tax credits and, 91, 92, 95
  and air pollution, 176
  Article V of the Constitution and,
    251–52
  and blueprint for change, 251–52
  checks and balances on, 45
  Citizens United v. FEC case and,
    60–61
  and Clinton emails, 5, 6, 11
  and dangers to democracy, 259–60
  and DOJ Civil Rights Division
    report, 160–61
  and DOJ prosecution of Stevens,
    135
  Earned Income Tax Credits and,
    98–99
  environmentalism and, 171, 176
  EPA rulemaking and, 178
  and FCC newsroom monitors
    controversy, 122, 222
  federal bureaucracy as subject of,
    229
  federal bureaucracy compared
    with, 29
  functions of, 22
  and gaps in laws, 31–33, 48–49
  gridlock in, 30–31
  and how bills become laws, 47, 49,
    57
  and how to resist, 226
  importance of legislative
    ratification by, 238–39
  IRS and, 24, 71, 84, 85, 86–88,
    109, 240–41, 256, 257–59,
    264–65
  Koskinen testimony before, 259,
    264–65
  and laws about government
    information, 18
  legislative veto by, 237–38
  National Park Service actions and,
    226
  Noble's testimony before, 257–59
  ObamaCare and, 104

  and Obama's 2010 State of the
    Union speech, 60–61
  oversight of federal bureaucracy
    by, 229, 237–39, 242
  Pigford case and, 155, 156
  power of, 22
  and presidential vetoes, 47, 238
  and prosecutorial misconduct, 136
  public anger at, 248
  and reform of federal bureaucracy,
    40
  and resistance, 208
  and rewards for bureaucratic
    failures, 129
  and rulemaking by agencies and
    departments, 181
  "rulemaking process" and, 49,
    178–79
  security for members of, 22
  Sekulow testimonies before, 256,
    257
  Shulman's comments about IRS
    to, 71
  and VA "bugging" of
    congressional investigators, 120,
    122
  VA wait-time scandal and, 114,
    115, 117
  and writing regulations, 145
  See also House of Representatives,
    U.S.; Senate, U.S.; *specific
    committee or legislation*
Congressional Review Act, 250
conservatives
  and Boeing–labor union–NLRB
    controversy, 197, 198, 199
  confidential information about,
    72–74, 163, 164, 165
  contributions to, 260
  criminal prosecution for tax
    violations by, 26
  and criminalization of
    conservative speech, 81–83, 84,
    86
  and delays in processing
    applications for tax-exempt
    status, 23–24, 25, 26, 73, 256–65

as DOJ employees, 158–65
and FCC newsroom monitors
  controversy, 218, 221
IRS audits of, 74–76, 227–28
IRS disclosure of confidential
  information about, 72–74, 229
IRS-DOJ collusion concerning, 24
as IRS targets, 23–24, 35, 45,
  61–89, 145–46, 150, 227–29,
  256–65, 267
and partisanship of federal
  bureaucracy, 37, 38
tax-exempt statistics about, 67
and Volkswagen-UAW-NLRB
  controversy, 201
See also Lerner, Lois: "apology" of;
  Tea Party; specific organization or
  person
Constitution, U.S.
  Article V of, 10, 20, 244–45,
    251–52, 259
  and blueprint for change, 232,
    238–42, 244–55
  and branches of government,
    23–24, 57, 232
  federal bureaucracy as danger to,
    30, 244–45
  federal bureaucracy as subject to,
    10, 20, 229, 244–45, 251–52, 259
  as framework for reform, 232
  functions of, 44
  and how bills become laws, 47, 57
  and image of Justice Department,
    260
  importance of, 244
  and limitations on power, 151
  ratification of, 60
  resistance and, 208
  restoration of, 40, 58, 238–42,
    244–55
  and targeting of Americans, 264
  See also shadow government; specific
    branch, clause, or amendment
Constitutional Convention (1787),
  44
Corker, Bob, 201
corporations

Citizens United v. FEC case and,
  59–61
and expansion of criminal laws,
  144–46
foreign, 60–61, 184, 193, 197
See also specific corporation
corruption
  and comparison of Congress and
    federal bureaucracy, 29
  in federal bureaucracy, 1, 3, 10, 29,
    30, 33–34, 37, 57, 58, 89, 149, 256
  potential for government, 199
  shadow government and, 28–29
  and Stevens prosecution, 132–35
  See also specific agency, department,
    or issue
Councilman, Bradford, 144
"creative destruction," 128–29
Criminal Division (Justice
  Department), 130–47
Criminal Investigation Unit (IRS),
  83, 96
criminalization of conservative
  speech, 81–83, 86
"cultural genocide": transracial
  adoptions as, 97–98
cyberattacks
  and Clinton emails, 13
  See also hackers

Dallas, Texas: EPA "Region 6"
  Office in, 182–83
DDT: banning of, 171–76, 184
Declaration of Independence, 244
Defense Department, U.S.
  partisanship in, 56
  and Petraeus case, 17
DeMint, Jim, 199
democracy
  "climate change" and, 176–81
  EPA and, 23, 166, 167–71, 176–81
  and partisanship in DOJ, 149, 150
  and partisanship in federal
    bureaucracy, 39
  questions about constitutional, 40
  reform and, 231, 237

democracy (*cont.*)
 restoration of constitutional, 40,
  58, 238–42, 244–55
 and sanctions for prosecutorial
  misconduct, 147
 threats to constitutional, 46, 89,
  259–60
 See also blueprint for change
Democratic Party
 and divisiveness among
  Americans, 246, 247–48
 DOJ and, 149
 environmentalism and, 180
 EPA and, 177
 federal bureaucracy as extension
  of, 38, 55, 56
 government "shutdown" and, 223
 IRS and, 155
 labor and, 194–95
 and "loss" of IRS email, 84
 National Park Service actions and,
  224, 226
 NLRB and, 204
 ObamaCare and, 125
 partisanship in federal bureaucracy
  and, 38, 55, 56, 109, 149, 155
 and rise of Tea Party, 59, 60
 socio-economic background and, 99
 See also liberals
despair
 and blueprint for change, 252–54
 importance of fighting against,
  252–54
"destruction creation" concept, 129
disability claims, VA, 117–18
discrimination
 and DOJ report about Voting
  Section operations, 160–61
 need for protection from political,
  165
 Pigford case and, 155–58
 and reform of civil service, 234–35
divisiveness, American: and need for
  change, 246–48
Docs4PatientCare, 75
Dodd-Frank bill, 48–49
drones: and Clinton emails, 11

drugs: and VA scandals, 119
due process, 211
Dunn, J. R., 127

Earned Income Tax Credits, 98–101,
  154, 155
Earthjustice, 152, 153
Ebola virus: doctor's fight against,
  254
Echols, Emily, 214–15
Economic Policy Institute, 193
Economist: and VA disability claims
  story, 117–18
economy
 environmentalism and, 177,
  178–79
 jobs and, 193
education
 and blueprint for change, 213, 242,
  249–50
 of children, 249–50
 and reform of public schools, 233
 resistance and, 213
 restoration and, 213, 249–50
Education Department, U.S., 56
efficiency: and how bureaucracies
  fail, 125
Ehrlich, Paul, 169
elections
 and *Citizens United v. FEC* case,
  60–61
 funding for, 60–61
 importance of, 29
 and need for reform, 268
 partisanship in federal bureaucracy
  and, 29, 55–56
 See also specific election
elections of 2004, 55
elections of 2008, 33–34, 55, 59, 133
elections of 2010, 26–27, 65
elections of 2012
 and Boeing–labor union–NLRB
  controversy, 197–98
 disclosure of conservatives'
  confidential information and,
  72–74

EPA and, 188, 245
gridlock and, 31
IRS activities and, 26–28, 72–74
partisanship in federal bureaucracy
   and, 55, 56
socio-economic class votes in, 99
elections of 2014, 267
elections of 2016, 13, 18
email
   classified, 4, 6, 7, 8, 11, 12, 17–18
   of Clinton (Hillary), 2, 3, 4–9,
      10–19
   EPA, 187–88, 245
   laws/regulations about
      preservation of, 14–15
   of Lerner, 13, 64, 81–83, 84–85,
      87–88, 258, 259, 260, 267
   of Powell (Colin), 7
   top secret, 4, 6, 12–13
employees, federal
   "absent without leave," 120
   on "administrative leave," 115
   appeals by, 236
   at-will, 165, 233, 234–35
   and blueprint for change, 241
   comfortable environment for EPA,
      189
   firing/termination of, 52–54, 115,
      121, 122, 135, 233, 234–35, 236
   ideology and, 155–65
   incentive structure for, 35–36
   liability of, 235
   "merit" system for, 36, 52
   oath of office for, 244
   overpayment of, 121, 122
   protections for, 54
   and reform of public sector
      employment, 232–33, 241
   "suspension without pay" of, 135
   See also civil service; job security;
      unions: government
energy sector, 184. See also oil and
   gas industry
Enron, 36, 137–38, 139
entitlements: and rise of Tea Party, 59
Environmental Protection Agency,
   U.S. (EPA)

accountability of, 176, 186, 187
alarmism of, 168
"climate change" and, 168, 176–81
complexity of issues facing, 166–71
cost-benefit analysis at, 185–86
court orders and, 185–86
creation of, 48, 175
and DDT banning, 171–76, 184
democracy and, 23, 166, 167–71,
   176–81
Democrats and, 177
destruction of evidence by,
   185–86, 187
DOJ collusion with, 152–54
e-mail scandal at, 187–88, 245
elections of 2012 and, 188, 245
ethics award at, 188
and FOIA requests, 187, 188, 190
funding for, 181, 189
and garnishment of citizen's
   wages, 190
greenhouse gas emissions and,
   177–78, 179
incompetency at, 189
and Landmark Legal Foundation,
   188
media and, 168
need for reform at, 205, 245
Obama administration and, 188
partisanship at, 150–55, 187, 188,
   229
power of, 23, 48, 176, 181, 182–90
resistance to, 229
as rogue agency, 182–90
rulemaking by, 178–81
science/scientists and, 168–71, 185,
   186–87, 188
as shadow government, 29
and sharing of confidential
   information, 189–90
and "sue and settle" cases, 152–54,
   166–67
See also environmentalism
environmentalism
   creation of modern movement
      about, 174
   DDT and, 171–76

environmentalism (*cont.*)
Democrats and, 180
economy and, 177, 178–79
and growth of federal bureaucracy,
36
liberals and, 171, 180–81, 186–87
and "sue and settle" cases, 152–54,
166–67
See also Environmental Protection
Agency, U.S. (EPA)
Equal Opportunity Act, 159
Establishment Clause (U.S.
Constitution), 216
ethics award, EPA, 188
evangelical adoption movement,
97–98
evidence
EPA destruction of, 185–86, 187
"exculpatory," 133
and fish-DOJ case, 143
IRS "loss" of, 84–89
and Sarbanes-Oxley Act, 143
in Stevens case, 133
exchanges, ObamaCare, 101–6
"exculpatory evidence," 133
executive branch. *See* presidency;
*specific person, department, or
agency*
Executive Order 12333, 10
Executive Order 13563, 231–32
Exxon, 61

fair tax (sales tax), 111–12
fairness
and civil service accountability,
233–37
and how bureaucracies fail, 125
Fairness Doctrine: and FCC
newsroom monitors controversy,
218–23
farmers
EPA sharing of information about,
189–90
Pigford case and, 155–58
Federal Bureau of Investigation
(FBI), 5, 8–13, 83, 119, 134

Federal Communications
Commission (FCC)
creation of, 48
need for reform of, 245
power of, 48, 217, 218
and saying no to newsroom
monitors, 217–23, 245
as shadow government, 29
Federal Election Campaign Act
(FECA), 64
Federal Election Commission (FEC)
Christian Coalition case and,
62–64
Citizens United case and, 59–61, 247
IRS and, 82, 83, 84, 85–86, 258–60
Lerner at, 258
and union contributions, 195
See also Noble, Lawrence
Federal Records Act (1950), 14
Federal Register, 49, 50, 51
Federal Rules of Criminal
Procedure, 133
Federalist Papers, 19, 60
First Amendment
Citizens United v. FEC case and,
59–61, 247
Echols case and, 214
IRS war on conservatives and, 64,
69, 261, 263
and National Park Service
blockade of National Mall, 225,
226
public officials' responsibility
when violating, 40
and reform of civil service, 235
fish: DOJ case about, 142–43
flat tax, 111, 112
Flax, Nikole, 81–83, 85–86, 88
Florida: legislative ratification in,
239
Forbes magazine
Armendariz story in, 182–83
EPA "sue and settle" story in, 153
Gibson Guitar story in, 141–42
Ford Motor Company, 193
foreign governments/organizations
adoption and, 90

Citizens United v. FEC and, 60–61
and economic competition among
  states, 197
and IRS war on conservatives,
  60–61, 65
jobs and, 193
oil and, 184
Forest Service, U.S.: and
  preservation of war memorial,
  215, 216–17
Foundations of Freedom (booklet), 249
Founding Fathers
and freedom of information, 5
need for restoration of vision of,
  242, 268
Fox News: and FCC newsroom
  monitors controversy, 221
Fox, Robin, 127
Franklin, Benjamin, 44, 255
Fraser Institute, 57–58
fraud
  DOJ's "Operation Choke Point"
    and, 146
  and fish-DOJ case, 143
  immigration and, 107–8
  and IRS audits of tax credits,
    95–96, 241
  Pigford case and, 155–58
  VA scandals and, 120
free speech
  American exceptionalism and,
    44–45
  anonymous, 59–61
  and blueprint for change, 208, 211,
    214–15
  bureaucracy's limitations on, 261
  and criminalization of
    conservative speech, 81–83
  FCC newsroom monitors
    controversy and, 218–23
  IRS and, 79–81, 227, 260, 262
  NAACP v. Patterson case and,
    69–70
  resistance and, 214–15
  right to, 210, 211
  tax-exempt organizations and,
    79–81

Tea Party and, 81
and Volkswagen-UAW-NLRB
  controversy, 201
See also Citizens United v. FEC
  case; political speech
Freedom from Religion Foundation
  (FFRF), 79–80, 216–17
freedom of assembly: *NAACP v.*
  Patterson case and, 69–70
freedom of association:
  bureaucracy's limitations on, 261
Freedom of Information Act
  (FOIA), 5, 187, 188, 190, 267
freedom of religion: and blueprint
  for change, 208
freedom of the press, 208, 221
Frezza, Bill, 141–42
fuel standards, 179, 180, 193
Fund, John, 51, 158

Gallup poll: and partisanship in
  federal bureaucracy, 56
Garland, Merrick B., 263
gas industry. *See* oil and gas
  industry
General Motors (GM), 193–94, 200,
  234
Germany: as origin of cyberattacks,
  13
Gettysburg Address, Lincoln's, 40
Gibson Guitar case, DOJ's, 140–42
Gibson, Sloan, 122
Gilligan's Island (TV show), 110
Gingrich, Newt, 197
global warming: predictions about,
  170–71, 177
Goeke, James, 135
Goldman Sachs, 61
Goodlatte, Robert, 146
Gore, Al, 170–71, 231
Government Accountability Office
  (GAO)
  EPA/DOJ "sue and settle" cases
    and, 153
  and fraudulent adoption tax
    credits, 96

Government Accountability Office (GAO) (*cont.*)
    and number of regulations passed in recent years, 250
    and reform of IRS, 265
    VA wait times for veterans and, 114
government, U.S.
    accountability of, 5
    American exceptionalism and, 43–44
    branches of, 23–24, 232
    complexity of, 199
    corruption of, 28
    deterioration of control by, 19
    fight for reform of, 268
    gridlock in, 30–34, 181
    growth of, 36–37, 59
    as instrument of ideology, 245
    limitations on, 206, 208
    Madison's comments about, 19
    mistakes of, 244
    and petition for redress of grievances, 44–45
    poor, 43–44
    and potential for partisanship and corruption, 199
    power of, 44, 47–48, 208, 247, 252, 256
    as problem, 199
    purpose/role of, 212–13, 243–44, 249, 268
    "reinventing," 231–32
    role in divisiveness among Americans of, 247, 248
    Russia compared with, 243–44
    "shutdown" of, 37, 223–27
    size of, 199
    three R's and, 39–40
    transparency of, 5
    truths about, 30–37
    vulnerability of, 208
    See also bureaucracy, federal; shadow government; *specific branch, agency, or department*
Graham, Billy, 75
Graham, Franklin, 75, 76

Graham, Lindsey, 198–99
Grassley, Chuck: IRS audit of, 76–77
grassroots associations: *Citizens United v. FEC* and, 61
greatness, American, 254–55
greenhouse gas emissions, 177–78, 179
gridlock, government, 30–34, 181
Gruber, Jonathan, 102–3
Gruhn, George, 141
Guardian newspaper, 168

hackers, 3–4, 19. *See also* cyberattacks
Hagerty, Bill, 201
Haldeman, H. R., 88
Hannity, Sean, 218
Haslam, Bill, 201
Hayes, Denis, 169
Health and Human Services, U.S. Department of (HHS)
    abortion-pill mandate and, 32–33
    and gaps in laws, 32–33, 48
    IRS collusion with, 104–5
    Obamacare and, 48, 104–5
    power of, 23
    as threat to democracy, 23
health care
    debate about, 123
    and growth of federal bureaucracy, 37
    IRS reshaping of, 48, 101–6, 240
    and Obama's health care initiative, 75
    private sector and, 125
    RAND Corporation study of VA, 124
    and rise of Tea Party, 60
    "single-payer," 123
    as socialized medicine, 123, 124
    VA as model for American, 122, 123–25
    See also Medicaid; Medicare; ObamaCare
Heinz, John, 185
Helman, Christopher, 182–83

Hendrickson, Mark, 185
Hill, The
  and Boeing–labor unions–NLRB
    controversy, 199
  IRS story in, 99–100
Holder, Eric, 24
Hollywood: Clintons as source of
  ideas for, 1
Home Depot: hacking at, 3
Homeland Security, U.S.
  Department of, 4, 141
House of Representatives, U.S.
  and Boeing–labor unions–NLRB
    controversy, 21
  environmentalism and, 180
  and EPA funding, 180, 181
  and how bills become laws, 47
  and impact of partisanship on
    elections, 29
  and Koskinen impeachment,
    264–65
  "Secret Science Reform Act of
    2014" proposal by, 186–87
  See also Congress, U.S.; *specific
    committee or legislation*
"How a Bill Becomes a Law" (song),
  46–47
Huffington Post
  and IRS disclosure of
    conservatives' confidential
    information, 72
  and overpayment of VA
    employees, 121
  Stein story in, 65
human nature: role in bureaucracies
  of, 127
Human Rights Campaign, 72–73

ideology
  and divisiveness in America, 246
  government as instrument of, 245
  and public ignorance and apathy,
    222, 223
  restoration and, 249
  See also partisanship
illegal aliens, 107–9, 238

Illegal Immigration Reform and
  Immigration Responsibility Act,
  108
immigration
  "additional child tax credits"
    (ACTC) and, 107–9
  American exceptionalism and,
    41–42, 43, 57, 58
  border control and, 106–7
  fraud and, 107–9
  illegal aliens and, 107–9
  IRS unilateral reform of, 106–9,
    239
  jobs and, 106
  national security and, 106
  Obama and, 47, 106
  Sekulow's family background and,
    41–42, 43, 57, 58, 108, 242, 243
Immigration and Nationality Act, 238
Immigration and Naturalization
  Service (INS), 108, 109
immunity, prosecutorial, 131, 147
incentives
  effectiveness of, 233
  employee, 35–36
incompetency
  and comparison of Congress and
    federal bureaucracy, 29
  of federal bureaucracy, 1, 3, 29,
    33–34, 36, 37, 57, 58, 189
  as systemic problem, 163
  See also specific agency or department
Individual Tax Identification
  Number (ITIN), 107, 108–9
information
  classification of, 8, 11–12, 16
  right to, 209–10, 211
  See also type of information
Information Quality Act, 231
INS v Chadha (1983), 238
Inspector General, DOJ, 160–62
Inspector General for Tax
  Administration, Treasury
  Department, 100, 108–9
Inspector General, of intelligence
  community: and Clinton emails,
  8

Inspector General, Treasury
   Department, 87
Inspector General, VA, 115
Intelligence Reform and Terrorism
   Prevention Act (2004), 9–10
intent, proving criminal, 144–46
Internal Revenue Code, 66, 91, 109
Internal Revenue Procedure 86-43:
   and AMEN, 79
Internet Service Provider story, 144
intimidation
   and IRS war on conservatives,
      70–71, 228
   and knowing your rights, 209
   and report about DOJ Voting
      Section employees, 162–63
   resistance to, 208
Iowa Coalition for Life, 77–79
Iran, and Clinton emails, 12
IRS (Internal Revenue Service, U.S.)
   abolishing the, 111–12, 205,
      239–42
   accountability at, 110, 257, 261,
      262, 264, 265
   ACLJ lawsuits against, 71–72, 80,
      150–51, 152, 227, 249, 256–57,
      261–63, 264, 267
   adoptions and, 90–98, 209, 210, 245
   American exceptionalism and, 28
   apologies by, 23–24, 25–26, 71,
      81–82, 95, 150
   and burden of proof, 240–41
   bureaucratic delays in
      investigation of, 13
   and characteristics of modern
      bureaucracies, 58
   Citizens for a Strong New
      Hampshire, Inc. v Internal Revenue
      Service and, 267
   Citizens United v. FEC and, 61
   computer crash at, 84–85, 86
   conferences of, 110–11
   congressional hearings about,
      257–59, 264–65
   conservatives/Tea Party as targets
      of, 23–24, 35, 45, 61–89, 145–46,
      150, 164, 227–29, 256–67

corruption in, 36, 89, 111, 112,
   260, 268
creation of, 48
credibility of, 85
Criminal Investigation Unit of,
   83, 96
and criminalization of
   conservative speech, 81–83, 84,
   86
data-keeping prowess of, 86–87
disclosure of confidential
   information by, 72–74, 229
DOJ as lawyers for, 150–51
DOJ collusion with, 24, 26, 82–83,
   84–85, 89, 145
DOJ investigation of, 89, 260, 264
and Earned Income Tax Credits,
   98–101, 154, 155
elections of 2012 and, 26–28,
   72–74
Exempt Organizations Division of,
   62, 76
FEC and, 82, 83, 84, 85–86,
   258–60
FFRF lawsuit against, 79–80
and FOIA requests, 187, 267
free speech and, 79–81, 227, 260,
   262
funding for, 189
and gaps in laws, 48
health care and, 48, 101–6, 240
HHS collusion with, 104–5
Holder's comments about, 24
immigration reform and, 106–9,
   239
incompetency at, 36
initiative of, 28
intimidation by, 70–71
investigations of, 260
ITIN and, 107, 108–9
job security at, 35, 36
and knowing your rights, 209
lawsuits against, 261
"line" workers at, 25–26
"loss" of evidence by, 84–89
Lynchpins of Liberty v. United States
   and, 266–67

mission statement of, 81
"mistakes" of, 73
need for change at, 245, 264,
    265–68
Nixon's use of, 88
Noble's comments about, 257–58
Obama and, 24, 26–28, 45, 65, 72,
    75, 104, 266
ObamaCare and, 48, 101–6, 223
outside pressures on, 258, 259–60
overpayment of tax payments by,
    99–101
oversight of, 87–88, 109
partisanship at, 45, 55–56, 64,
    77–79, 96–98, 99, 101, 104–5,
    109, 155, 158–59, 227, 228–29
as personification of shadow
    government, 29
as "piecing together" prosecutions,
    24, 82–83, 89, 145
"poor management" at, 265–66
power of, 23, 48, 65, 112, 183, 240
and presidential directives, 28
pro-life movement and, 77–79,
    249
Procedure 86-43 of, 79
processing of tax-exempt
    applications by, 23–26, 61–72, 84,
    249–50, 256–65
public anger at, 248
reform of, 111, 112, 205, 236–37,
    239–42
reputation of, 94
resistance to activities of, 227–29
and rule of law, 264
and Schuelke review of DOJ, 134
Sekulow commitment to fight
    against, 256
Sekulow's job with, 3, 25, 39, 45,
    159
Taxpayer Advocate Service of, 92,
    94–95
as threat to democracy, 23, 245,
    260
unpopularity of, 45
and war with Tea Party, 59, 60, 61,
    65–69, 71, 74, 76, 77, 81, 83, 87

welfare policy and, 239
whistle-blowers at, 158
and Z Street v. Koskinen case,
    261–63
See also audits, IRS

Jackson, Lisa, 187
Jefferson, Thomas, 244
Jim Crow, 45, 244
job security
    accountability and, 34–35, 233–37
    in federal bureaucracy, 35, 36,
        51–54, 57, 65
    in private sector, 35–36
    reform and, 233–37
    shadow government and, 28–29
    USA Today story about, 34
    See also employees, federal
jobs
    in automobile industry, 192–95
    and Boeing–labor union–NLRB
        controversy, 198
    comparison of private and public
        sector, 232–33
    economy and, 193
    and foreign governments/
        organizations, 193
    immigration and, 106
    manufacturing, 192–95
    protection of, 232
    in South, 192–93
    and Volkswagen-UAW-NLRB
        controversy, 200
    See also job security; National
        Labor Relations Board; unions
Johnson (Lyndon) Amendment, 80
Johnson, Lyndon B., 80, 176
Joyce, Kathryn, 97
judges: relationship between lawyers
    and, 163–64
Judicial Watch, 81–82
judiciary
    and ACLJ fight for justice, 257
    EPA and, 181, 185–86
    and FFRE case, 217
    and how bills become laws, 47, 57

judiciary (*cont.*)
importance in bureaucratic
overreach cases of, 202
and IRS targeting, 261–65
and need for reform of
bureaucracy, 266
power of, 22
See also Circuit Court of Appeals;
Judiciary Committee, House;
Judiciary Committee, Senate;
Supreme Court, U.S.
Judiciary Committee, House, 106,
146
Judiciary Committee, Senate, 257,
258–59, 264
Justice Department, U.S. (DOJ)
accountability of, 165
and ACLJ-IRS lawsuits, 150–51,
152, 264
appointment of special counsel for,
264
Arthur Andersen LLP case and,
139
banks as targets of, 146
Civil Rights Division of, 149–65
and Clinton emails, 5, 6, 7, 8–9,
10, 12, 13
conservatives as employees at,
158–65
corruption at, 164–65
creation of, 48
credibility of, 150
criminal law issues in, 130–47
and criminalization of
conservative speech, 82
Democrats and, 149
EPA collusion with, 152–54
and expansion of criminal laws,
144–46
fish case of, 142–43
and Gibson Guitar case, 140–42
image of, 260
and immunity of prosecutors,
131
Inspector General's report about
Voting Section of, 160–62
investigation of IRS by, 89

IRS and, 24, 26, 82–83, 84–86, 89,
145, 260, 264, 265–66
liberals and, 149
mission of, 159–60
need for change at, 245
ObamaCare and, 132–35
partisanship in, 33–34, 56, 89,
149–50, 158–65, 205
as "piecing together" prosecutions,
24, 82–83, 89, 145
and Pigford Giveaway, 155–58
and pop culture views of
prosecutors, 130
power of, 23, 48, 135–40, 146, 183
and power of prosecutors, 130–31,
183
and proving intent, 144–46
public anger at, 248
radicals' collusion with, 150–55
reform of, 165, 236
Schuelke investigation of, 134–35
Sekulow on legal faculty of, 131
as shadow government, 29
sharing of confidential
information by, 163, 164
Stevens prosecution by, 33–34,
132–35, 245
"sue and settle" pattern at, 51,
150–58, 163, 164
as threat to democracy, 23, 245
Voting Section of, 161–63
whistle-blowers at, 158
See also Civil Rights Division;
Court of Appeals; *specific person*
Juszkiewicz, Henry, 141–42

Kelley, Colleen, 55
Kennedy, Anthony, 60
Kerry, John, 55
King, Alexander, 173
King, Martin Luther Jr., 254
Klein, Ezra, 123
Korean War: despair during, 254
Koskinen, John, 85, 259, 264–65
Kozinski, Alex, 136
Kristof, Nicholas, 123–24

Krugman, Paul, 124–25
Kyoto Protocol, 177

labor
    Democrats and, 194–95
    Obama administration and, 195
    See also Labor Department, U.S.;
        National Labor Relations Board;
        unions
Labor Department, U.S., 23, 195
Lacey Act: and Gibson Guitar–DOJ
    case, 141–42
Landmark Legal Foundation, 188
Landover, Maryland: EPA
    comfortable warehouse in, 189
Law & Order (TV show), 130
"law of group polarization," 38
laws
    about accountability, 14
    American exceptionalism and,
        43–44, 57
    bills becoming, 46–51, 57
    challenges to, 47
    Clinton's (Hillary) violation of, 2,
        8–9, 13–19
    enforcement of, 48
    expansion of criminal, 144–46
    federal leaders as following, 14–19
    gaps in, 31–33, 48–49
    and image of Justice Department,
        260
    limitation of prosecutable, 147
    "rulemaking process" and, 48–51
    about transparency, 14
    See also rules; specific law
lawsuit. See litigation; specific lawsuit
lawyers
    and DOJ lawyers for IRS, 150–51
    judges' relationship with, 163–64
    and legal advice about rights, 210
    at NLRB, 196
    ObamaCare and, 104–5
    partisanship of, 56, 104–5
    and sharing of confidential
        information, 163
    and "sue and settle" cases, 154

See also American Center for Law
    and Justice (ACLJ); judiciary;
    prosecutors, federal; specific case
Left. See liberals
legislative branch. See Congress,
    U.S.; House of Representatives,
    U.S.; Senate, U.S.
legislative veto, 237–38
Lerner, Lois
    "apology" of, 23–24, 25–26, 71,
        81–82
    and Christian Coalition
        investigation, 78
    and Citizens for a Strong New
        Hampshire, Inc. v Internal Revenue
        Service, 267
    and criminalization of
        conservative speech, 81–83, 84
    DOJ relationship with, 26
    elections of 2012 and, 27–28
    elections of 2014 and, 267
    emails of, 13, 64, 81–83, 84–85,
        87–88, 258, 259, 260, 267
    at FEC, 258
    Flax and, 81–83
    and Grassley audit, 76–77
    and image of Justice Department,
        260
    and IRS war on conservatives, 62,
        64, 71, 74, 81–83, 84
    "loss" of email of, 84–85, 87–88
    Noble and, 258
    partisanship of, 64, 258
    professional background of, 62
    targeting of conservatives by,
        258–59, 260, 267
    and tax-exempt organizations,
        23–24, 25–26, 62, 64, 71, 84
    and Tea Party, 65, 81–82, 87
Levin, Mark, 188, 251
Lewis, David, 120
liberals
    and American exceptionalism,
        42–43
    Citizens United v. FEC case, 59–61
    and dangers to democracy, 259–60
    and DDT banning, 175

liberals (*cont.*)
  divisiveness in America and,
    246–47
  DOJ partisanship and, 149, 162,
    163, 164
  environmentalism and, 171,
    180–81, 186–87
  FCC newsroom monitors
    controversy and, 218
  and fixing problems of
    bureaucracies, 128
  IRS audits of adoption tax credits
    and, 97
  and IRS disclosure of confidential
    information, 74
  ObamaCare and, 105
  and partisanship in federal
    bureaucracy, 56, 149, 162, 163,
    164, 181
  public anger at, 248
  reform and, 229–30
  and rise of Tea Party, 59, 60
  sharing of confidential
    information between DOJ and,
    163
  and socialized medicine, 123
  and "sue and settle" cases, 163
  tax-exempt organizations of, 24,
    25, 66
liberty
  ACLJ efforts to expand, 46
  and blueprint for change, 208, 211,
    212, 213, 244–46, 255
  and corruption in DOJ, 165, 245
  Declaration of Independence and,
    244
  IRS activities and, 245
  and knowing your rights, 211
  partisanship in federal bureaucracy
    and, 57
  and power of federal
    bureaucracies, 190
  and purpose of government,
    243–44
  restoration of, 206, 249
  and sanctions for prosecutorial
    misconduct, 147

slavery and, 244
  See also type of liberty
*The Liberty Amendments: Restoring
  the American Republic* (Levin),
  251
Life magazine: air pollution
  comments in, 169
Lincoln, Abraham, 40, 113
litigation
  and reform of civil service, 236
  resistance and, 227
  See also specific litigation
The Living Wilderness: and Hayes
  prediction about starvation, 169
Lorrie, Karen (pseud.), 161
Lynch, Loretta, 18
Lynchpins of Liberty, 249–50,
  266–67
Lynchpins of Liberty v. United States,
  266–67

Mademoiselle magazine: Ehrlich's
  comment about food supply in,
  169
Madison, James, 19
malaria, 171, 173, 174, 176
manufacturing jobs, 192–95
Martinek, Susan, 77–78
Maslowski, Wieslaw, 171
McCain, John, 55
McMahon, Emily, 104
McNulty, Patrick, 119
media
  and blueprint for change, 250
  and Clinton emails, 5, 8–9, 13
  elections of 2010 and, 65
  EPA and, 168
  and FCC newsroom monitors
    controversy, 217–23
  and how to resist, 226
  injunction against Obama
    administration and, 227–28
  IRS audits of adoptions and, 93, 95
  and IRS decisions about tax-
    exempt status, 24, 72
  IRS "loss" of evidence and, 89

and prosecutorial misconduct, 136
and shadow government in U.S.,
    28–29
and VA wait-time story, 115
See also specific organization or person
Medicaid, 101
Medicare, 125
"merit" system, 36, 52, 54
Merit Systems Protection Board, 53,
    164
Microsoft Office Communications
    Server, IRS, 86–87
military
    as federal bureaucracy, 126–27
    and fight for freedom, 268
    functions of, 233
    incentives in, 233
    reasons for leaving, 126
    See also Army, U.S.; Veterans
    Affairs (VA), U.S. Department of
Mills, Cheryl, 11
Mitchell, Katherine, 114
Monaco, Lisa, 137, 138, 139–40
Moses, 21, 22
MoveOn.org, 25, 66
Müller, Paul, 173
"Multi-Market Study of Critical
    Information Needs," FCC. See
    newsroom monitors

NAACP v. Patterson case (1958),
    69–70
National Academy of Sciences,
    174–75
National Affairs: Wilson's article
    about bureaucracies in, 127–28
National Archives: regulations about
    email at, 15
National Association for the
    Advancement of Colored People
    (NAACP), 69–70
National Education Association, 194
National Fish and Wildlife
    Foundation, 142
National Highway Traffic Safety
    Administration (NHTSA), 179

National Journal: ObamaCare story
    in, 103
National Labor Relations Board
    (NLRB)
    and Boeing "Dreamliner" plant,
        195–99
    creation of, 48
    Democrats and, 204
    funding for, 198
    legal staff of, 196
    need for change at, 245
    Obama administration and, 197,
        198–99, 202–5
    Obama appointments to, 202–5
    overreach of, 202–5, 245
    partisanship in, 56, 193–201, 229
    power of, 48, 190, 195, 200
    public anger at, 248
    relitigation of actions of, 204–5
    resistance to, 222, 229
    as shadow government, 29
    and Volkswagen-UAW
        controversy, 200–201
National Mall
    amnesty rally in, 37–38, 226
    World War II Memorial in, 37–38,
        224–27
National Park Service, 37–38,
    223–27
National Review
    firing of federal employees story
        in, 53
    IRS criminalization of
        conservative speech story in, 83
    Williamson stories in, 38, 168
national security
    and Clinton emails, 3, 6, 13, 14
    FBI authority concerning, 9–10
    and hackers, 4, 19
    immigration and, 106
    laws concerning, 15–16
    levels of classified information
        about, 8, 16
National September 11 Memorial &
    Museum, 253
National Treasury Employees
    Union, 55

National Voter Registration Act, 160

NATO (North Atlantic Treaty Organization): Clinton emails about, 12

Natural Resources Defense Council, 153

New Atlantis: Zubrin's comments about DDT in, 172

New York Observer: prosecutorial misconduct stories in, 136–38

New York Times, The
and Boeing–labor union–NLRB controversy, 196
and Clinton emails, 6, 8
and IRS decisions about tax-exempt status, 24
Kristof article about health care in, 123–24
Krugman article about VA reform in, 124–25
Pigford story in, 156
and prosecutorial misconduct, 136
Stevens prosecution story in, 135

newsroom monitors: saying no to FCC, 217–23, 245

Nixon, Richard M., 28, 88, 89

no, saying
and FCC newsroom monitors controversy, 217–23
power of, 212
See also resistance

Noble, Lawrence, 257–59

nonprofit corporations
advocacy issues and, 66
See also tax-exempt organizations; *specific organization*

North Korea, 11

North, Oliver, 64

nuclear programs, 11, 12

oath of office, 244

Obama, Barack
access to, 55
and American exceptionalism, 43
appointments of, 182, 199, 202–5
bailouts and, 59
and *Citizens United v. FCC*, 60–61
Dodd-Frank bill and, 49
elections of 2008 and, 55, 59
elections of 2010 and, 65
elections of 2012 and, 26–28, 55, 56, 72, 99, 188
and EPA misconduct, 185
and Graham's threats about commerce secretary appointment, 199
gridlock and, 31
health care initiative of, 75
immigration and, 47, 106
and IRS, 24, 26–28, 45, 65, 72, 75, 104, 266
and Lerner's "apology," 24
Monaco appointment by, 139
new rules during administration of, 50
NLRB and, 202–5
and ObamaCare, 34, 125
and partisanship in federal bureaucracy, 55, 56, 258
and permanent executive branch, 148
popularity of, 138–39
power of, 182
and prosecutorial misconduct, 136–37
socio-economic background and support for, 99
State of the Union speech (2010) speech of, 60–61
and VA wait-time scandals, 115–16, 118

Obama (Barack) administration
ACLJ fight against, 256–57, 265
and Boeing–labor union–NLRB controversy, 197, 198–99
Clinton emails and, 10, 12
and DOJ abuses, 163
and DOJ investigation of IRS, 89
EPA and, 188
and fuel standards for cars, 180
and government reform, 231–32
injunction against, 227–28

and IRS criminalizing of
conservative speech, 81
and IRS "loss" of evidence, 85,
88
and IRS targeting, 263, 264
and knowing your rights, 210
labor and, 195
and Lerner emails, 88
and "sue and settle" cases, 154
VA funding during, 114
ObamaCare
abortion-pill mandate and, 32–33
Citizens United v. FEC and, 61
cost of, 125
court challenges to, 105–6
Democrats and, 125
DOJ and, 132–35
enforcement of, 48
exchanges for, 101–6
funding for, 223
and gaps in laws, 48
goals of, 101–2
and government "shutdown," 223
individual mandate in, 103
and IRS criminalizing of
conservative speech, 83
IRS rewriting of rules about,
32–33, 101–6, 223
and liberals, 105
need for reform of, 266
Republicans and, 125
Senate votes for, 133
socio-economic background and,
102–6
states and, 101–6
Stevens and, 33–34, 133
tax credits and, 102–6
VA as model for, 122, 123–25
Obama's Enforcer: Eric Holder's
Justice Department (Fund and
von Spakovsky), 51, 158
Office of Chief Counsel, IRS/
Treasury Department
and rewriting of ObamaCare law,
104
Sekulow as employee in, 3, 25, 39,
45, 159

Office of Management and Budget
(OMB): and hackers, 4
Office of Personnel Management
(OPM): hacking at, 3–4
oil and gas industry:
environmentalism and, 170, 179,
183, 184
Opensecrets.org, 194
"Operation Choke Point," DOJ's,
146
Operation Christmas Child, 75
Oversight Committee, House,
86–87, 198

Pai, Ajit, 220–21
Paine, Thomas, 43
partisanship
American exceptionalism and,
57–58
and blueprint for change, 246–48
in civil service, 235
and divisiveness in America,
246–48
elections and, 29
in federal bureaucracy, 29, 30,
37–40, 54–58, 65, 109, 149, 181,
205, 251, 256, 258
and reform, 40, 229, 235
and size of government, 199
as systemic problem, 163
three R's and, 40
See also *specific department or agency*
Partnership for Public Service,
232–33
pastors: and IRS scrutiny of
conservatives, 63–64
Pawlenty, Tim, 197
Pelosi, Nancy, 32
Pendleton Act, 53
Perciasepe, Bob, 189–90
Perry, Mark: list of wrong scientific
predictions compiled by, 168–71
persistence: resistance and, 226–27
petition for redress of grievances:
American exceptionalism and,
11, 45

Petraeus, David, 17
Pew Research Center for the People and the Press, 246, 247
Pigford Giveaway, DOJ's, 155–58
Pilger, Richard, 82
Planned Parenthood, 24, 25, 66, 77–79, 91
political speech
anonymous, 59–61
Citizens United v. FEC case (2010), 59–61, 247
funding for, 60
See also free speech
Politico
appeal about firing of federal employee comment in, 53
Graham's comments about IRS audits of conservatives in, 75
PolitiFact, 61
Ponnuru, Ramesh, 180
popularity: as protection, 138–39
Powell, Colin, 7
Powell, Sidney, 137–38
power
abuse of power as path to, 135–40
and Article V of Constitution, 251–52
and blueprint for change, 246
of Clinton (Hillary), 1–2
constitutional limitations on, 151
danger of unrestrained, 259
and divisiveness among American people, 247
in federal bureaucracy, 19, 29, 57, 58, 65, 111, 128, 190, 199, 229, 232, 251–52, 256, 264
of federal government, 44, 47–48, 208, 247, 252, 256
of federal prosecutors, 130–31, 147
and how bureaucracies fail, 128
of saying no, 212
and number of rules and regulations passed in recent years, 251
of Obama, 182
and potential for partisanship and corruption, 199

presidential, 22–23, 47
and reform, 229
in a republic, 44
separation of, 48, 152
and "sue and settle" cases, 151, 152
See also specific branch of government, agency, or department
power plant standards, 179
prayers
and IRS delays in processing tax-exempt applications, 25, 63, 64–65
and IRS pro-life investigations, 78
presidency
appointments by, 148–49
blame on, 132
checks and balances on, 45
as figurehead, 30
and how bills become laws, 47, 49, 57
and job security in federal bureaucracy, 52
and permanent executive branch, 148
power of, 22–23, 47
reform efforts of, 231–32
vetoes by, 47, 238
private sector
civil service compared with, 233–37
health care and, 125
and how bureaucracies fail, 125
job security in, 35–36
merit system in, 54
and reform of public sector employment, 164–65, 232–33, 241
pro-life movement
and ACLJ lawsuit against IRS, 71–72, 249
adoption and, 90–98
Citizens United v. FEC and, 61
and delays in processing applications for tax-exempt status, 23–24, 25
IRS and, 23–24, 25, 35, 77–79, 249
Lerner's "apology" to, 23–24

prayers of, 25
See also abortion; specific group
The Progressive: and Ehrlich's prediction about "Great Die-Off," 169
Progressive organizations: tax-exempt statistics about, 67
ProPublica: and IRS disclosure of conservatives' confidential information, 73
prosecutors, federal
  and abuse of power as path to power, 135–40
  accountability of, 137, 147
  discretion of, 130–31
  immunity of, 131, 147
  and limitation of prosecutable laws, 147
  misconduct among, 135–40, 147, 165, 236
  as "piecing together" prosecutions, 24, 82–83, 89, 145
  pop culture view of, 130
  power of, 130–31, 147
  and proving intent, 144–46
  and reform of civil service, 236
  rogue, 132, 139
  sanctions for misconduct of, 147
  standards for, 165
  See also specific person or case
public advocacy organizations and Clinton emails, 5
  See also specific organization
public, American
  anger of, 248
  divisiveness among, 246–48
  ignorance and advancement of ideology of, 222, 223
public schools: reform of, 233

race
  Pigford case and, 155–58
  and transracial adoptions, 97–98
RAND Corporation: health care study by, 124
Range Resources, 183, 184

Reagan, Ronald, 45, 98, 234
recess appointments, Obama's, 202–5
Reed, Ralph, 63
reform
  and accountability, 40, 165, 205, 229, 231–32, 233–37
  and blueprint for change, 205–6, 212, 229–30, 231–37, 239–42
  of civil service, 40, 164–65, 233–37
  constitutional framework for, 232
  democracy and, 231, 237
  difficulties of, 229–30
  of DOJ, 165, 236
  of elections, 268
  of EPA, 205
  of federal bureaucracy, 39–40, 197, 205–6, 212, 229–30, 231–37, 239–42, 256, 266–68
  fight for government, 256, 266–68
  goal of, 229
  importance of, 206, 229–30
  of IRS, 111, 112, 205, 236, 239–42, 264, 265
  and job security, 233–37
  and liberals, 229–30
  of ObamaCare, 266
  as one of three R's, 39–40
  partisanship and, 229
  power and, 229
  presidential efforts at, 231–32
  of public schools, 233
  simplicity of needed, 205
  unions and, 232–33, 234
  of VA, 205, 236
refugees
  American exceptionalism and, 43
  See also immigration
regulations
  need for fight against, 256
  and number of regulations passed in recent years, 250–51
  role of, 212–13
  rules as, 49–51
  significant, 238–39
  See also rules; specific regulation, agency, or department

regulators. *See* bureaucracy,
    federal; *specific agency, or
    department*
Reilly, William, 185
religion
    and blueprint for change, 208, 210
    and evangelical adoption
        movement, 97–98
    FEC war on, 62–64
    freedom of, 208
    and IRS audits of conservatives,
        76
    and knowing your rights, 210
    See also churches; pastors; religious
        liberty; *specific organization*
religious liberty
    abortion-pill mandate and, 32
    American exceptionalism and,
        44–45
    and growth of federal bureaucracy,
        36
    and IRS war on conservatives, 64,
        227
    and partisanship of federal
        bureaucracy, 38
Renewable Fuel Standard (RES)
    program, 179
republic
    characteristics of, 44–45
    definition of, 44
    improvement of, 44–45
    power in a, 44
Republican Party
    and divisiveness among
        Americans, 246, 247–48
    elections of 2012 and, 26
    and IRS audits of conservatives,
        74
    ObamaCare and, 125
    "Secret Science Reform Act of
        2014" proposal by, 186–87
    See also specific person
resistance
    accountability and, 208
    awareness and, 225–26, 227
    and blueprint for change, 208, 212,
        213, 214–29

Boeing–labor unions–NLRB
    controversy and, 195–99
and bureaucratic overreach,
    195–99
and call to action, 225–26, 227
and education, 213
to EPA, 229
and FCC newsroom monitors
    controversy, 217–23
and FFRE controversy, 216–17
formula for, 225–27
free speech and, 214–15
futility of, 207–8
and how to resist, 226–27
to IRS, 228–29
litigation and, 227
to National Park Service actions,
    223–27
to NLRB, 222, 229
and peaceful civil disobedience,
    225–27
persistence and, 226–27
victory in, 228–29
and Volkswagen-UAW-NLRB
    controversy, 200–201
restoration
    and blueprint for change, 208, 212,
        213, 237–39, 242, 249–55
    of constitutional democracy, 40,
        58, 238–42, 244–55
    education and, 213
    goal of, 206
    of liberty, 206
    and need for reform, 206
retaliation: and knowing your rights,
    211
Rice, Susan, 137
Richards, Ms. (alias), 77, 78
Richmond Tea Party, 27
right(s)
    and blueprint for change, 208,
        209–11, 235–36, 242, 245–46
    and congressional oversight of
        federal bureaucracy, 242
    to information, 209–10
    knowing about, 208, 209–11
    legal advice about, 210

and oath of office for federal
employees, 244
penalties for violation of
constitutional, 235–36
and reform of civil service, 235
See also Bill of Rights; *specific
right*
Romney, Mitt
and Boeing–labor union–NLRB
controversy, 197
elections of 2012 and, 26, 55, 56,
72–73, 99, 188, 197
and EPA email scandal, 188
IRS audits of conservative donors
to, 74–75, 76
and IRS disclosure of
conservatives' confidential
information, 72–73
and political contributions of
federal employees, 55, 56
socio-economic class support for,
99
and Tea Party's impact on
elections, 26
VA reform plan of, 124–25
R's, three, 39–40, 207–13. *See also*
blueprint for change; reform;
resistance; restoration
Ruckelshaus, William D., 175
Ruemmler, Kathryn, 137–38,
139–40
rule of law, 1, 6, 7, 18, 89, 101, 136,
150, 164, 264
"rulemaking process," 48–51,
178–81
rules
in Federal Register, 49
"notice and comment" period for,
49
and number of rules and
regulations passed in recent
years, 250–51
as regulations, 49–51
See also regulations
Russia
and Sekulow's family background,
41–42, 43, 57, 58, 242

U.S. government compared with,
243–44
Rwanda: American response to
genocide in, 137

sales tax (fair tax), 111–12
Salon: anti-adoption review in, 97
Samaritan's Purse, 75, 76
San Diego, California: EPA letter
about sewage in, 186
Sarbanes-Oxley Act (2002), 143
Sasse, Ben, 4
Saturday Night Live (TV show), 47
Scherz, Hal, 75
Schoolhouse Rock (TV show), 46
Schuelke, Henry F., 134–35
Schweiker, Richard, 185
science/scientists
EPA and, 168–71, 185, 186–87, 188
fallibility of, 176
and "Secret Science Reform Act of
2014" proposal, 186–87
wrong predictions of, 168–71
Scott, Robert, 193
"Secret Science Reform Act of 2014"
proposal, 186–87
Section 521(c)(4) (IRS code), 66, 73,
75–76, 77, 80. *See also* tax-exempt
organizations
Sekulow, Jay
as committed to IRS fight, 256
congressional testimonies of, 256,
257
and Echols case, 215
family background of, 41–42, 43,
57, 58, 108, 242, 243
and FCC newsroom monitors
controversy, 221
legal background of, 3, 21–22, 25,
39, 45–46, 131, 150–51, 158–59,
164, 176, 203, 225, 256
motivations of, 45–46
as victim of hackers, 3
Sekulow, Jordan (son), 225
Sekulow, Sam (grandfather), 41, 42,
43, 57, 58, 242, 243

self-correction: bureaucracy as
   incapable of, 229
Senate, U.S.
   and Boeing–labor unions–NLRB
      controversy, 198
   elections of 2008 and, 34
   environmentalism and, 180
   and EPA funding, 181
   and how bills become laws, 47
   and Kyoto Protocol, 177
   and Obama appointments, 202–5
   ObamaCare vote in, 34, 133
   office building for, 22
   "pro forma session" of, 202–5
   security for, 22
   and Stevens allegations, 34
   See also Congress, U.S.; specific
      committee or legislation
separation of power, 48
September 11, 2001, 22, 253
shadow government
   corruption and, 28–29
   examples of, 29
   growth of, 28–29
   job security and, 28–29
   media and, 28
   See also bureaucracy, federal
Shinseki, Eric, 115, 116, 117,
   121–22
Shulman, Douglas, 71
"shutdown," government, 223–27
Sierra Club, 153
significant regulations, 238–39
Silent Spring (Carson), 174
Silvergate, Harvey, 144, 145
slavery, 244
social media, 221, 225, 226, 242, 247,
   248, 249
Social Security, 223
socialized medicine, 123, 124
socio-economic background
   adoption tax credits and, 94–95
   Democratic Party and, 99
   and Earned Income Tax Credits,
      98–101
   ObamaCare and, 102–6
Solomon, Lafe, 196, 198, 199

South
   economic and population changes
      in, 191–92
   jobs in, 192–93
   labor unions in, 193–99
   taxes in, 192
   wages in, 194
South Carolina: Boeing
   "Dreamliner" plant in, 195–99,
   201
South Korea, 13
Spakovsky, Hans von, 51, 158
special interests: Citizens United v.
   FEC and, 60–61
spoils system, 52
Star Trek (TV show), 110, 207
State Department, U.S.
   and Clinton emails, 6, 7, 8, 11,
      12–13
   and Clinton's (Hillary) aides, 6
   regulations about emails/records
      at, 4, 14–15
   See also Clinton, Hillary
states
   and Article V of the Constitution,
      252
   economic competition among, 197
   limitation of federal power over,
      252
   and need for reform of state
      bureaucracies, 206
   ObamaCare and, 101–6
Statue of Liberty, 42
Statute 18 U.S.C., 15–18
steel industry, U.S., 185
Stein, Sam, 65
Stevens, Ted: prosecution of, 33–34,
   132–35, 245
Stewart, Jon, 86
Strassel, Kimberley, 103–5
"strong emotional feelings": and
   IRS decisions about tax-exempt
   status, 24
"sue and settle" pattern, DOJ's,
   51, 150–52, 155–58, 163, 164,
   166–67
Sunstein, Cass, 38

Supreme Court, U.S.
  and Arthur Andersen LLP case, 139
  building for, 21
  checks and balances on, 45
  Citizens United v. FEC and, 59–61,
    247
  climate change decision of, 178
  Echols case and, 214, 215
  and fish-DOJ case, 143
  functions of, 22
  importance in bureaucratic
    overreach cases of, 202
  and *INS v. Chadha*, 238
  and IRS questions for tax
    exemptions, 69–70
  legislative veto and, 238
  NAACP v. Patterson and, 69–70
  and need for reform of
    bureaucracy, 266
  ObamaCare and, 106
  and Obama's 2010 State of the
    Union speech, 60–61
  and Obama's appointments to
    NLRB, 203
  power of, 22
  and public parks case law, 225
  Sekulow's cases before the, 21–22,
    39, 42, 45–46, 215, 225
Sweeney, Edmund, 175

Target: hacking at, 3
tax credits
  "additional child," 107–9
  adoption, 91–98, 209, 210, 240
  earned income, 98–101, 154, 155
  fraud and, 95–96, 241
  immigration and, 107–9
  IRS overpayment of, 99–100
  ObamaCare and, 102–6
tax-exempt organizations
  free speech and, 79–81
  House Ways and Means
    Committee chart about, 66–67
  IRS delays in processing
    applications for, 23 26, 61–72,
    73, 84, 249–50, 256–65

IRS questions concerning, 67–71,
    249–50
  and IRS war on conservatives,
    23–26, 61–72, 73, 84, 229,
    249–50, 256–65
  Lerner's "apology" concerning,
    23–24, 25–26, 71, 81–82
  liberal, 24, 25, 66
  NAACP v. Patterson case and,
    69–70
  need for reform of determination
    of, 266
  Section 501(c)(4) of IRS code and,
    66
  and *Z Street v. Koskinen* case,
    261–63
  See also specific organization
Tax Foundation, 100
Taxpayer Advocate Service (IRS),
    92, 94–95
Tea Party
  Citizens United v. FEC and, 61
  elections of 2012 and, 26–27
  free speech and, 81
  influence on elections of, 26–27
  intimidation of, 71
  and IRS audit of Grassley, 77
  IRS audits of donors to, 74, 76
  and IRS criminalization of
    conservatives' speech, 83
  and IRS decisions about tax-
    exempt status, 23 24, 25, 27, 65,
    66 69, 229
  and IRS "loss" of evidence, 87
  IRS war with, 23–24, 27, 35, 59,
    60, 61–72, 74, 76, 77, 81, 83, 87,
    150, 164
  issues of concern to, 59
  Lerner's "apology" to, 23 24,
    81–82
  liberals concern about, 59
  rise of, 59, 60
  and "Tea Party cases" of IRS, 61
technology
  benefits of, 3
  and "creative destruction" concept,
    128–29

technology (*cont.*)
   disadvantages of, 3
   hackers and, 3
   and proving criminal intent,
      144–45
Ten Commandments Monument,
   21, 22
Tennessean: Womack's comment
   about Volkswagen-UAW-NLRB
   controversy in, 201
Texas Railroad Commission, 183
Three Felonies a Day: How the Feds
   Target the Innocent (Silvergate),
   144, 145
three R's, 39–40, 207–13. *See also*
   blueprint for change; reform;
   resistance; restoration
Tijuana River Valley: EPA letter
   about sewage in, 186
Top Secret information, 8, 16
Toyota, 193
"training videos," IRS, 110
transfer of wealth issues:
   partisanship in IRS and, 99
transparency, 5, 14, 88, 186, 189,
   268
Treasury Department, U.S., 45, 84,
   100, 104. *See also* IRS

Uniformed and Overseas Citizens
   Absentee Voting Act, 160
unions
   auto industry and, 193–95,
      200–201
   Boeing "Dreamliner" plant and,
      195–99
   decline in membership of, 193,
      194, 200, 233
   Democrats and, 194
   government, 56, 232–33, 234
   and partisanship of NLRB, 56,
      193–201, 229
   political contributions of, 194–95
   private sector, 193–201, 232–33,
      234
   and reform, 232–33, 234

   in South, 193–99
United Automobile Workers
   (UAW), 193, 194, 200–201
USA Today, 34, 52, 136
Utility MACT Rule, IRS, 154

VanderSloot, Frank, 74–75
VECO Corp., 134
Veterans Affairs (VA), U.S.
   Department of
   "absent without leave" employees
      at, 120
   accountability at, 122
   audit of facilities at, 115, 116
   bipartisan public support for, 114
   and "bugging" of congressional
      investigators, 120, 122
   Coburn's top-ten scandals at,
      118–20
   corruption at, 33, 114, 117, 118–20,
      121, 125, 245
   disability claims at, 117–18
   disciplinary actions for employees
      at, 115
   funding for, 114, 117, 120
   Gibson's defense of employees at,
      122
   incompetency at, 33, 114, 117, 118,
      122, 230, 245
   job security at, 35
   mission of, 113
   as model for American health care
      system, 122, 123–25
   need for reform of, 205, 245
   overpayment of employees at, 121,
      122
   power of, 23
   reform of, 122, 124–25, 236
   security incidents at, 119–20
   Shinseki's replacement at, 121–22
   as threat to democracy, 23
   wait-time scandals at, 33, 35,
      113–18, 125, 129
   whistle-blowers at, 158
Veterans Health Administration,
   123

veto
  governor's, 239
  legislative, 237–38
  overriding of, 238
  presidential, 47, 238
Veuger, Stan, 26–27
victory: in resistance, 228–29
Volkswagen Corp.: UAW-NLRB
  controversy with, 200–201
Voting Accessibility for the Elderly
  and Handicapped Act, 160
Voting Rights Act, 159, 161, 162
Voting Section (DOJ), 161–63

Waco Tea Party, 27
wages
  and Boeing–labor unions–NLRB
    controversy, 199
  EPA garnishment of citizen's, 190
  in South, 194
wait-times scandal, VA, 33, 35,
    113–18, 125, 129
Wald, George, 168
Walker, Toby Marie, 27
Wall Street Journal, The
  auto industry story in, 193
  and Clinton emails, 8–9
  Pai alarm about FCC newsroom
    monitors in, 220–21
  and political donations of
    organized labor, 194–95
  proving intent story in, 144
  Strassel story about ObamaCare
    in, 103–5
  wiretap story in, 144
Washington Post
  and divisiveness among American
    people, 248
  IRS conferences story in, 110
  Klein article about health care in, 123
  and VA wait-time story, 117

Washington Times: immigration
  story in, 107
Watergate, 28, 88
Watt, Kenneth, 170
Ways and Means Committee,
  House, 66–67, 75–76, 84, 85,
  265
welfare policy: IRS transformation
  of, 239
Wheeler, Tom, 222
whistle-blowers, 158. See also specific
  person
Whitefish Mountain Resort
  (Montana). Jesus statue and,
  216–17
Whitehouse, Sheldon, 82
WikiLeaks, Clinton emails about,
  12
Will, George, 252
Williamson, Kevin, 38, 168
Wilson, James Q., 127–28
Windsor, Richard (aka Lisa
  Jackson), 187, 188
wiretap story, councilman, 144
Womack, Todd, 201
"works councils," 200
World War I, 41
World War II
  DDT during, 171–72, 173
  despair during, 253–54
  and preservation of Jesus war
    memorial, 216–17
World War II Memorial (National
  Mall), 37–38, 224–27

Yates, John, 143

Z Street v. Koskinen case, 261–63, 267
Zerbe, Dean, 77
Zubrin, Robert, 172, 173, 174, 175